'*Neither Here Nor There: A Guide for Immigrants and the Therapists who Walk With Them* is just excellent! It outlines the major challenges facing immigrants and describes specific techniques that these individuals and their therapists can use to overcome them. Dr. Porcu draws from many different psychotherapies and other psychotherapeutic approaches, with great creativity and expertise, to create a comprehensive approach to help immigrants thrive.'

Judith Beck, *president of the Beck Institute*

'*Neither Here nor There* is a much needed resource for people coping with the many challenges of immigration. Leide Porcu is herself an immigrant who has built a successful career as a therapist. She draws on her own lived experience to help others learn how to successfully master the experience. This book will give readers the knowledge to normalize the experience of coming to a new land. Dr. Porcu provides a uniquely well-informed insight into this experience. Highly recommended.'

Robert L. Leahy, *director, the American Institute for Cognitive Therapy, clinical professor, Weill Cornell Medical College, New York.*

'*Neither Here nor There* is a companion for those who cross borders in hope, finding new layers of emotional and cultural terrain to navigate—and a bridge for the practitioners and healers who walk beside them.'

Sharon Salzberg, *author of* Lovingkindness *and* Real Life.

'*Neither Here Nor There* is a compassionate, clear, and empowering guide for anyone navigating life between cultures. With deep psychological insight and a therapist's grounded wisdom, Leide Porcu gives voice to the emotional, relational, and spiritual complexities of migration. What makes this book truly stand out is its invitation to reclaim agency—to move from disorientation to empowerment. Whether you are an immigrant, a child of immigrants, or someone who walks beside them, this book offers not just understanding, but tools for healing, belonging, and rising.'

Neelu Kaur, *author of* Be Your Own Cheerleader, Speaker, *organizational psychologist*

Neither Here Nor There

This book looks at the psychological experience of being an immigrant and offers strategies to foster resilience, adaptation, and wellbeing.

At a time when over 250 million people live outside their countries of origin, this book responds to a global need among psychotherapists working with a growing, often distressed, immigrant population by emphasizing cultural awareness, trauma sensitivity, and cultural humility. This accessible and deeply empathetic guide explores the emotional complexities of migration by drawing on decades of clinical experience and the author's own story of cultural dislocation. It examines topics such as anxiety, cultural grief, and impostor syndrome and addresses the financial, systemic, linguistic, and legal struggles many immigrants face. It also empowers immigrants to take an active role in their healing and growth, especially in today's political climate, where mental health funding and services for immigrants are increasingly limited.

With friendly and inclusive guidance on how to work with problems experienced by immigrants, this is an essential reading for psychoanalysts and therapists as well as anyone who has experienced immigration or any type of cultural or social dislocation.

Leide Porcu, PhD LP is a New York-based psychotherapist and psychoanalyst with a background in anthropology. A graduate of IPTAR and the Beck Institute, she holds a PhD in Anthropology from Columbia University. Her writing explores healing, identity, language, and humor. She is passionate about helping people thrive across cultures.

Neither Here Nor There

A Guide for Immigrants and the Therapists Who Walk With Them

Leide Porcu

R Routledge
Taylor & Francis Group

LONDON AND NEW YORK

Designed cover image: Roksolana Tkach

First published 2026
by Routledge
4 Park Square, Milton Park, Abingdon, Oxon OX14 4RN

and by Routledge
605 Third Avenue, New York, NY 10158

Routledge is an imprint of the Taylor & Francis Group, an informa business

© 2026 Leide Porcu

British Library Cataloguing-in-Publication Data
A catalogue record for this book is available from the British Library

Library of Congress Cataloging-in-Publication Data
A catalog record has been requested for this book

ISBN: 978-1-041-09149-3 (hbk)
ISBN: 978-1-041-09118-9 (pbk)
ISBN: 978-1-003-64870-3 (ebk)

DOI: 10.4324/9781003648703

Typeset in Optima
by Taylor & Francis Books

To Gabriela, who keeps showing me new steps just when I think I have learned the dance.

Contents

Illustrations

Figures

Tables

Acknowledgments

This book could not have been written without the support of a phenomenal community of mentors, colleagues, and friends. I am especially grateful to my former supervisor at IPTAR, Debra Schnall, who was instrumental in helping me soften the rough edges of my unconventional psychoanalytic style. She first taught me how to pass, then how to adapt, without giving up my voice. Because of her, I managed my impulsivity, stayed in the program, and ultimately learned a great deal.

Lucia Imbesi, one of my supervisors at the Western Queens Consultation Center Clinic, has remained a steadfast supporter and trusted friend over the years. John Lavin and James T. McQuade gave me a work opportunity that sealed my clinical interest in immigration.

Meditation groups and teachers accompanied me throughout this journey, especially the Meditative Writing Group led by Therese Ragen, and the Psychoanalytic Meditators Group guided by Sara Weber and William Auerbach. Other important teachers have been Robert Peng, Lin Wang Gordon, Sharon Salzberg, and Space2Meditate led by Jon Aaron and Upayadhi.

I received much support from my colleagues, analysts, and friends, including readings, ideas, and connections. They include Isabella Abbonizio, Jama Adams, Stefania Boi, Martha Bragin, Luca Caldironi, Stefania Calabrese, Carlos Campetta, Diana Carretero, Alexandra Cattaruzza, DC Cymbalista, Eleanor Esposito, Gabriella Giuggioloni, Alfio Gliozzo, Vicky Gluhosky, Richard Grose, Desales Harrison, Marvin Hurvich, Danielle Knafo, Saverio Lo Monaco, Natalia Kurchanova, Robert Leahy, Peter Meiland, Tod Mijanovich, Alessandro Mongili, Michal Moskowitz, Samera Nasereddin, Carlos Padron, Patricia Palacios, Elena Perazzini, Roberto Pieraccini, Valentino Porcu, Stefania Puxeddu, Anna Eva Radicetti, Evelyn Rappaport, Barbara Reichenthal, Amir Rezaizadeh, Patrizia Ricciardi, Kim Rosenthal, Alessandra Sabbatini, Ron Scapp, Guglielmo Schinina, Bob Silverstein, Ellen Simpao, Pamela Thorp, Isaac Tilym, Tuba Tokgoz, Matthew von Unwerth, Maria Grazia Verardi, and Elena Visconti.

I also want to honor the foundational teachings of Sigmund Freud and his followers, as well as the transformative contributions of Aaron Beck, whom I had the privilege of meeting. Their ideas continue to shape my way of thinking.

To IPTAR, the Beck Institute, and the Academy of Cognitive and Behavioral Therapies, thank you for being intellectual and professional homes that inform and inspire me. A heartfelt thanks goes to the Silberman School of Social Work, CUNY, where teaching the course Social Work Practice with Immigrants and Refugees opened a new perspective for me. It deepened my appreciation for the field of social work. If I were to start over, I would become a social worker first. The opportunity to meet young, passionate students—bringing fresh ideas and energy—has been a gift. We grow together in mutual exchange.

Finally, I wish to acknowledge my Aunt Olga, the matriarch of my family, whose prayers and steadfast love have accompanied throughout this journey. The cover artwork is by Roksolana Tkach. It was created with inspiration from Maria Lai, Cristina Bernazzani, and old Japanese paintings with broken frames.

Preface: An Invitation to Think Together

This book was started in pre-pandemic times, when the dramatic events outlined in Project 2025[1]—a proposed political agenda aimed at restructuring the U.S. government and rolling back immigrant rights—and the current level of targeting of immigrants still was unthinkable. When I distributed surveys during the first Trump administration, asking immigrants, schoolteachers, and therapists about the immigrant experience, the responses, more often than not, did not focus on politics. Despite the policy and ideological shifts from the Obama era, only a few individuals emphasized the first Trump Administration or its damaging effects on immigrant lives.

Today, however, immigration and politics are intertwined. They occupy center stage in both national debate and daily life—both for immigrants and American citizens. Immigration has become a flashpoint used to justify policies, drive spending, and consolidate power. These narratives create unprecedented stress—and at times, disgrace and humiliation—for all immigrants, whether documented or undocumented. But they also harm American families and businesses.

The fight against "illegals" has become a tool to incite and polarize. This black-and-white thinking—blaming and scapegoating—is powerful. It can unite people behind a leader, give them a target, and solidify group identity around the task of criminalizing and expelling "the other." But this collective act, as if it could wipe away complexity, is profoundly damaging for all.

A ghostly feeling has spread: as if someone had pulled the carpet out from under us. Rights we thought were secure now feel contingent. When fear becomes overwhelming, survival overrides thought. Silence spreads. People comply—or act without reason. And those who break the silence face even more perilous consequences.

When emotions are triggered at such an intensity as we see today, people lose the ability to think clearly. And in groups, this kind of blind emotional response multiplies. As a therapist, I often see something similar on an individual level. When someone comes into my office in a state of rage—thinking in extremes, urgently needing to discharge emotion—I focus first on creating space. I validate and contain the feelings. But the next step must be to reengage the mind: to examine thoughts and distortions, to strategize, and to move toward a more balanced and empowered position. Making decisions based solely on feelings—without enough research or awareness of consequences— rarely serves us well. It can diminish our position, not strengthen it. We have all done things impulsively. We have all, at times, given authority a blind nod. But each time we do, we lose a piece of ourselves. We become more vulnerable.

Let us try something else. Let us think together. Let us approach social problems as we would personal ones. When we are angry or dissatisfied— say, about our job, our relationship, or where we live—what do we do? Do we pack the car and leave? Do we throw the other out the window? No. We stop. We think. We talk. We explore the cause of our anger and ask if there is space for discussion or change. If we do decide to leave, we weigh the losses. We ask, what good things might we be leaving behind? What would the aftermath look like? Before we throw out the baby with the bathwater, we pause.

This is what we need right now:
Stop.
Ground ourselves.
And think.

That means creating space for the people we dislike—or do not under- stand: the people on "the other side": the reds, the blues, the immigrants. They are all part of the same body. Even the most recent immigrants are part of the body. They keep it going—they are vital.

For me, this is not, first and foremost, a question of ethics or morality. It is also not only about helping the poor, protecting the children, or welcoming people fleeing natural and political disasters (many of which were fueled by American and international politics and economics). It is a matter of national and individual self-interest—the bread and butter of the American perspective.

To take the immigrants out is like cutting off your nose to spite your face. I say this not because I am a somewhat recent immigrant (30 years in), but because I know immigrants. I see the work they do. "Purifying" the country by removing recent immigrants—or even all undocumented people—will not solve American problems. It will make them worse.

Let us ask: What would we lose if all immigrants left? Do we want our tax dollars to fund detention centers, prisons, and bounty hunters? Or would we prefer to educate our children, improve our cities, ensure safe flights and hospitals, and with discernment, overhaul the immigration system?

Let us come to a calm place. Let us explore our values, our threats, and our needs. Let us ask: How can we help ourselves and one another?

Let us move beyond polarization at the micro level. Let us invite the other to the table and talk—enough to understand one another, enough to soften the edges, enough to see the humanity in one another and our inter- dependency. Only a small percentage of people are truly sociopathic. The rest are emotionally reactive, misguided, or in need of tools to grow and understand. Only a small percentage of immigrants are criminals. The majority bring value. Perhaps we should pause to reflect on the very concept of criminality—what it means, who defines it, and whose interests it serves. What are the different types of harm and offense in our society? Who truly damages our social fabric? What function does it serve to focus public outrage on 'criminals'—especially when that label is disproportionately applied to immigrants or marginalized groups? And who escapes scrutiny while this attention is diverted? When we reduce complex individuals to stereotypes and blame, we often fail to tackle the issues and actors causing the most systemic, large-scale forms of harm—environmental destruction, financial fraud, political corruption. Who are the big criminals we are not naming?

As you read this book, you will not find a polemic against the current administration. That is not what this book is about. We must work with whatever administration is elected. Our task as therapists is helping people find their way: to help develop people's capacity to think critically, to sort information with care, and to build mature emotional and ethical lives. As social beings, our task is to use persuasion and lead by example to promote the world we want to live in.

My hope is that by lowering the volume, we lower defensiveness. And when defensiveness goes down, conversation becomes possible.

Following are a few foundational truths—often ignored in public discourse—that this book keeps in view.

Immigrants Are Not a Monolith

It is important to remember that immigrants are not a homogeneous group. Their stories, resources, and vulnerabilities vary widely. Depending on the political agenda of the moment, they can be portrayed as either heroes or criminals. But the reality is much more complex, and as we know, these generalizations help no one.

Immigrants Clean Our Messes and Do the Low-Pay, Dirty Jobs

It is important to highlight, that it is precisely undocumented individuals who clean up our messes. They were on the front lines after Ground Zero and during our environmental disasters, often for very little money. They got sick often without receiving proper medical care and were ultimately forgotten. Migrants were essential workers during COVID-19, and they have increasingly filled low-paying agricultural jobs, once held by U.S. workers. These jobs are particularly strenuous, dangerous, and lacking in benefits.

Crime and Public Perception

Yes, some immigrants are involved in criminal activity or gangs, but statistical data contradict the idea that immigration increases crime:

- Immigrants commit fewer crimes than the native-born population.[2]
- Second-generation immigrants show higher rates of crime than first generation, but they are still lower than some segments of the general population.
- It is essential to distinguish between perceived fear—amplified by politicians and media—and actual risk.

Resilience and Suffering Coexist

Many immigrants and refugees experience deep suffering. Those who arrive and settle here have often already faced very difficult circumstances; the longer the detention in the interim period, the higher the risk to one's mental health and to one's future prospects. In neglecting and persecuting these communities, we risk weakening one of our most vital sources of renewal. Yet, despite of all of this, immigrants are, in many cases, particularly resilient.

Economic and Social Contribution

It is true that immigrants come with an initial cost to a host society. But it is equally true that, over time, they give back much more than they receive.[3] They are not just poor people standing in line at the border or criminal gangs—they are first and foremost essential workers, silent pillars of the American economy. We must resist simplistic portrayals.

The Undocumented: Invisible Taxpayers

Even immigrants without legal status pay taxes through their work. For years, immigration services remained separate from our tax system precisely to allow these individuals to pay taxes. However, they do not receive full access to benefits in return: they pay into Social Security but will not be able to use it. A notable example: as temporary agricultural workers, they are often paid with a check. They pay taxes but despite being extremely poor, they do not request a tax refund.[4] Consider this: We often pay them little (despite laws demanding equal pay for all), and they contribute to Social Security benefits without even being able to access them. Could it be that, perhaps, we actually owe them money?

Case in Point: A Contract for Living Together

During a classroom discussion on integration and cultural preservation, I asked my students to imagine a scenario I often encounter in my clinical work: an elderly immigrant woman, isolated in her apartment, who speaks only her native language—neither English nor Spanish—and refuses all attempts at engagement or support. A passionate debate unfolded. Some students empathized deeply. They spoke of cultural trauma, linguistic alienation, and the right to self-determination. "Maybe she is holding onto what little of her culture she has left," one said. "Why should we impose our idea of integration on her?"

Others took a more pragmatic—and at times ageist—stance: "She is old. She made her choice. Should we continue investing resources if there is no return?"

Still others challenged the very framework of integration. "Why are certain communities, like the Amish or Hasidim, allowed to live in parallel worlds while other immigrant groups are pressured to assimilate?" one student asked. "Is integration (or separation) a privilege granted only to some?"

Even among therapists—professionals trained to hold complexity, listen deeply, and bracket their assumptions—the conversation became quickly polarized. It brought to the surface unconscious biases that had gone unexamined until that moment. For instance, the idea that clinicians should support a client's optimal level of integration into the host culture was not universally accepted. Several practitioners viewed the possibility of completely separate, coexisting cultural groups as socially acceptable. In their view, the therapist's role was not to guide individuals toward a modicum of integration but to support the client in identifying their own optimal level of connection, including separation. At most, they would clarify the potential benefits and trade-offs of remaining isolated, such as missed job opportunities due to limited English, but would not intervene further.

Even within a relatively homogeneous group like therapists, we discovered deep divergence. Up until that moment, we believed we were aligned, but as the discussion unfolded, it became clear that many of our shared assumptions were untested. We realized that what felt like common ground could dissolve the moment it was scrutinized. We held different ideas not only about what integration meant, but also about what kind of society we wanted to live in. This moment of rupture forced us to ask: What other biases do we carry? How do our own values shape what we believe is "best" for others? And what do we do when someone's choice conflicts with our idea of wellbeing?

This led to a deeper question: What is the implicit contract between immigrants and the host society? And should it be made more visible? Perhaps what we need is not rigid enforcement or complete cultural assimilation, but a shared agreement—a humane and mutual social contract that includes:

- The right to preserve one's identity and traditions
- The responsibility to learn enough about the host culture to navigate it with dignity
- A joint effort to promote communication, empathy, and functional coexistence.

This is of concern to all of us, not only the elderly women who sparked this debate: It is about how we choose to live together, not in dominance or detachment, but in ongoing dialogue.

Integration, Ambivalence, and the Therapist's Dilemma

My bias—if I am being honest—is to help patients integrate. I believe in learning the language of the host country. For me, this means building independence, preventing victimization, developing a voice for advocacy and self-advocacy, and gaining access to better jobs. But this does not mean erasure of one's culture and language. It is also important to keep, at least in part, one's traditions and cultures and maintain pride in them. Our richness as immigrants is when we have creative access to both. Learning the dominant language is often a privilege—not everyone has the time, resources, or capacity to do it. But at times, it is not just a privilege; it is a necessity. It was for me. Learning Spanish quickly—beyond the basics—became essential to maintaining my legal status. After a bad experience in the class I was teaching as an adjunct, I was feeling I was in a dead end, paid little, with no prospect of getting the papers, and unappreciated by the students. Out of anger and impulsivity, I quit on the spot and found myself with very little time to secure a job to keep my legal status—talk about acting out of angry feelings! I was on the brink of becoming undocumented. A possibility presented itself to work in a clinic that was short-staffed in Spanish-speaking therapists. All of a sudden, I realized: No Spanish, no papers. So, I improved enough of my rudimentary Spanish and was hired. Other immigrants—past and present—have had to do the opposite: to forget or hide their languages because they were stigmatized. Italian immigrants in earlier waves, like so many others, made sure their children did not speak their native tongue so they could blend in, be accepted, and avoid discrimination. Still, every language holds power. Languages are something you can work on for free if you have even a bit of time. They can become an asset, a jewel, a way in—and sometimes, a weapon.

But then I ask myself, how tightly should I hold on to this bias—the belief that a strategic embrace of American culture is inherently good? How much should I try to raise the English question with a client who does not want to even think about learning English? Or, more subtly, can I be aware of my foundational preferences—ones that are not only my own but based also on research—and suspend that orientation and see what unfolds for the patient? As a therapist, perhaps I should sit back and resist the impulse to educate, fix, or even help. Instead, I can explore: What are the client's feelings? Their desires, values, hopes? Is English, with all its potential for wider communication and connection, something they want or need? Is integration a value for them? Because learning a new language is not neutral. It can be an act of transformation. It can shift awareness, unsettle relationships, and bring to light emotions and perspectives that were previously dormant. The play *English* by Sanaz Toossi[5] (an Iranian American writer) captures this complexity beautifully. It shows how learning English can feel liberating and humiliating at the same time—how it can open up the world and also estrange you from it. So maybe it is not about persuasion at all. It is about approaching the conversation—with patients and with ourselves—with humility, curiosity, and reflection. We do not need to erase our values to honor someone else's. And the same holds true for anyone, immigrant or not.

There is a difference: therapists are trained to be mindful of the subtle forms of influence we carry. Outside the clinic, persuasion flows unchecked— through media, institutions, and communities. So we—therapists, immigrants, allies, and hosts—must confront a crucial question, especially in light of ideological and cultural pressures: *What must be kept, and what must be given away in the process of integration?* Keeping everything can lead to rigidity and confusion. Giving everything away would be a profound loss—and is, in truth, impossible. Integration can be a shared process, but it is not a stage on which people are forced to perform a single version of acceptability or passing.

And yet, even within the clinic, we are not immune. Therapists are trained to be self-reflective—but no amount of self-reflection allows us to fully step outside of the dominant ideology. Psychology itself has long served a normalizing function, shaping people toward prevailing cultural ideals and often pathologizing those who fall outside them. Foucault's work on power, surveillance, and the classification of deviance reminds us of this legacy. I wonder: was the bias I uncovered in that class not just a personal blind spot, but a symptom of a deeper structure? In the absence of a nearby home-country community, I had, perhaps unconsciously, favored a culturally dominant view of integration—and of learning English as essential, and maybe Spanish at a minimum (the second unofficial language of the United States)—even for an elderly patient.

At the time, I believed that encouraging her to learn English would help her feel more connected and less isolated. But I later realized that my wish for her to integrate may have reflected *my own values* more than hers. The goal was well-intentioned, but it carried a subtle pressure to adapt in a particular way— one that might not have felt necessary or even possible for her. Rather than asking, *"How can I help her integrate?"* the more ethical question became: *"How can I help her feel whole—on her own terms—in this context?"*

The more we engage with diverse voices, the better we can clean our own mirrors. But we must also ask: What values are embedded in the therapeutic work itself? When working in a country with foundational cultural norms, is it our role to gently nudge clients toward them? Are we doing so uncon- sciously, even when we believe we are simply helping them clarify where they stand in relation to those norms?

A Statement of House Rules

I am thinking of the founding principles of a country—those shared foundations that make coexistence possible despite difference. Perhaps it is hard to define what they are now, especially in a time of polarization and fragmentation. But I do think that common language, public education, democratic principles, and a few shared holidays matter. These are not small things. They are symbolic anchors.

Perhaps we should all agree that in our country, we accept diversity, but we all respect a few fundamental principles: the official language is English, and we should all find a way to learn it (which also means we must give people the opportunity and tools to do so. If people work below minimum wage and for extra-long hours, learning English cannot be a priority); freedom of speech; equality; respect for women and for all people; no physical punishment of children. We should put these things into a kind of contract of cohabitation—"house rules," if you will. We should commit to them, even if we Americans are not always proficient in them ourselves, because they are what we strive for. I created this list not because immigrants necessarily break these rules, but because these are often the fears projected onto immigrants. Naming them clearly might help move us toward "meeting in the middle," easing both the fear of erasure and the fear of invasion.

And yet, meeting in the middle is not an easy point to establish; even within the USA there is much debate on values and ideals. It is not only immigrants or minorities who have their own different values. It is Americans themselves—through book bans, attacks on multicultural education, and politicized battles over school curricula. There are foreign aspects of diversity and there are internal ruptures. So, in pluralistic societies, the challenge is not whether to accept diversity, but how to build a common life without erasing difference.

We cannot melt into one another, and we should not pressure newcomers into full assimilation. But how *can* we live alongside one another, not closed in silos, but learn and appreciate the values of all cultures without fear of being erased?

At the risk of sounding simplistic, I would add a small booklet, or a video, or a Podcast to the citizenship process. It should be a product that draws people in, that speaks of their issues. In fact, I would hand it to immigrants at the very start, upon arrival. A welcome booklet (I know this sounds unrealistic in this historical moment or raids and incarcerations, but I am thinking about the near future, and I am optimistic). It would be not just about laws, historical facts, and logistics, but about the core values this country aspires to uphold: what we hope to offer, and what we ask in return.

Practical Integration to Strive For

This is how I think about therapy—and about integration: not as fixed ideologies, but as processes shaped by pragmatism, curiosity, and care. As an immigrant, I find myself drawn to what is practical—what keeps the world moving forward. In therapy, I remember blending cognitive-behavioral techniques with psychoanalytic insight, and all sorts of other tools even when others claimed it was theoretically incompatible. But I did it because it worked. It helped people. It made space for both reflection and action.

I feel the same way about integration. We do not need rigid ideologies. We need clear, workable frameworks. Some "house rules." We need basic but thoughtful orientations and programs that actually help people navigate and engage. In Sardinia, for example, we spoke Sardinian at home for generations—until television arrived. No one forced us to stop speaking Sardinian. But the allure of Italian-language TV—its stories, its rhythm, its window into another world—slowly shifted our speech patterns. That change came not through imposition, but through emotional persuasion and cultural seduction. (At the same time it is fair to acknowledge that shaming was also present.)

But integration should not happen at the level of McDonald's—or the cultural and gastronomic garbage America too often exports. It should not be about replacing richness with uniformity or seducing people with the cheapest, loudest version of belonging. If we are to invite people in, let it be through what is best—through quality, depth, and meaning.

Integration, at its most powerful, should engage, persuade, and elevate. It should draw people into a shared project that is intellectually and emotionally nourishing: civic participation, public libraries, compelling education, ethical dialogue, and meaningful cultural exchange.

If immigrants are to adapt, let it be to the highest aspirations of American life—not its lowest common denominators. Let the integration process be one of mutual growth, not erasure. Let it lift us all.

The Uncanny Valley of Culture: Where Shared Identity Ruptures

And yet, the question is not only what the immigrant—or immigrant patient—wants, but also what the host society can tolerate or is prepared to welcome. In recent years, I have noticed a phenomenon that I would cautiously liken to the "uncanny valley"—a concept borrowed from robotics. The uncanny valley refers to the discomfort people experience when something non-human appears almost—but not quite—human. This near similarity becomes unsettling, because it challenges the brain's categories of familiarity and difference.

A comparable response sometimes arises around immigrants in the United States, particularly among monolingual Americans. I call this the *uncanny valley of culture*. One version of it appears when an immigrant who seems fully assimilated—fluent in English, behaviorally indistinct—suddenly code-switches, speaking in another language to a family member or customer. In that moment, the illusion of shared identity is punctured. The listener may feel confused, surprised, even betrayed. The person they assumed to be "one of us" is revealed to possess an invisible dimension: a second language, another cultural system, perhaps even a greater degree of cognitive flexibility. The reaction is not always hostile, but it often carries a charge—unsettling, destabilizing, difficult to name.

A second form of an uncanny valley with respect to culture emerges not from the individual but from the collective: the visible transformation of public space. Many native-born Americans—especially those who are monolingual—express discomfort when the landscape of their daily lives begins to change. When stores carry too many unfamiliar foods, when public signs include multiple languages, when the faces, garments, or rituals of neighbors no longer mirror their own, a silent sense of dislocation can take hold. The place that once felt like "home" begins to feel unfamiliar. This is not always articulated in political terms, but it is deeply emotional. It speaks to the human need for continuity, predictability, and symbolic cohesion.

But this discomfort, like all forms of the uncanny, is also an opportunity. It reveals the boundaries of our comfort zones and forces us to confront the assumptions we carry about identity, language, and belonging. It challenges both immigrants and hosts to think critically: What do we expect from one another? What do we fear losing—and why? And can we imagine a form of integration that acknowledges difference without demanding erasure?

As guests in a country, should immigrants be made aware—explicitly or implicitly—that some values are not up for debate? And how do we navigate the tensions that arise when a person enters into a social contract out of necessity (to work, to remain legal, to survive) but does not agree with the foundational beliefs of the host country?

Newcomers often initially observe the host culture with distance—through a sort of one-way mirror, sometimes with a critical eye. They may not feel inclined to adopt its values or even engage with them. But later, when work requires interaction or when they become parents of American children, they face a reckoning. They must reconcile their own worldview with the expectations of the society they now live in.

So what is the role of therapy in all of this? What should therapists be aware of? First and foremost, we need to be aware of our hidden biases and assumptions, but we also need to be cognizant of the needs and limits of tolerance of the host country, the ways we might unknowingly act as agents of normalization, even when our intention is simply to help. Are we—perhaps quietly, gently—encouraging integration, and with it, a certain version of belonging that may not be right for everyone?

These are not easy questions. But they feel essential to ask if therapy is to be a space of genuine reflection rather than soft persuasion. They feel essential to ask of yourself as an immigrant if you intend to stay and make America your own land.

Reflective Questions for the Reader

Whether you are an immigrant, a therapist, or both, consider:

- What assumptions have shaped your view of integration and identity?
- Which values do you feel are essential to hold onto, and which might you be open to questioning or revising?
- Where does your sense of belonging, agency, and freedom reside—in preserving what you know, in adapting to something new, or in creating a balance between both?

Whether you are American or an immigrant—at any stage of integration or resistance (and perhaps also a therapist trying to help others feel at home in this culture)—ask yourself:

- From your perspective, what values do you see as foundational to American identity today?
- Which values were once considered core to America but now feel outdated or irrelevant—and for whom? Which values are forcefully imposing themselves in recent times and how is it affecting your point of view, your sense of belonging, and your safety?
- Which aspects of this culture do you cherish and align with? Which do you reject?
- Is there enough common ground between your values and those you identify as "American"?
- How do you see yourself, your family, and your community within the larger tapestry of American culture?
- What metaphor best describes your relationship to this cultural landscape? Two parallel rivers? A rivulet that flows in a larger river? A field and its plants? Something else entirely?

Let us think together about what truly matters for this country—and whether the original principle, that this is a nation of immigrants, still holds. If not, what are the emerging metaphors? Where are we going? Then, together, let us formulate new texts, materials, and a statement that reflect the complexities of our current times.

The Oath of Allegiance is poetic; the citizenship booklet for the naturalization exam provides important historical and civic facts. But could we also create more practical, inclusive documents—something that speaks to shared expectations and everyday mutual responsibilities? A new kind of foundation, simple and accessible from the start, that invites participation without demanding erasure?

Let us all engage in creating a "treatment of welcome," a set of house rules on how we want to be treated and treat others, rather than act out our sense of overwhelm with erasure and expulsion. Let's reflect on what the fundamentals of being in this country should be.

Even Moses had ten commandments. Why should we not try drafting ten shared principles for immigration and coexistence—clear, accessible, and rooted in mutual respect? We do not need rules carved in stone, but we may benefit from something equally grounding: a shared understanding of what it means to live together across difference. Not rigid ideology, but something usable—something that helps people orient themselves in a new place while respecting where they come from.

I invite you all—reds, blues, immigrants, Indigenous, and citizens—to write me at immigrants@leideporcu.com with your ideas of what a statement of welcome for immigrants and temporary residents should include. What does mutual engagement, rights, and responsibility look like to you? I would be glad to share your visions and create a first draft.

Notes

1 Cecilia Esterline et al., *Project 2025: Unveiling the Far Right's Plan to Demolish Immigration in a Second Trump Term* (Washington, DC: Niskanen Center, 2024), www.niskanencenter.org/wp-content/uploads/2024/02/Project-2025-Unveiling-the -far-rights-plan-to-demolish-immigration-in-a-second-Trump-term-1.pdf.
2 Ariel G. Ruiz Soto, *Immigrants and Crime in the United States* (Washington, DC: Migration Policy Institute, 2024), www.migrationpolicy.org/content/immigrants-a nd-crime, 1–5.
3 National Academies of Sciences, Engineering, and Medicine, *The Economic and Fiscal Consequences of Immigration* (Washington, DC: National Academies Press, 2017), https://nap.nationalacademies.org/catalog/23550/the-economic-a nd-fiscal-consequences-of-immigration.
4 Jorge Durand and Douglas S. Massey, eds., *Crossing the Border: Research from the Mexican Migration Project* (New York: Russell Sage Foundation, 2004), 252–253.
5 Sanaz Toossi, *English/Wish You Were Here: Two Plays* (New York: Theatre Communications Group, 2024).

References

Durand, Jorge, and Douglas S. Massey, eds. 2004. *Crossing the Border: Research from the Mexican Migration Project*. New York: Russell Sage Foundation.
Esterline, Cecilia, et al.2024. *Project 2025: Unveiling the Far Right's Plan to Demolish Immigration in a Second Trump Term*. Washington, DC: Niskanen Center.
National Academies of Sciences, Engineering, and Medicine. 2017. *The Economic and Fiscal Consequences of Immigration*. Washington, DC: National Academies Press.
Ruiz Soto, Ariel G. 2024. *Immigrants and Crime in the United States*. Washington, DC: Migration Policy Institute.
Toossi, Sanaz. 2022. *English*. New York: Concord Theatricals.

Introduction

> I am trying to make peace with the uncertainty of whether to stay abroad or go
> back to my home country. I want to feel more at ease with where I am now
> and less anxious about what the future holds.
>
> —Anonymous contributor (country withheld)

The Immigrant's Journey: My Story

As I held the letter of admission to study anthropology at Columbia University
30 years ago, pride and excitement washed over me like the waves of the
Mediterranean Sea that sits on the coast of my town. As the daughter of a fish
seller from Sardinia, Italy, I was an unlikely candidate for the honor of
attending one of North America's most elite institutions: an Ivy League university. Although I had graduated from an Italian undergraduate program with
honors, it was not an elite school, and I was not a native English speaker. My
first language was Italian, of course, and my second language was French.
Back then, I was living between Cagliari and London, where I was attending
English courses. It took a great deal of effort to navigate the extremely complicated application process in English, a language I was barely proficient in at
the time, take the required graduate program exams, the Test of English as a
Foreign Language (TOEFL) and the Graduate Record Examination (GRE), and
gain admission into one of the top anthropology programs in the world.

While it was deeply gratifying to achieve such an incredible goal, my joy
was soon overshadowed by an extremely unsettling experience. My body
and mind began to fail me, as if they had suddenly ceased to function. I had
just landed in Paris to celebrate with my boyfriend—who was also accepted
to a prestigious school in New York—the Pratt Institute in Brooklyn. However, immediately upon landing, I did not feel like myself. I woke up on that
Saturday morning feeling strange and afraid. I felt extremely tired, I could not
tolerate the city noise, I felt nauseous, vomited several times, and I couldn't
eat. At one point I thought I was going mad. In another moment, I thought I
was about to die. I couldn't even tolerate my boyfriend's voice or his frenetic
bustling around me. Although I didn't have the slightest idea of what was
wrong with me, I knew clearly that I needed immediate attention. He took

DOI: 10.4324/9781003648703-1

me to the emergency room. The doctor in attendance, however, was not overly concerned. The diagnosis seemed so worry-free that I can barely recall what he said I was suffering from—it was either anxiety or panic—I don't remember which.

I recently found the old doctor's note where he noted that I was very suggestible and prescribed some over-the-counter Valerian, recommending that I follow up with a doctor once I returned to my hometown. Suddenly, I felt dependent and vulnerable. I shortened my long weekend and had my boyfriend take me home.

My family has always been leery of doctors, and we were utterly unaware of psychological and emotional issues. So, there was no follow-up with a psychologist. Instead, I went into my bedroom to partake of our family's prescription for any and all ills—bedrest. But this colorful room with all the shelves crammed with mementos and books was too intense for me. I moved to the guest room which was painted white, with sparse white furniture, and empty shelves. In that monochromatic harmony my overactive mind found comfort. I lay on the bed, staring at the ceiling.

I was concerned for myself but also inconsolable and a jumble inside because I knew I needed to get well soon, catch a plane, and start a new life in America. As I continued to observe the room, I decided that this would be the safest place for me to be for now; so, I simply stayed home. After a few weeks, I eventually took up gardening. Weeding in particular was of great help. I weeded my garden so much that I started to dream of weeding, and my dreams became very green.

That episode was among the scariest experiences of my life. Up to that moment, my life had been low-key and manageable. The world I was about to enter seemed too big for me, and I felt completely unprepared. At the time, however, I didn't see the connection between my attack and my upcoming move. Undoubtedly, I had some anxiety all along, but I wasn't aware of it and had no idea what it was. It took me a long time to understand the fear I had about leaving the sense of safety that my routines, my family, and my life in Europe provided. I was ill-equipped to face what lay ahead. Nevertheless, I was determined to go to America, so I summoned the strength to see a psychiatrist. I was prescribed a low but effective dose of selective serotonin reuptake inhibitors (SSRIs), and after a few weeks, I felt okay. After two months, I felt ready to leave for the US.

I boarded a plane.

The day I landed in the United States, I was overwhelmed by a sense of dislocation. Every street felt unfamiliar. The city was dirty and chaotic—a never-ending work-in-progress billowing with smoke rising from the ground. Every face was a reminder that I was no longer home. Navigating the simplest tasks, like grocery shopping or making small talk, felt like learning to walk again. Loneliness wasn't just a feeling; it was my constant companion. Accustomed as I was to dining in company, I couldn't bear the thought of having lunch after lunch alone. I buried my fears by throwing myself into my work. I still barely spoke English, yet I was required to read several complex theoretical books in the language each week. While I was driven to perform at an Ivy League level without showing emotion or revealing any weakness, inside, I was trying to translate the world around me solely on my own—often leading to misunderstanding and confusion.

The first time—and the thousandth time—I was asked, "Where are you from?" I hesitated. It wasn't the question itself that stung but the underlying message that I didn't quite belong, as though I was neither here nor there. My accent, my appearance, my habits—everything seemed slightly out of place. I felt like a puzzle piece forced into the wrong puzzle; almost fitting, but not quite. However, I also knew I wasn't alone in these feelings of isolation and not belonging. I was aware that many of my classmates—despite their composed expressions and determined efforts to fit in—were also struggling. Some quietly dropped out of the PhD program, while those who stayed were visibly stressed and strained.

Remarkably, despite my language limitations, I finished my master's degree and graduated first in my class in the PhD program in anthropology. Like a damaged apple, I ripened fast. But I felt miserable, overworked, anxious, and isolated.

Seeking Therapy and Becoming a Therapist

My personal immigration experience pushed me to seek therapy for the very first time in my life. There, I discovered a safe place to discuss my difficulties, gain insight about the origins of my distress, which, as you may suspect, went beyond the stressors accompanying immigration. I also argued with my therapist. She questioned my ambivalent dependency toward my parents. I maintained that she could not understand Italian cultural subtleties. And while I benefited from her empathetic, validating, and insightful support, I also needed practical tools that could empower me to manage strong emotions and survive in a competitive environment, one in which I barely spoke the language and did not know the rules. I found that the tools and techniques she offered were insufficient to help me cope with immediate problems.

Although I recognized the lack of practical tools to support me at the stage I was in as a newcomer in the US, my experience as a patient nevertheless was very positive and inspired my journey to becoming a therapist. I began training to become a psychoanalyst while simultaneously attending my anthropology PhD program. As a result, my approach to psychotherapy lies at the intersection of anthropology, psychoanalysis, as well as the practical techniques I first explored to improve my own wellbeing, ranging from CBT and body-centered practices to mindfulness. In 2006, I became a certified psychoanalyst, and from 2006 to 2010, I worked at a low-fee clinic in Jackson Heights, Queens, where I served a vulnerable population comprising of, in large part, Latino and Asian populations. I realized that many of the issues that had affected me as an immigrant affected other immigrants as well.

However, as a therapist, I was at a disadvantage because my patients' collective distress was extreme, and material conditions and immigration status largely contributed to their psychological malaise. My tools could only go so far. I had to keep recentering myself to avoid joining them in their feelings of hopelessness and despair.

My colleagues at the clinic were mainly immigrants, like me. We experienced a great deal of stress from long working hours, as well as the vicarious trauma that therapists experience from continuously bearing witness to their patients' traumas without sufficient resources to cope. I offered my patients a sympathetic ear, words of compassion, and de-stressing techniques, and when possible, highlighted patterns connected to earlier family dynamics that contributed to their distress. However, I secretly wished that I could give them more: material security, social equality, and a decent job. I wished they had more time to invest in themselves. I realized that while I had more privilege and comfort than my patients did, neither my patients nor I had the luxury of spending years processing deep-seated experiences and everyday challenges through traditional talk therapy.

When my analyst would ask me to lie down, slow down, and free associate in psychoanalytic sessions, there were times I'd get angry at her and felt she was condescending and out of touch, at best. She invited me to enter a process that may well have been the royal road to getting to the bottom of my issues, but at that moment, I felt the road was blocked more by practical concerns than by psychological defenses. How could I allow myself to relax and explore my unconscious when the present felt so uncertain? I didn't know how I would maintain my legal status in the United States after getting my PhD—or even at the end of each semester teaching anthropology as an adjunct professor. I was unsure of how to work and continue to build a life. In that present state of mind, I lacked the safety to relax and dissect my history, even if it was clear that my history was quite relevant and was affecting my present.

The lack of security I felt, despite my visible achievements, was not unique but reflects the sense of precariousness faced by millions of newcomers in this country. The United States is a land of immigrants. In 2019, immigrants numbered 44.9 million, making up 13.7% of the total population.[1] Some newcomers are forced to migrate under great duress. Others come to further educational or professional goals or to join family members or partners. We immigrants exhibit exceptional grit and resilience and often thrive by making significant and profound changes in our lives, despite difficult situations. We also significantly contribute to the host country through our work: We build infrastructure, harvest and deliver food to American tables, fill essential service positions, and open and manage thriving businesses. Even when relocation is planned and executed with relative ease, confusion, fatigue, and self-consciousness can arise after geographical and cultural dislocation. Such disorientation is intensified by the loss of daily contact with loved ones and the erosion or reduction of previous professional and existential knowledge. Yet, we immigrants often have an unrealistic expectation of ourselves, and placed upon us, that we should integrate seamlessly and painlessly into the American way of life.

It is important to keep in mind that in the present global system, migration is the norm, rather than the exception. According to Steven J. Gold and Stephanie J. Nawyn's 2019 *Routledge International Handbook of Migration Studies*, "250 million *individuals* today are said to live outside their country of origin. That number tallies to approximately one in thirty individuals living on earth."[2] If we reflect on these data for a moment, we can appreciate the force of this statement. There is much that differentiates people on the move worldwide, both socio-politically and geographically, including the ways they are welcomed in the new country. Language, for example, plays a significant role in the integration process. Terms like illegal, immigrant, migrant, and expat, both self-applied or imposed by others, also indicate class distinctions. For instance, Europeans living in New York are quick to specify they are not "immigrants" but "expats," thus claiming a different pedigree and privilege, distinct from immigrants coming from less privileged backgrounds or countries in disarray.

These linguistic distinctions reflect global hierarchies shaped by deeper forces that are frequently rooted in the historical and ongoing actions of wealthy nations and multinational corporations that drive migrants to leave their homelands in the first place. These actors have long resisted acknowledging their role in the exploitation of resource-rich countries; they often operate through political alliances with local elites that undermine possibilities for autonomous growth. The potential of these nations has not been absent—it has been systematically eroded.

Therefore, it is important that we all acknowledge that if migration today represents a global crisis—often overwhelming in scope—it also entails a shared global responsibility. If we enjoy the fruits of privilege, we must also bear the discomfort, and the moral weight, of complicity. In wealthier societies, primitive psychological defenses, such as denial, projection, and willful ignorance, often emerge when confronted with the so-called "threat" of immigrant arrivals. The blame is redirected onto immigrants themselves or their homelands, thereby obscuring the long-standing benefits that richer nations have gained through the extraction of labor, displacement, and systemic underdevelopment.

Neither Here Nor There: A Guide for Immigrants and Those Who Walk With Them is a guidebook designed for immigrants who move in search of a better life yet struggle to navigate the psychological and cultural complexities of their new environments. As a therapist, I have sat with many immigrants who found it difficult to articulate their sense of dislocation. As an immigrant myself, I understand the silence that often speaks louder than words.

This book also aims to serve as a bridge between immigrants and the therapists who accompany them. In a globalized world, even clinicians who are not explicitly trained to work with immigrant populations will, inevitably, encounter immigrants among their clients. While therapists bring effective tools to the work, these tools are not always transferable across cultural contexts. For example, Western psychology tends to emphasize individuation and personal autonomy, often overlooking the value of community, interdependence, and collective identity—elements that are central to many immigrants' lives. Without reflection, these cultural blind spots can lead to misattunement or even harm.

Throughout the book, I adopt a dialogic narrator stance. That means I speak from different positions: sometimes as a clinician, sometimes as an immigrant, sometimes addressing therapists, sometimes speaking directly to immigrants themselves, and at other times, to both. I do not conceal these shifts; instead, I mark them clearly and intentionally. This allows each reader to feel addressed and included, either directly or by witnessing the conversation unfolding across perspectives.

While immigrants are the central focus of this book, I also welcome secondary audiences: second-generation immigrants, educators, and professionals who work within immigrant communities. And although I do not offer a specialized guide for those who have fled war or persecution, many of the reflections and tools offered here may also be of value to asylees and refugees, particularly when trauma and dislocation are part of their story.

Among the different categories of immigrants, there is also common ground. Recognizing both the similarities and the differences could make immigrants a transnational force of international weight. If a common global migrant identity could take hold, we could have a stronger grassroots voice. We could establish a pact of mutual support and mentoring among diasporic people, creating powerful links between the country of origin and the host country, and lending a hand to other diasporic people beyond our national identities.

I have one deceptively simple goal for this book: to draw from my own experience—as both an immigrant and a therapist—to offer insight into the themes and tensions that often shape the immigrant journey. Addressed to immigrants and therapists alike, this book aims to foster personal and collective empowerment within the context of life in the United States. Alongside reflections, I offer practical tools to help manage the anxiety, shame, loneliness, and emotional strain that can accompany everyday life in transition.

What follows is a preliminary map of the immigrant experience, touching on the phases of premigration, transit, and postmigration adjustment. Future volumes may explore these phases in greater depth, with particular attention to the unique challenges of aging, youth, and intergenerational dynamics within immigrant families.

Neither Here Nor There: A Guide for Immigrants and Those Who Walk With Them is written for those who find themselves caught between worlds—struggling to feel at home in a new country, negotiating the pressure to adapt while attempting to hold onto what was left behind. It offers a path forward for immigrants navigating the friction of straddling two cultures, and the quiet ache of feeling out of place in both.

The book is divided into six modules. Part I: The Immigrant's Experience, which consists of Chapters 1–3, introduces the psychological and emotional terrain of migration, highlighting the profound impact of dislocation, loss, and identity shifts. Through stories, clinical reflections, and practical tools, these first three chapters offer a foundation for understanding how immigration challenges and reshapes individuals and families. Rather than viewing migration through a purely sociological or policy lens, this section focuses on the inner life of immigrants and second-generation individuals, illustrating how external transitions spark internal reckonings. It also sets the stage for the rest of the book by calling attention to the therapeutic needs and cultural knowledge necessary to support those who straddle multiple worlds. Chapter 1 maps the terrain of the immigrant journey by exploring common psychological challenges, including imposter syndrome, cultural dissonance, and acculturation stress. Through vignettes and theory, it examines how race, legal status, family history, and social pressure shape mental health and self-perception. Chapter 2 turns to the theme of loss, naming the layered griefs of migration, such as separation from loved ones, loss of language or ritual, and the invisibility of mourning in exile. It offers ways to honor these losses and to reconnect with continuity. Chapter 3 explores the feeling of being "neither here nor there," a phrase that captures the liminal space many immigrants inhabit. Using Akhtar's five coping strategies and a therapeutic lens, it provides reflections on identity fragmentation, intergenerational tensions, and the possibility of growth through integration. Together, these chapters frame migration as both an external journey and an internal process—one marked by rupture and resilience, and worthy of nuanced, culturally attuned care.

Part II: Integrating and Adapting explores the psychological and cultural work involved in adapting to a new society. As immigrants navigate unfamiliar norms and expectations, they encounter shifting values, altered family roles, and new definitions of success. This section explores aspects underlying the surface of apparent integration, revealing the internal negotiations required to find balance between cultural inheritance and adaptation. Through case examples, reflection prompts, and clinical insights, the chapters in this section frame adaptation not as a simple act of assimilation, but as an ongoing, multidimensional process involving identity, time, and stress management. Chapter 4 introduces the *immigrant paradox*, a pattern in which some first-generation immigrant groups show better health outcomes than their native-born or second-generation peers. The chapter explores how structural racism, cultural loss, and internalized expectations erode these initial strengths over time. The chapter urges both therapists and immigrants to recognize resilience without ignoring the mental health risks that often accompany the experience of immigration. Chapter 5 uses the metaphor of a broken gear box to describe the disorientation immigrants may feel as they adjust to new models of time, productivity, and emotional expression. It examines how perfectionism, guilt, and confusion may arise—not from personal deficits but from cultural mismatch. Chapter 6 focuses on the daily and cumulative stressors that can overwhelm immigrants, including paperwork, financial insecurity, and caregiving burdens. It reframes these challenges as systemic and relational rather than individual, offering tools for setting boundaries, managing demands, and cultivating resilience. Together, these chapters underscore the idea that adaptation is not linear: it requires compassion, flexibility, and support from both within and outside the immigrant community, including therapists who can meet clients with humility and insight.

Part III: Finding Your Voice, consisting of Chapters 7–10, focuses on the often-overlooked task of reclaiming voice and agency in the wake of migration. As immigrants navigate cultural dissonance, shifting norms, and internalized expectations, communication becomes more than language use; it becomes a site of identity negotiation, emotional survival, and self-expression. This section explores how internalized "shoulds," intergenerational tensions, and linguistic dynamics can lead to silence, fragmentation, or misunderstanding. It offers pathways toward reasserting one's voice, both literally and metaphorically, while honoring complexity and difference. Chapter 7 begins this section, exploring how immigrants internalize conflicting cultural voices and expectations, which can often result in inner conflict and a drive for perfection. The chapter provides tools to identify, challenge, and reintegrate these voices into a more coherent and self-directed narrative. Then, Chapter 8 investigates the emotional tug-of-war between obligation and longing, which is particularly salient across generations and cultural value systems. Through personal reflection and therapeutic guidance, it encourages readers to find a "third space" between inherited duties and authentic desire. Chapter 9 proceeds with these themes by delving into the emotional and identity-based dimensions of language, revealing how different tongues hold different aspects of the self. It highlights the psychological effects of language loss, code-switching, and interpretation, offering both immigrants and clinicians new ways to listen for meaning underlying words. Chapter 10 extends this inquiry into cross-cultural communication, unpacking how tone, non-verbal cues, and social dynamics shape understanding. It offers practical tools to help both immigrants and therapists engage more consciously and respectfully across cultural divides. Together, these chapters affirm that voice is not merely about fluency, but about power, belonging, and recognition. Reclaiming it is an essential step toward integration, relationship, and healing.

Part IV: Teasing Out Feelings and Connecting Body and Mind, consisting of Chapters 11–15, invites readers to slow down and listen—to their emotions, their bodies, and the often-silenced parts of themselves that migration has taught them to hide. The immigrant journey often requires emotional suppression, a survival-based strategy that leads one to disconnect from feeling, authentic self-expression, and physical presence. This section addresses the emotional cost of disconnection and offers ways to gently reintegrate what has been compartmentalized or neglected. Chapter 11 explores how pushing aside your emotions is done through numbing or mislabeling distress under the weight of cultural and systemic pressures. The chapter offers tools for identifying and integrating emotions through somatic awareness, cognitive techniques, and self-compassion. Chapter 12 traces the complexities of guilt and regret across cultural and intergenerational lines, particularly around family, loyalty, and success, and reframes these emotions as opportunities for growth and relational repair when engaged consciously. Chapter 13 turns to shame and imposter syndrome, showing how they often operate invisibly within immigrant narratives. The chapter offers therapeutic tools to support identity repair and encourages clinicians to examine their own cultural countertransference. Chapter 14 reframes anger from being viewed as a character defect to being recognized as an adaptive signal. It provides strategies for recognizing, regulating, and transforming anger into a constructive, boundary-setting force, especially in contexts where it has been punished or misunderstood. Finally, Chapter 15 focuses on the body as both a site of trauma and healing. It examines how stress and historical wounds are stored somatically and introduces embodied practices for reconnection, rest, and transformation. Together, these chapters encourage both immigrants and therapists to recognize the intelligence of emotional and physical responses and to move from mere survival toward embodied healing and wholeness.

Part V: Exploring Your Unconscious includes Chapters 16 and 17 and guides readers into the symbolic, imaginal, and sensory dimensions of healing that often lie beyond words. It reveals ways that immigrants, whose experiences may be fragmented by trauma, language loss, or cultural displacement, benefit from therapeutic tools that engage one's creativity, one's body, and one's unconscious. Each of these chapters offer immigrants and therapists accessible ways to tap into deep internal landscapes, using metaphor, imagery, and multisensory practices to process emotion, reclaim agency, and restore coherence. The chapters show how healing does not rely on language or logic alone but can emerge through metaphor, sensation, and imagination where memory is fluid, and meaning can be reshaped. Chapter 16 introduces symbol-based healing through anthropological reflection and therapeutic vignettes. It shows how clients can transform emotional burdens through imagination, movement, and play. Readers meet Barbie, Charlie, and Dada, who use metaphor and guided imagery to reclaim their strength, identity, and purpose. Chapter 17 focuses on dreams as portals to hidden fears, longings, and insights. It provides interpretive guidance and therapeutic exercises while respecting cultural variations in dream meaning. A group practice called the Dream Circle illustrates how dream work can become a communal and culturally grounded tool for reflection and healing. Chapter 18 offers a diverse set of awareness-based exercises, including visual art, sound, food, and tactile lifelines, to help readers integrate emotion and identity across time, cultures, and generations. Each activity is trauma-informed and adaptable to therapy or self-guided exploration. Therapist reflections underscore the need for flexibility, humility, and embodied presence when working across linguistic or cultural boundaries. Part V reminds us that the unconscious, when approached with respect and creativity, holds not only our pain, but also the seeds of our renewal.

Part VI: Reframing and Organizing includes Chapters 19–23, bringing the book to a close by offering cognitive, behavioral, and planning-based tools that help immigrants and therapists transform insights into sustained, purposeful action. These chapters center on agency, reframing, and structure, not as rigid formulas, but as culturally adaptable strategies that honor both emotion and intention. Whether grappling with negative self-talk, anxiety, procrastination, or ambivalence, readers are offered frameworks to untangle thought patterns and build a future rooted in clarity and cultural continuity. Chapter 19 introduces core principles of culturally responsive cognitive behavioral therapy (CBT), showing how distorted beliefs, which are shaped by past trauma, acculturation stress, and internalized bias, can lead to fear, isolation, and self-sabotage. Through accessible tools and metaphors, therapists and immigrant clients alike are invited to garden their minds with care, rooting out unhelpful beliefs with strategic kindness. Chapter 20 expands on CBT, providing a comprehensive, culturally aware framework: the Nine-Lens Reflective Tool. Through Emi's story, readers learn to trace distressing thoughts across dimensions of body, belief, history, and context, emerging with a personalized action plan that bridges insight with behavior. Chapter 21 offers a toolkit of creative CBT strategies, such as the Folded Page and Worry Container, designed for moments of emotional overload, ambivalence, or uncertainty. These tools help readers counter the automatic pull to catastrophize and reclaim a sense of grounding, so they can navigate inner conflict with both compassion and cultural relevance. Then, Chapter 22 takes up organization as an act of self-authorship. Using planning techniques like the ABC method and calendar mapping, and through the case of Angelo, it highlights how procrastination and disorganization often conceal deeper emotional or cultural struggles and how small steps toward order can unlock energy and clarity. Chapter 23, the final chapter in the book, weaves all these threads together. It guides readers through the psychological and symbolic process of integrating identity, vision, and commitment. The story of Andrei offers a fitting example. The chapter illustrates how engaging in creative planning, emotional integration, and community supports the capacity to take resilient action in uncertain terrain. The chapter closes with an invitation to walk deliberately, if even imperfectly, toward what lies ahead. Together, these chapters affirm that healing is not only an internal process; it is embodied in habits, goals, and the courage to move forward. Part VI offers structure: not as constraint, but as a flexible vessel—capable of holding uncertainty, story, and transformation.

The contents of these chapters echo the conversations I often have with my patients. They are indelible stories—traces of wisdom that linger, like guideposts on a highway, hopefully offering a sense of where you are.

The language, tools, and practices shared throughout these chapters are drawn from years of clinical work, supervision, teaching, readings, and, most importantly, dialogue with fellow therapists, friends, and patients. They also reflect insights from a global survey I conducted, which gathered voices from across borders and backgrounds. While I have introduced a few techniques here (and therapist readers will agree with me), the majority are drawn from techniques that are available in the field and are increasingly becoming general knowledge. They are evidence-based techniques informed by models incorporating mindfulness and meditation. As therapists, we are not inventors or revolutionaries. We work with the received body of knowledge, tailoring it to meet the needs of our patients, which sometimes leads to something genuinely new—not merely a repackaging, but an original contribution. I believe that everyone holding this book will find these techniques to be accessible and actionable. I would be thrilled if therapists wrote to me to share what works best for their immigrant populations and what kinds of take-home exercises and reflection pieces they offer.

Beyond the concrete tools like CBT and mindfulness, the stories themselves offer therapeutic power. While this book doesn't provide therapy or a high-brow academic or clinical perspective tailored to specialists, it contains stories and story fragments that are fundamental to my experience and will likely resonate with you, the reader. We often live distracted lives, unaware of how our emotions are shaped by personal history and broader cultural dynamics. As a result, we can feel isolated—alone in our lives and with our stories. In therapy, we begin to share and reexamine those stories. Whether you are telling your own or listening to another's, something profound happens when a story is spoken aloud—often again and again, until its edges begin to soften and shift. Sometimes, we also retell stories we have heard, from others, from films, or from dreams, because they carry something we need to process. Whether we are living the story or bearing witness to it, something essential is at work. Gradually, we begin to link feelings and thoughts, connect the disjointed pieces of history, and gain insight. Over time, the meaning of our experiences becomes clearer. In therapy, we often repeat our stories until we find an "exit to the highway," so to speak.

The voices we hear in this book form a kind of chorus, enriching the dialogic structure of the text. If you are an immigrant, you may recognize elements of your own experience in these stories. If you are a therapist, these stories may help you attune more closely to the emotional landscapes your patients inhabit. Recognizing yourself in these stories, whether as an immigrant or as someone accompanying one, may offer an opportunity for deeper reflection. I believe these narratives can resonate in a healing way—with those who live them and those who bear witness to them.

They resonate with me as an immigrant, and with my patients, who often present similar stories no matter where they are from. The stories connect readers to their immigrant experiences, even to the parts they may not have fully processed or considered. Readers may feel less alone because of this shared chorus of stories, and more integrated in their experience of living between "here" and "there." For example, Jo's story (in *Feeling Guilt*, Chapter 2) illustrates this point. When she opened a box containing mementos and fragments of her story in the new country, she was deeply moved, even to the point of vertigo. All those stories flooded her mind; but she was also able to connect with her immigrant experience in a profound way, realizing how time and space can feel fragmented for someone living between two worlds. She was able to experience how much time had passed in those two worlds. She was able to acknowledge feelings she had previously not been able to express so clearly. The integration of her stories into a coherent whole was fostered by her telling and retelling, linking all the stories together.

Maritere,[3] an immigrant and a patient of mine, made the following comment about how psychotherapy helped her manage her emotions and relationship:

> In many ways, I am becoming "American," like in the way I deal with anger. I used to fight all the time around the table, or debate, whatever you want to call it. Now I get to a point that I can say: "let's continue the conversation another time." And I learned this here, but it's also helping me when I go back home. For me, having these frames of reference, these schemas on how to think and how to talk is very useful. Because I know there is a problem, I keep on getting into trouble with people, but I don't know where to go with it. These schemas give me a way to order things and a possible outline. People get upset with me but do not tell me how to act differently. My parents were no different. They would get upset and lash out, but did not take me aside to tell me calmly: "Listen, I need you to do this and that." I feel I came a long way. Just the other day at work I was so angry, and I was right. But then I remember the structure on how to give feedback. I prepared myself with that in mind, and when I spoke, it was well received. The following week my boss called me in for counsel, asking me how I would tackle a difficult issue. That gives me a lot of satisfaction. It may be that these schemas are made for Americans in mind. But I do not think of it as a colonization of the mind. Whatever can help me not to get so angry and have better relationships at home and outside is welcomed, even if it's made in China!

Maritere's comment about finding these tools welcome wherever they come from underscores an important point. While this book is sourced from and designed for people from different walks of life, it also emerges from a psychotherapy perspective—which is largely a Western endeavor. It must be recognized that therapeutic tools developed in Western contexts do not always align with the values, communication styles, or lived realities of immigrant communities. This tension can be apparent in conversations outside the therapy room as well. When discussing this book project with some of my seemingly well-adjusted immigrant acquaintances, they squirmed, as if I had introduced a forbidden topic. Their attitude changed, however, once I removed my therapist/writer's hat and admitted that I too have experienced problems with adjustment. Then, with relief, they laughed and said, "I could write this book!"

While the ideas presented in this book may not be entirely novel, they are uniquely assembled here with the specific purpose of helping immigrant populations navigate and make sense of their experiences and build a bridge with their therapists. I humbly believe this book makes a valuable contribution.

The Research for This Book

The examples and vignettes presented throughout *Neither Here Nor There: A Guide for Immigrants and Those Who Walk With Them* are composites that have been created from actual patient experiences. Names and identifying elements have been altered to honor privacy and preserve anonymity.

In addition to collecting my patients' observations and experiences as immigrants, I conducted surveys with immigrants globally and interviewed colleagues. Of the 117 participants, more than 90% either immigrated themselves or were the children of immigrants to the United States. The second most common country participants immigrated to was Canada. Some responses are also from United States citizens who relocated abroad.

The individuals sharing personal narratives, reflections, and survey responses have been given pseudonyms to protect their anonymity. No real names or identifying details have been used. In cases where written consent to publish direct quotations was not obtained, original statements have been paraphrased, summarized, or reconstructed from memory and field notes. In some instances, narratives represent composite or fictionalized voices informed by recurring themes across multiple individuals. When included, regional or country identifiers serve only to provide cultural context and are not intended to reveal identity. All materials have been handled with professional discretion and in accordance with established ethical standards. The goal is to honor lived experience while prioritizing the safety and dignity of those whose stories have informed this work.

Among the respondents of my survey, more than 85% of them are first generation, 75% of whom consider themselves financially stable or affluent, with at least a bachelor's degree. They came to the United States mainly to seek professional development and expand their social and cultural opportunities. 60% of respondents identified as married or in long-term relationships; 46% said their life had improved with immigration. Very few respondents were in dire straits. Because this survey does not lend itself to the participation of poor and/or undocumented immigrants who may be suspicious of online data collection, and/or who may not be able to offer 20 to 30 minutes of their time, this survey is composed of responses from immigrants who were privileged at the time of the survey. But it is important to note that even at an upper level of financial comfort, the respondents acknowledged a high level of stress connected with immigration.

When asked what kinds of tools would help immigrants with their specific difficulties, survey participants underscored the need for tools that would foster emotional and practical coping, assertiveness, and adaptation. The following summarizes their integration and cultural tools.

Integration and Cultural Tools

- 74% of respondents indicated that immigrants would benefit from learning about cultural differences and how to communicate with people of different cultures to minimize misunderstanding and adjust expectations.
- 62% indicated that immigrants would benefit from having better opportunities to learn the language of the host country.

Psychological Tools

- 54% of respondents indicated that immigrants would benefit from tools that would help them increase self-confidence.
- 54% indicated that immigrants would benefit from learning strategies to protect oneself, stand up for oneself, and become more assertive.

Practical Support

- 51% of respondents indicated immigrants would benefit from practical support, such as learning how to manage money, debt, and credit cards and having better access to legal support for immigration issues.

Stress Management

- 47% of respondents indicated that immigrants would benefit from learning skills that would help them relax, manage stress, and get organized.

While this survey reflects the perspectives of mostly financially stable, educated immigrants, their expressed needs echo themes I have repeatedly observed in my clinical work with a much broader population, including those facing economic hardship, undocumented status, and limited access to care. The stressors named in the survey—language challenges, cultural navigation, emotional strain, and the need for assertiveness and coping tools—are not exclusive to the privileged. Rather, they are universal struggles within the immigrant experience, which are often compounded for those with fewer resources. Including these results helps anchor the book in the lived concerns of real people, while amplifying the broader relevance of the strategies offered here.

A Message to You

The intention of *Neither Here Nor There: A Guide for Immigrants and Those Who Walk With Them* is to help immigrants who struggle to maintain a connection between their country of origin and their adopted country and who grapple with how to manage a sense of loss and displacement; it is intended to help you navigate the complexities of integration, double belonging, and hybridity.

Immigrants often face profound and ongoing social inequalities. *Neither Here Nor There: A Guide for Immigrants and Those Who Walk With Them* can name those forces, but it cannot dismantle them. Still, naming matters. Despite widespread conversations about human rights, intersectionality, and social justice, pain often turns inward. Many people, especially when vulnerable, internalize harmful social narratives. They may blame themselves for their struggles, believing that their stress, failures, or exhaustion are signs of laziness, inadequacy, or personal defects, rather than recognizing the larger systems at play.

Psychology itself has often contributed to this dynamic. Many therapeutic approaches prioritize the intrapsychic world—the individual's internal thoughts, emotions, and past—while treating the external world as background noise rather than a central part of the picture. The social, cultural, and political dimensions of suffering are too often minimized, leaving individuals to carry what should be collective burdens.

It is essential to understand that the challenges you face may not originate solely within you. Yes, some difficulties are genetic, psychological, or rooted in personal or family history. However, others are systemic, historical, and social. These external forces often produce internal effects that undermine wellbeing, self-worth, and even physical health. On the other hand, some may tend to avoid personal accountability by attributing every hardship to external causes. It is important to recognize the role of personal agency in healing while being realistic when assessing the effects of broader systems.

This book invites you to reduce stress, improve focus and organization, and strengthen your mental and physical health. Keep doing your best, but do not carry everything alone. Seek rest without guilt. Be strategic, not reactive. Unashamedly ask for support, mentorship, and the presence of kind people. Become your own advocate and inner ally. And be realistic about what is humanly possible under your current circumstances.

This book should be used as a resource and a starting point for readers to decide for themselves which ideas and tools are most useful to them or their patients. As an immigrant reader, you decide which concepts to embrace and how you want to integrate them with your cultural perspective and healing practices, including your religion and spirituality. Use it to complement the healing practices you bring from home. Use the parts of this book that intuitively make sense to you. This book is for anyone who feels somehow "neither here nor there." It's the book I wish I'd had when I first came to the US 30 years ago.

If you are a therapist reading this, I hope these reflections will support your work and serve as a reminder that the world outside the consulting room is not separate from the patient's distress but deeply entangled with it. Our therapeutic relationships are also shaped by intersectionality, privilege, and often-unspoken power dynamics. We may forget this, especially when guided by genuine care and the desire to help. Yet our position as helpers can carry an authority that risks silencing, intimidating, or invalidating our patients, especially when left unexamined. Unless we address these dynamics consciously, they may become a harmful undercurrent in the room.

I hope you find comfort, clarity, and strength in these pages. I would be honored to hear your thoughts. You can write to me at immigrants@leideporcu.com.

Notes

1 Jeanne Batalova, Mary Hanna, and Christopher Levesque, "Frequently Requested Statistics on Immigrants and Immigration in the United States," *Migration Information Source*, February 11, 2021, www.migrationpolicy.org/article/frequently-requested-statistics-immigrants-and-immigration-united-states-2020.
2 Steven J. Gold and Stephanie J. Nawyn, *Routledge International Handbook of Migration Studies*, 2nd ed. (New York: Routledge, 2019), 2.
3 All patients who appear in this book have been given pseudonyms to protect their anonymity.

References

Batalova, Jeanne, Mary Hanna, and Christopher Levesque. 2021. "Frequently Requested Statistics on Immigrants and Immigration in the United States." *Migration Information Source*, February 11. www.migrationpolicy.org/article/frequently-requested-statistics-immigrants-and-immigration-united-states-2020.
Gold, Steven J., and Stephanie J. Nawyn, eds. 2019. *Routledge International Handbook of Migration Studies*. 2nd ed. New York: Routledge.

Part I
The Immigrant's Experience

1 The Challenges of Immigration

High school was tough. I stood out in ways I could not change, and sometimes teachers made comments that embarrassed me in front of everyone. I would shrink inside, and other times I was angry—really angry. Things began to change when we moved to New York. It was the first time I felt less alone. In a city where people come from everywhere, I could finally choose who to be around. Joining a local dance group helped me feel part of something.

—Anonymous contributor

Four Immigrant Stories: Four Forms of Dislocation

Maria is a second-generation immigrant whose parents emigrated from Mexico. They are smart and humble people who have worked hard in blue-collar jobs to build a life for their family. Maria is now a college graduate and a successful businesswoman—a trailblazer in her family. Yet, not having had familial reference points for navigating either academia or the professional world contributes to chronic self-doubt. Her unease intensifies when faced with routine changes or unfamiliar challenges, such as expanding her business, a venture she is just beginning. Although her results are consistently strong, Maria struggles to internalize her accomplishments. She lives with a persistent fear of being found out as an "impostor," convinced her success is a fragile illusion. This internalized insecurity, shaped by both her family history and societal expectations, keeps her from seeking the recognition she deserves. Despite her upward mobility, Maria's psychological positioning remains constrained by the unspoken ceiling of her upbringing.

Biba, a 1.5-generation (that is, someone who immigrated during childhood or adolescence) Latina woman with DACA status, is juggling a full-time job and full-time studies. Her parents never had the chance to attend college, and her current achievements, while significant, are accompanied by exhaustion and financial stress. Biba's economic precarity is acute: Without a master's degree, she cannot access the salary bump she needs. She adopts a more assimilated version of herself at work, where she suppresses aspects of her identity in order to "fit in," but she reclaims her cultural self in private, where she feels safe. This tension between survival and authenticity is a

DOI: 10.4324/9781003648703-3

daily negotiation. Her story highlights the complex intersection of immigration status, socioeconomic pressure, cultural identity, and the emotional cost of striving within systems that were never built with her in mind.

Julie is a French woman who recently began a graduate program at an Ivy League university and is overwhelmed by her weekly assignments. She is expected to read several books, write papers, and contribute to class discussions, all in English. The competitive, non-collegial environment leaves her feeling incompetent, lonely, and sad, leading to frequent tears. Overwhelmed by the pressure to meet deadlines, she grows increasingly depressed and anxious. She has difficulty sleeping and is falling behind in her work.

Mario is a middle-aged, first-generation immigrant who emigrated from Italy many decades ago. Although financially stable and fluent in English, he has never felt truly at home in the United States. He speaks of Italy with nostalgia and yearning, but when he visits, he is met with indifference or mild condescension; locals see him not as one of their own, but as an American pretending to be Italian. Neither place offers full belonging. This fractured sense of home also complicates his romantic life. He finds it difficult to connect with American women, whose assumptions and lifestyles often clash with his sensibilities. At the same time, he does not feel aligned with Italian Americans, whose cultural reference points differ from his own. Mario's identity floats between fixed categories, shaped by emotional exile more than by economic hardship. His case underscores that social positioning is not only a matter of class or language, but also of emotional and existential dislocation.

The Weight of Positioning: Family, Class, and Identity

These four individuals occupy markedly different social positions that shape their inner lives and external possibilities. Maria and Biba are both Latinas whose families immigrated with limited resources, but Maria's second-generation status and business ownership provide her with relative stability, though not without psychological cost. Biba still struggles to finish college while working fulltime under DACA status; she faces economic, legal, and emotional precarity that renders advancement not only difficult but elusive.

Julie, although privileged in terms of class and education, finds herself culturally marginalized in an Ivy League environment that offers less than adequate support to meet the needs of international students. Her case highlights that elite status does not always protect against emotional distress or cultural exclusion. Mario, by contrast, has financial security and citizenship but remains emotionally displaced, caught between two cultures neither of which fully claim him. His story reveals that even legal and economic stability does not guarantee belonging.

What these four cases show is that social positioning is more than having class or credentials—it is about access to emotional resources, cultural capital, legal protections, and the felt sense of home. When therapists understand these intersecting factors, they can better address the hidden labor of adapting to a new culture and the emotional toll of navigating multiple, often conflicting, worlds.

While factors, such as socioeconomic status, education, and familial influences, do not fully determine a person's potential for successful adaptation, they have an important impact on their experiences. Immigrants face the challenge of navigating these external forces, and to do so, they must draw on internal resilience. Emotional and cognitive dispositions play a key role in their ability to form meaningful connections and integrate into their new environments. Those who can build strong relationships and create networks are often better equipped to handle the emotional strain of navigating two worlds.

Ultimately, social positioning, shaped by one's relationships and personal dispositions, has a strong influence on emotions, self-perception, and sense of belonging. The hope for acceptance, both by one's immigrant community and the broader society, is crucial for developing active agency in the world. For each of these individuals, finding that balance between two worlds requires more than just external adaptation; it involves an internal reconciliation of their identity, emotions, and aspirations.

You Are Not Alone

I feel more in sync with any immigrant, no matter where they come from, than with any White American. There is something that brings us into common ground in the diaspora.

—Ellie, an Italian patient

Othering, Projection, and the Psychology of Exclusion

The feeling of being different and not belonging is often intensified by subtle and overt acts of exclusion. Immigrants, depending on the stage of immigration, personal circumstances, social context, and age, can often find themselves ostracized and *othered*. In response, they may distance themselves from the local population as a form of self-protection. At times, immigrants may also "other" local residents or fellow immigrant groups, projecting negative traits onto them; this is a phenomenon known as *projection* in psychoanalysis. It's not uncommon for in-groups to highlight internal similarities while attributing negative qualities to outsiders. As an immigrant, you may be perceived as a threat to the values, beliefs, practices, or economic opportunities of the local community, leading to your feeling isolated. While bonding with fellow immigrants can be comforting, doing so by othering locals is counterproductive. The act of othering, whether experienced or inflicted, benefits no one. Closing ourselves off from local residents deprives us of the potential for positive connections. Instead, remaining curious and open to relationships with kind and welcoming people from all backgrounds can enrich our experience.

It is also important to keep in mind that the challenges immigrants face are common—regardless of an individual's intelligence, financial achievement, or educational success. However, too often, we interpret these struggles as personal shortcomings rather than recognizing them as the result of complex historical, economic, and social dynamics, many of which lie beyond an individual's control. This misinterpretation may lead us to spiral into negativity, shame, and self-doubt that can impair our lives and careers, making us overly self-critical and unkind to ourselves.

These patterns are complex but not unchangeable. Therapeutic tools, including cognitive-behavioral strategies, can help interrupt negative spirals of thought and restore a more balanced view. For therapists, recognizing these dynamics, such as projection, othering, internalized blame, is essential when supporting immigrants through the layered process of integration.

Letting Go of the Need to Be Exceptional: When "Good Enough" Is Enough

One client, Masa, a 32-year-old man from Japan, came to therapy exhausted from overworking and plagued by self-doubt. Despite receiving consistent praise at his tech job, he feared that any mistake would expose him as a fraud. "If I am not exceptional, I am failing," he often said. We identified this as all-or-nothing thinking and began testing small shifts, like submitting work with fewer revisions. When the work was well received, Masa began to question his assumptions. Over time, he adopted more balanced thoughts like, "Good enough is still good," and "I can grow without being perfect." This reframing helped him take more risks and build stronger connections both professionally and socially, while reducing his anxiety.

As people who have left their home country in pursuit of safety, dignity, or opportunity, and have managed to make a life elsewhere, immigrants tend to be strong-willed individuals. As trailblazers, either the first in their family to leave in hopes of improving circumstances, or, in the case of second-generation immigrants, the children of those who did, we are often expected to fulfill the promise of upward mobility.

Yet even when this advancement is achieved through hard work, a sense of legitimacy often remains elusive. Without a lineage of professional status or a history of belonging in the new context, many immigrants lack what sociologists call *status legitimation*. As the first in a family to graduate from college, hold a professional job, or move in spaces unfamiliar to previous generations, there may be no legacy of success to look to for assurance—no beaten path to follow.[1] This can generate the feeling of being an undeserving fraud, someone who is not entitled to their newly achieved status.

The Silent Struggles of First and Second Generations

Many first- and second-generation immigrants share the following experiences

- You find yourself in a new country, unfamiliar with its systems and societal norms.
- You attempt to chart a path forward, but the road ahead is convoluted, full of choices, with no clear direction.
- You lack direct role models to guide you through this terrain.
- Your career, education, or social class differs markedly from that of your parents.
- You no longer have the certainties or pre-established paths that shaped previous generations.
- You experience fear and feelings of incompetence.
- Self-doubt plagues you.
- Even when opportunities arise, the sheer magnitude of work required leaves you overwhelmed and exhausted.
- Even when praised, recognized, or promoted, part of you feels undeserving—as if you are an imposter, waiting to be exposed and sent back to where you came from.
- You carry guilt for not doing more for the loved ones you left behind—or for not supporting others from your community who are struggling.
- You worry about fulfilling the cultural expectations placed on you by your country of origin—sometimes at the expense of your own wellbeing.
- You become acutely aware of the privileges you left behind by emigrating.
- You feel like a guest or a stranger in your homeland, sensing that old friends now see you as somewhat foreign.
- You experience a deep and persistent sense of nostalgia.
- As a child of immigrants, you may feel shame for not knowing your family's language or customs and simultaneously feel frustrated or embarrassed regarding your parents' behavior or attitudes.
- Having built a life in your new country, you may struggle to maintain a relationship with a partner who has different cultural expectations.
- If you immigrated with a partner from your home country, you may feel disillusioned—either because they have changed and become more "Americanized," or because they have not changed at all, creating a widening disconnect.
- With respect to your children, you may feel the growing tug-of-war between cultural traditions (e.g., Italian, Irish, Korean, American), often leading to conflict with the people you love most.
- As a first- or second-generation immigrant who has somewhat integrated, you may feel uncomfortable or even distressed when coworkers make stereotypical or disparaging remarks about people from your country of origin.

Despite its length, this list is incomplete. And although it looks like a lot to contend with, remember that you are not alone; these situations and feelings are part of the process for people who leave the familiar for the unknown and who take risks to seek positive change. They are part of the experience of people who live in between cultures and who, as partial outsiders, can question more objectively their culture's mandates and choose another life.

At a conference held at the Italian Consulate in the Spring of 2024, a young Italian man attending an Ivy League university took the microphone during the Q&A and shared his feelings about pining for his village in Southern Italy, despite the tremendous opportunity he was given in the United States. He asked the speakers what he should do with his emotional burden. The speakers, a panel of distinguished Italian immigrants committed to giving back to their native southern Italy, were quick to reassure him that the feelings he was experiencing were normal, temporary, and would ease over time. However, the truth is, the trajectories of these feelings of longing are complex and not univocal.

The cultural contexts within the United States shape our experiences in important ways, often disrupting our sense of connection, identity, and continuity. In my psychotherapy practice, I often encounter stressful or painful situations that are not the result of a patient's individual short-comings but are due to broader social, cultural, and material conditions. Race, ethnicity, age, ability, and gender are especially salient and often compounding factors in the US. They can influence the degree to which immigrants access opportunities, adjust to the culture, and feel a sense of belonging. When I remind people who have immigrated to a new country how hard it can be to live as an immigrant, they feel a sense of profound relief. Their pain can be understood and put into context.

The dilemma of the young Italian student attending an Ivy League university who longed to return home speaks to a broader challenge many male immigrants face—how to acknowledge and navigate emotional struggles in cultures where notions of masculinity discourage vulnerability and same-gender connection. In many places around the world, men are told throughout their lives to pull themselves up by their bootstraps and hide their emotions. Heterosexual men are also less likely to maintain deep emotional connections with other men, often leaving them isolated in their struggles. I often recommend that these men join an amateur sports team or spend time at a sports bar, if possible. These are some of the few socially accepted settings where heterosexual men can form comfortable connections with other men.

The sense of longing, which in young males may be complicated by the inability to find intimate male companionship, is not limited to the young. Feeling fulfilled and wanting to stay in the host country, or desiring to go back, is a common concern that is filled with ambivalence. Over time, the question of return can become more pressing, especially as people age and their circumstances shift. Not all immigrants can realistically plan a return, while others cannot sensibly commit to staying. As Salman Akhtar discusses in *Immigration and Acculturation*, middle and old age—a phase that is challenging for anyone—is particularly difficult for immigrants.[2]

In their later years, individuals become more vulnerable, facing an increased number of losses. They not only lose loved ones and a deep sense of place but also fragments of their power and identity, such as their professional identities. Having experienced numerous losses and disconnections, immigrants often find it challenging to maintain a healthy balance of connection and separation in their new country. For elderly immigrants, this struggle is even more difficult compared to those who have not emigrated. The act of giving back to their home country, when possible, can help older immigrants feel more relevant while alleviating lingering feelings of guilt and regret about leaving. Building this bridge between the two countries not only eases feelings of personal vulnerability but also fosters a deeper sense of integration.

The undocumented elderly face even greater risks than other older immigrant populations, as their lives have often been marked by exploitation and insecurity. In her book *Undocumented Americans*, Karla Cornejo Víllavícencío interviews undocumented individuals, including the elderly.[3] Víllavícencío captures this reality when she states: "This country takes their youth, their dreams, their labor, and spits them out with nothing to show for it."[4] Notably, she highlights in her reports on disasters like Hurricane Sandy, Ground Zero, and the Flint water crisis that undocumented immigrants are often the first to step forward for dangerous cleanup work. They do so for little pay, with no protections or insurance. As they age, these individuals not only lose their physical strength and labor power but also face the biases associated with old age. Lacking financial security and a robust social safety net, they are often left in poor health due to years of overwork without adequate protection.

The United Nation's *Universal Declaration of Human Rights*,[5] which has been ratified by the United States, upholds the principle that migrant workers should receive the same wages as citizens. However, this is not always done in practice. According to Saverio Lo Monaco, an immigration lawyer based in New York, undocumented workers pay contributions to Social Security, but they do not receive a pension or other benefits at the end of their working life. They are not issued a regular Social Security Number but an ID number that allows them to lawfully contribute to the US coffers while barring them from receiving benefits. It's not only hardworking and contributing undocumented immigrants who face financial loss; workers with temporary visas often do not receive benefits either. Temporary visa holders are required to contribute to Social Security, yet many do not qualify for benefits because eligibility requires accumulating a total of 40 credits. Since one can earn a maximum of four credits per year, a worker must be employed in the United States for a minimum of ten years to claim benefits. Therefore, individuals working under a three-year H1B visa, for example, won't receive benefits unless they can renew their visa and remain in the country for at least ten years. In summary, the money deducted from undocumented immigrants and temporary visa holders for Social Security benefits will not be returned to them at the end of their working life and will remain in U.S. government coffers. This practice may sound like a scam, but that's truly how the system works.[6] This structural betrayal compounds the emotional strain of migration.

Víllavícencío's older immigrant interviewees spoke of wanting to go back to their original country in old age. Life there is more affordable, allowing them to continue working in a more relaxed manner while also feeling more welcomed. If they cannot return in time, often the family collects enough money to have the body transported to the country of origin for burial, honoring the wishes of the deceased.

Not All Long to Return: Ambivalence and Adaptation

While many immigrants long for a return to their homeland, either in old age or after experiencing isolation in their host country, not all share the same sentiment. In the *Immigrant's Journey* survey that I conducted worldwide, respondents were generally optimistic about their immigration experiences. Although most indicated that the beginning of their journey was difficult, they also noted the long-term rewards. Many appreciated the U.S. meritocracy, which allowed them to pursue careers that would have been unattainable in their less developed or more structurally rigid countries of origin. For many LGBTQ+ individuals and women, safety, freedom of expression, and equality, although still imperfect, were more accessible in the United States than in their homelands.

In addition, respondents often spoke of the joy of reuniting with family during holidays and the renewed appreciation for their heritage. They also took pride in reflecting on their struggles and feeling a deep connection with the families they had built, finding unity in their shared experience of navigating a foreign world. It is important to note, however, that in the *Immigrant's Journey* survey, the elderly and undocumented were underrepresented. The respondents tended to be relatively privileged, often well-educated, and in the early or middle stages of their careers.

As these perspectives reveal, although immigrants share many common experiences, there is no single immigrant experience. People emigrate for different reasons and receive varying levels of welcome in their new country. Moreover, even for the same individual, perceptions of life before and after migration, as well as feelings of allegiance to the old and new countries, can evolve over time.

If you are a therapist reading this, you may recognize that many of these experiences lie close to the surface of what brings immigrants into your practice. They may not be named explicitly, but they shape how your patients show up—how they speak, trust, cope, strive, and sometimes, withdraw. These dynamics are not merely personal; they are embedded in history, social structures, and the push-pull of belonging and exclusion. Recognizing these undercurrents allows for more attuned, culturally sensitive work. Even widely used tools like CBT become more effective when applied with an understanding of the invisible burdens many immigrants carry— burdens that may look like anxiety or depression but are rooted in layered histories of dislocation, aspiration, and identity tension.

The Phases of Immigration

> In the beginning, it was hard to find my footing. I struggled not just with the language, but with the unspoken rules of how people connect and compete in this new place. Applying for jobs felt overwhelming, and once I started work- ing, I often felt like I was a few steps behind. Still, I kept going. I made mis- takes, got discouraged, and cried more than I ever had before—but I always came back the next day, ready to try again.
>
> —Anonymous contributor

Mapping the Journey: Sunnen's Four Phases of Immigration

According to the French psychiatrist and hypnotist Gerard Sunnen,[7] who immigrated with his family from France to New Jersey as a child, there are four phases of immigration:

- Anticipatory anxiety and plain fear, particularly before leaving one's home country:
- I am going to do great things: a phase marked by creativity and the flow of adrenaline. The *creativity and adrenaline* phase is an emotional roller coaster, with moments of hope and enthusiasm, and moments in which one feels incapable and ill-equipped.
- Loss and realization of loss: After the initial enthusiasm, the loss of the home country sets in.
- Adaptation to life in the new country: This phase involves intense inter- nal work, both during the day and at night, when the dreaming mind struggles to solve problems and adjust.

Amir, Sara, Juan, Ana: Four Lives, Four Phases

Using Gerard Sunnen's four phases of immigration as a framework, we can better understand the emotional journeys of my patients, Amir, Sara, Juan, and Ana, each of whom demonstrates how the immigration process is both universal in its stages and deeply individual in its impact.

Amir, a graduate student, embodies the early phases of immigration. He initially experienced anticipatory anxiety and plain fear, yet his excitement outweighed these concerns. In the "I am going to do great things" phase, Amir fantasized about his life in the United States with the adrenaline-fueled optimism typical of newcomers. Now, however, he finds himself in the second phase, realizing his loss. Life in the United States is more complicated than he imagined, and he now regrets not weighing the pros and cons more carefully before leaving home. Amir's enthusiasm has given way to a strong desire to return to his home country once he finishes his degree, highlighting the emotional rollercoaster that marks the early stages of immigration.

Sara, a middle-class Italian woman in her first decade of immigration, reflects on the intense internal work required during the adaptation phase. Like many immigrants, she spent her early years in survival mode, narrowly focused on maintaining legal status and staying afloat. In therapy, she now recognizes that she had suppressed her emotions for years, not realizing the weight of the stress she was carrying. For Sara, the "creativity and adrena-line" phase was more about endurance than excitement. Only now, as she begins to settle into her life in the United States, does she reflect on the toll this period took on her mental health. Her experience shows how the intense demands of adaptation can delay immigrants' emotional processing.

Juan, a brilliant academic, is also in the adaptation phase but faces unique struggles with identity and expectations. Despite his academic success in the United States, Juan feels torn between the external admiration he receives from those back home and his internal turmoil. His reflections on the tra-jectory he was placed on, academia, versus his personal desire to work with his hands, speaks to a deeper existential conflict. While others see him as a "Rockstar" for teaching at Harvard, Juan remains haunted by feelings of judgment, shame, and regret, all of which keep him tethered to his past, despite his geographical relocation. Juan's critique of both his upbringing and American culture reflects his struggle to find a balance between the two worlds, where neither fully satisfies him.

Ana, who is now in the phase of loss and realization, mourns the emo-tional dislocation she feels from her country of origin, Peru. Having spent most of her life in the United States, she experiences a deep attachment to Peru, yet the people there no longer view her as one of them, leaving her feeling alienated from both countries. Her mourning is further complicated by the loss of family members she has had to grieve from a distance, which constitutes a profound emotional burden for many immigrants. Ana's story also illustrates one of the unique challenges faced by those who immigrated as children, having had no choice in the move. She not only mourns her relatives but also the person she might have become had she remained in her homeland. This dual sense of loss, both personal and cultural, exem-plifies the complexities of the immigrant experience in later stages of life.

An older woman who moved to the United States with her family when she was a young girl still maintains strong ties to Italy. She often compares the attitudes, values, and lifestyle of the two countries. Her best friends are Italians. She does not feel fully at home in the United States despite having spent the majority of her life here. She wishes she could move back, telling me, "If it weren't for my American family and the medical system, which is better in the United States, I would move back." She is in a phase of deep longing for reunion with her—perhaps idealized—motherland:

> I do not own a home anymore neither here nor there. My ashes will be divided half in Italy, with my dad, and half here, with my mom. The initial feeling of loss never goes away, despite the fact I have been in this country more than seventy years. When I am in Italy, especially when I am in my native town, I remember and recognize the old places, but I also see all the changes that took place in my absence and which I did not have an opportunity to live through. It is my town but at the same time I do not really feel at home. I did not grow up in Italy in my formative years even though, in my heart and in my memories, I feel exceptionally close to Italy. And yet, I also feel lost there.

Her reflections show that even after decades, immigrants may still be in a phase of deep longing for their homeland. Despite spending most of her life in the United States, she continues to feel a strong connection to Italy and struggles with a sense of belonging in both countries. Even after having lived 70 years in the United States, her longing for her idealized motherland persists, although the thought of returning to Italy also leaves her feeling out of place. This duality captures the lasting emotional complexity of immigration, where neither the old nor the new country fully feels like home. Her reflections on her ashes being divided between the two countries symbolize the permanent split many immigrants feel.

These individuals, each in different stages of the immigration journey, illustrate the varied and deeply personal experiences immigrants face. From the early excitement of new opportunities to the enduring sense of loss and longing, each story underscores how immigration is an ongoing process that reshapes identity and belonging over time.

You Are Not Alone: A Chorus of Immigrant Voices

You are part of a chorus of immigrant voices. A chorus is a powerful thing. At the very least, it can lead to personal insight as you may recognize yourself in these stories, and at best you may feel part of something larger: a collective consciousness. It is power. Take time to reflect on your own history and the generational struggles of your family. Be aware of how your personal history and class is nested in the struggles of your country of origin and how that country is positioned vis-à-vis your current host country and the global economy.

Trauma, Migration, and the Need to See the Whole Story

Often, for immigrants, stress and trauma—both emotional and physical—begin long before arrival. For some, the difficulties start in the country of origin; for others, the migration journey itself is an ordeal. After arrival, challenges are likely to continue through legal insecurity (especially for undocumented individuals), or through marginalization, discrimination, economic exploitation, and in the challenges of cultural adaptation.

When taking stock of your life, it is important to look beyond the present moment. Consider the full arc of your experience: premigration, migration, and settlement, as well as your hopes for the future. If you are a therapist, you may find it helpful to become familiar with stage- or process-based models[8] and to orient yourself with temporal frameworks when collecting a patient's history—keeping in mind, of course, the unique path of every individual and the distinct contours of their sociocultural situation.

The Weight of Silence: When Immigrant Stories Are Missed in Care

The present moment cannot be considered in a vacuum. A culturally informed mindset that attends to premigration experiences, trauma histories, and cultural context is essential in supporting immigrant clients. Joseph Westermeyer and Jerome Kroll, in "Handling Cultural Differences Between Patient and Clinician"[9] offer a number of case studies that demonstrate this. One of them stands out: the case of a boy who immigrated to the United States and was evaluated by the medical, psychological, and school systems, but in a rushed manner. No one took the time to thoroughly investigate his premigration history or ask the right questions. Finally, he was reevaluated by the team led by the authors. During the various assessments, it was eventually discovered that he had suffered not only psychological trauma but also head trauma years earlier in his home country. By taking a thorough examination of his history, the treatment was adjusted, and the boy began to improve.[10]

This story highlights the importance of considering all the details of an individual's history. It serves as a reminder not only for immigrants navigating the medical and mental health systems, but also for professionals working with them. As immigrant patients, we must try to provide a complete and detailed account of our preimmigration, transit, and postimmigration experiences to our primary care providers, schools, and specialists involved in our care and that of our families. Even the best professionals can be rushed due to bureaucratic demands or a lack of resources. We need to be assertive, remain unintimidated by credentials or authority, and insist on being heard and given the time necessary for a proper evaluation. Studies have shown that people of color and immigrants often receive differential treatment. We must therefore make an extra effort to demand attention and explanations whether at the doctor's office or in the therapy room.

At the same time, if you are a clinician or therapist reading this, it is essential to recognize how often critical information is left unspoken—both out of resistance or avoidance, but also because time has not allowed it or the right questions were not asked. Patients may need space, prompts, and a sense of trust to speak about what truly shaped them.

As we've seen, understanding the full scope of one's history is crucial in navigating the challenges of immigration and seeking appropriate support. This principle of engaging in thorough reflection and communication not only pertains to Westermeyer and Jerome Kroll's case of the boy but also to our personal journeys, as we are each shaped by a unique sociocultural context. Gaining insight is a key component of reclaiming power and fostering emotional wellbeing.

With that in mind, take your time to reflect on these questions, piece by piece. This won't be the last time I ask you to consider them—and be patient with me if I repeat myself. Each time you consider them, you may discover a deeper layer of understanding or recall something previously forgotten. Reflection is how awareness deepens.

1   Where was I born?
2   How was my childhood, adolescence, and early adulthood?
3   What kinds of people were my parents, siblings, and other important people in my life?
4   How was growing up in my family?
5   What are my earliest memories? (Even if these are reconstructions inspired from pictures, they may give you a vibe of the emotions and experiences of your childhood).
6   How was school?
7   How was work?
8   How was my experience of colleagues and all the other people and institutions that were relevant along my journey?
9   Where and how did immigration enter into my mind as an idea, a desire, or a necessity?
10 What were the expectations of my parents and society?
11 Was there immigration in my family in the previous generations?
12 How has the commingling of my age, gender, socioeconomic status, and my level of intelligence and the family dynamics affected my immigration?
13 Are the latter still affecting the way I am in the world?
14 What facilitated my growth, hindered me, and overall shaped me?
15 Was there any trauma, physical or psychological, endured, witnessed, or experienced by loved ones or more generally by my people?
16 How did I adapt to the challenges?

Understanding Assimilation: Three Paths for the Second Generation

For second-generation immigrants, scholars envisage different pathways of assimilation. For instance,[11] one pathway is *straight-line assimilation*, which entails upward mobility with an incremental loss of the original culture. Another pathway to assimilation is *segmented assimilation*, which takes into consideration that society is stratified, and the second generation assimilates not only to a higher standing social group, but possibly to a humbler one, suffering downward mobility vis-à-vis the family of origin. Downward mobility does not happen because of a failure to Americanize but often because the children of the immigrants, for whatever the reason, have to integrate too fast; this entails learning the language and culture much faster than their parents. This overly fast integration can deprive these children of much-needed parental support. Another possibility of assimilation is called *selective acculturation*: Immigrants' children maintain a connection to their ethnic community and precisely because of this helpful ethnic buffer and sustenance, they manage upward mobility and maintain biculturalism.

As you reflect on your family of origin and/or yourself or the family you are forming, ask yourself if the types of assimilation described above—straight-line assimilation, segmented, and selective—can be helpful in understanding your life and how it's taking shape.

Support Matters: How Communities Shape Immigrant Adjustment

In "Psychological Acculturation: Perspectives, Principles, Processes, and Prospects," Marc H. Bornstein et al.[12] talk about how immigrant communities fare depending on the welcome they receive from the host country and from settled immigrants. If the settled community has willingness, time, and resources to put at the newcomers' disposal, the new immigrants fare much better. Bornstein et al. offer the following example:

> Recent migrants from the Dominican Republic are much more likely to have family members in the United States with residency or citizenship and accompanying language and systems navigation skills than recent migrants from Mexico. Mexican parents and their young children have lower availability of supports for childcare and finances as well as fewer multi-generational family networks. For children, this means that grandparents and other older family members with English-language skills are far more likely to be present in Dominican households than in Mexican households. As can be seen, individual acculturation patterns are influenced by group histories of migration.[13]

Fragmented Belonging: When Cultural Identity Offers No Refuge

The native community that is already established in the United States can be a valuable resource and offer a safe haven for many newcomers. However, for others, it can present challenges. For example, consider a Nigerian gender nonconforming person who was already marginalized in their country of origin. Those who are nonconforming with respect to gender may not be warmly welcomed by members of their own cultural community in the United States, and at the same time, they may struggle to fully connect with the LGBTQ+ community here due to differences in language, worldview, or cultural understanding. As a result, they may face multiple layers of isolation both from the world they left behind and the one they're trying to adjust to.

Reflecting on the excerpt above, how would you position yourself and your family in terms of social capital? Has your experience been more like Dominican immigrants, Mexican immigrants, or the LGBTQ+ Nigerian immigrant?

If you are a therapist reading this, you might consider how these dynamics play out in your clients' sense of belonging; or in how supported (or unsupported) they feel by their broader cultural environment.

These questions of social capital and belonging are not only theoretical, they shape how immigrants live, relate, and adapt every day. Whether you are navigating these issues yourself or supporting others through them, taking time to reflect can open space for new insights and actions. The following exercise is an invitation to begin that process.

Takeaway Exercise

Therapists: You may wish to offer the following reflection as a take-home exercise, if it fits your style of work and your client's needs. It is designed to foster self-awareness and encourage intentional community-building.

To the Reader Reflecting on Your Own Journey

"Know thyself" is a fundamental step in your development as both an immigrant and a human being—and it is the guiding theme of this book. As a therapist, I consider helping people come to know themselves the most meaningful part of my work.

In the section above, I offered a few lenses you can use to explore different aspects of your own experience, and to better understand the experiences of others in migration.

With the evolving picture of your immigration journey, both personally and globally, do you want to make any strategic adjustments to align yourself with a community for support and growth?

If you wish to make a stronger effort to connect with people who can help you thrive, who might they be? Would they come from your immigration cohort, other parents and teachers at your children's school, or your religious community? Would your group be based on gender, race, ethnicity, hobbies, sports, art, or volunteer work? Which other communities would you like to network with? What additional resources could you leverage?

If you feel hesitant about seeking connections strategically, ask yourself why. If it feels too transactional or exploitative, consider whether you can reframe networking as a mutually supportive opportunity.

Notes

1 On the topic of being the first in the family to attend college and the challenges of lacking an educational legacy, see A. Portes and R. G. Rumbaut, *Legacies: The*

Story of the Immigrant Second Generation (Berkeley, CA: University of California Press, 2001).

2 Salman Akhtar, *Immigration and Acculturation: Mourning, Adaptation, and the Next Generation* (Lanham, MD: Jason Aronson, 2011), 141–162.

3 Karla Cornejo Víllavícencío, *The Undocumented Americans* (New York: One World, 2020), 236.

4 Personal communication with immigration Lawyer Saverio Lo Monaco July 22, 2024.

5 See Article 23 of the *Universal Declaration of Human Rights*, available at: www.un.org/en/about-us/universal-declaration-of-human-rights#article23. It affirms that: Everyone has the right to work, to free choice of employment, to just and favourable conditions of work and to protection against unemployment. Everyone, without any discrimination, has the right to equal pay for equal work. Everyone who works has the right to just and favourable remuneration ensuring for himself and his family an existence worthy of human dignity, and supplemented, if necessary, by other means of social protection. Everyone has the right to form and to join trade unions for the protection of his interests.

6 The models developed by Gonsalves, Berry, Sluzki, and Yakushko may serve as a preliminary framework: J. W. Berry, "Immigration, Acculturation, and Adaptation," *Applied Psychology: An International Review* 46, no. 1 (1997): 5–68, doi:10.1111/j.1464-0597.1997.tb01087.x; C. J. Gonsalves, "Psychological Stages of the Refugee Process: A Model for Therapeutic Interventions," *Professional Psychology: Research and Practice* 23, no. 5 (1992), 382–389, doi:10.1037/0735-7028.23.5.382; C. E. Sluzki, "Migration and Family Conflict," *Family Process* 18, no. 4 (1979), 379–390, doi:10.1111/j.1545-5300.1979.00379.x. (Also see: C. E. Sluzki, "Disruption and Reconstruction of Networks Following Migration," in *Ethnicity and Family Therapy*, 2nd ed., edited by M. McGoldrick, J. Giordano, and J. K. Pearce (New York: Guilford Press, 1992).)

O. Yakushko, "Stress and Coping in the Lives of Recent Immigrants and Refugees: Considerations for Counseling," *International Journal for the Advancement of Counselling* 30, no. 3 (2008), 167–178, doi:10.1007/s10447-008-9054-0

7 Dr. Sunnen declined to participate in the survey but agreed to an interview, which was conducted in New York on March 5, 2020, focusing on his professional and personal experiences related to immigration.

8 Joseph Westermeyer and Jerome Kroll, "Handling Cultural Differences Between Patient and Clinician," in *Migrant Psychiatry*, ed. Dinesh Bhugra (Oxford: Oxford University Press, 2021), 459–465.

9 A 10-year-old refugee boy was initially thought to have psychological or developmental issues because he was not learning English in school, and counseling was recommended. But he showed little improvement. When he was later seen by a new team, they learned he had been hospitalized for two weeks during the war in his home country. Further tests revealed a brain injury from shrapnel sustained during a military attack years earlier. This discovery changed the course of treatment, and the boy made significant progress. The case is a clear reminder: attending to both the body and the personal history is essential, even when there are no visible signs. What is not seen can still have a deep and lasting impact. Joseph Westermeyer and Jerome Kroll, "Handling Cultural Differences Between Patient and Clinician," in *Oxford Textbook of Migrant Psychiatry*, eds. Dinesh Bhugra, Susham Gupta, and Rachel Tribe (Oxford: Oxford University Press, 2021), 462, doi:10.1093/med/9780198842190.003.0011.

10 M. C. Waters, V. C. Tran, P. Kasinitz, and J. H. Mollenkopf, "Segmented Assimilation Revisited: Types of Acculturation and Socioeconomic Mobility in Young Adulthood," *Ethnic and Racial Studies* 33, no. 7 (2010), 1168–1193, doi:10.1080/01419871003624076.

11 Marc H. Bornstein, Judith K. Bernhard, Robert H. Bradley, Xinyin Chen, Jo Ann M. Farver, Steven J. Gold, Donald J. Hernandez, Christiane Spiel, Fons van de Vijver, and Hirokazu Yoshikawa, "Psychological Acculturation: Perspectives, Principles, Processes, and Prospects," in *Routledge International Study of Migration Studies*, eds. Steven J. Gold and Stephanie J. Nawyn (New York: Routledge, 2019), 19–31.
12 Bornstein et al., 20–21; 25–26.
13 Bornstein et al., 20–21.

References

Akhtar, Salman. 2011. *Immigration and Acculturation: Mourning, Adaptation, and the Next Generation*. Lanham, MD: Jason Aronson.

Berry, John W. 1997. "Immigration, Acculturation, and Adaptation." *Applied Psychology: An International Review* 46 (1): 5–68. doi:10.1111/j.1464-0597.1997.tb01087.x.

Bornstein, Marc H., Judith K. Bernhard, Robert H. Bradley, Xinyin Chen, Jo Ann M. Farver, Steven J. Gold, Donald J. Hernandez, Christiane Spiel, Fons van de Vijver, and Hirokazu Yoshikawa. 2019. "Psychological Acculturation: Perspectives, Principles, Processes, and Prospects." In *The Routledge International Handbook of Migration Studies*, 2nd ed., edited by Steven J. Gold and Stephanie J.Nawyn, 392–407. New York: Routledge.

Cornejo Víllavícencío, Karla. 2020. *The Undocumented Americans*. New York: One World.

Gonsalves, C. J. 1992. "Psychological Stages of the Refugee Process: A Model for Therapeutic Interventions." *Professional Psychology: Research and Practice* 23 (5): 382–389. doi:10.1037/0735-7028.23.5.382.

Portes, Alejandro, and Rubén G. Rumbaut. 2001. *Legacies: The Story of the Immigrant Second Generation*. Berkeley, CA: University of California Press.

Sluzki, Carlos E. 1979. "Migration and Family Conflict." *Family Process* 18 (4): 379–390. doi:10.1111/j.1545-5300.1979.00379.x.

Sluzki, Carlos E. 1992. "Disruption and Reconstruction of Networks Following Migration." In *Ethnicity and Family Therapy*, 2nd ed., edited by Monica McGoldrick, Joe Giordano, and John K. Pearce. New York: Guilford Press.

United Nations. n.d. "Universal Declaration of Human Rights, Article 23." www.un.org/en/about-us/universal-declaration-of-human-rights#article23.

Waters, Mary C., Van C. Tran, Philip Kasinitz, and John H. Mollenkopf. 2010. "Segmented Assimilation Revisited: Types of Acculturation and Socioeconomic Mobility in Young Adulthood." *Ethnic and Racial Studies* 33 (7): 1168–1193. doi:10.1080/01419871003624076.

Westermeyer, Joseph, and Jerome Kroll. 2021. "Handling Cultural Differences Between Patient and Clinician." In *Migrant Psychiatry*, edited by Dinesh Bhugra, 327–340. Oxford: Oxford University Press.

Yakushko, Oksana. 2008. "Stress and Coping in the Lives of Recent Immigrants and Refugees: Considerations for Counseling." *International Journal for the Advancement of Counselling* 30 (3): 167–178. doi:10.1007/s10447-008-9054-0.

2 The Hidden Losses of Immigration
Emotional and Practical Costs

Reflection for the Therapist

Even for immigrants who left their home country under relatively stable conditions, the depth of loss may nevertheless be unfathomable—becoming fully apparent only years later, in moments of therapeutic witnessing. Be attentive to where the mourning is stuck and where it quietly persists.

Only years after immigration did author and psychoanalyst Lama Zuhair Khouri, a Lebanese immigrant to the United States, understand the depth of her loss of connection to her country, culture, family, and parts of herself:

> My concern is with an internal space where the immigrant feels as if he is attending a never-ending funeral of land, culture, language, relationships, and life… How does it feel to "go back home" and not find the one you left? What is the impact of realizing that the relationships the immigrant held in his mind, and for which he longed, are no longer there?[1]

Even when immigration is not the consequence of a human manufactured or natural catastrophe, it is nonetheless the outcome of a breakdown. Something must have gone awry if someone leaves their home country. In the best-case scenario, it is the failure of the homeland to nurture the needs, talent, identity, or aspirations of the person. One leaves a birthplace in search of stimulation or a place where they can be accepted and grow. But immigration does not guarantee a soft landing. It takes time to build a better life; there is a gap between expectations and reality.

On the other side of the immigration continuum are the people who flee untenable conditions: asylum seekers, refugees, and undocumented people. The experience of being forced out, enduring hardship, trauma, and significant losses, coupled with the lengthy process of obtaining legal status (or the ongoing insecurity of being undocumented), along with the dangerous or traumatic conditions faced both in and outside this country, and the pain felt for one's own people, all contribute to a complex and prolonged psychological, physical, and social adjustment.

DOI: 10.4324/9781003648703-4

Life is about loss for everyone. Being well adjusted—at least for Western psychology—means leaning into loss. It's an experience that we've all done since childhood.

We relinquish our desire for psychological oneness with our mother and accept a diminished role—as one member among others within the family; we learn to accept eventually that we are not the center of the world and cannot be and do everything we want. We accept and even learn to enjoy work and accept giving our hard-earned money for taxes. We painfully give up our feelings of omnipotence. The more we age, the more we lean into losses, accepting and making do with the physical and social injuries of aging. Increasingly we lose strength, beauty, power, and our loved ones. But if loss is part of the human experience, immigrants must endure more of it than others, leaving behind homes, loved ones, communities, identities, language, and an integral sense of being at home in the world. Therefore, we need to be better at it. Here are a few vignettes.

An emigrant from the Global South, who was faring relatively well compared to the poverty standards of his country of origin, left his country and his family behind in search of a better life in Europe. He recounts:

> I miss the nearness of my family, the noise, the closeness, the food. I left hoping for something better, but life here has worn me down. I work hard but feel invisible, underpaid, and undervalued. I only hope my children stay close, that they build something stable. If I could start over, I would not leave.

Barbie, a patient originally from Europe, said the following about the experience of loss:

> It's been more than five years since I have not gone home. First, I was busy, then I had my visa issues, and now there is the coronavirus and the travel ban. I do my thing; I go on, but I think I am burying my feelings. The holidays are particularly stressful. It is particularly hard not to know where I stand. When I speak with my family, it feels like watching a show I am no longer a part of. I am drifting farther from them, and there is nothing solid left to hold onto. First, my mother passed away. Then my father married someone close to my own age. Now the house I grew up in—the one I walk through in my mind when I need comfort—is gone. Sold. What once grounded me has become a ghost held together by memory. Sometimes I think I should just let it all go, sever the ties, and stop looking back. I am tired of wrestling with something that cannot be fixed.

The pain of longing for loved ones abroad can be so strong that it can produce a desire to completely discontinue contact altogether and to focus solely on the relationships developing in the new country. However, obliterating one's loved ones from one's life to suppress the longing would constitute further loss.

If you are an overly optimistic or unreflective immigrant (as I once was), leaving your country without giving some thought to the value of what you are leaving, knowing about the losses inherent in immigration will balance out naïve enthusiasm. The cultural loss and feeling of missing one's country of origin may be easier if you are doing well in the new country and there are no family dramas and deaths. But at some point, the loss catches up with you. For example, you may feel like you are becoming a partial stranger to the many significant people you love from a distance, as they have no sense of what your daily life is like or what you do for a living. They may not know your children as well as they know the children of your siblings who remained behind. Your children, who are growing up in a mixed culture, may at times be a bit of a mystery to you as well. You will lose loved ones and mourn them from a distance. You will lose the comfort and effortless understanding of your home country's rituals and national events. This is the unpleasant counterpart to the freedom and possibilities you acquire by immigrating to a new place.

At the same time, new and good things begin taking root in the United States. For instance, partners and friends who are more established may open new horizons for you, and your children may develop a rich social world. Remember to take the time to reflect on these gains and losses; they help you to place the losses in perspective. Previous generations had to erase much of their history and knowledge in order to blend in. Many did not even teach their children their native language. But it does not have to be this way.

Author and psychoanalyst Zuhair Khouri,[2] the Lebanese first generation immigrant quoted above, understood the depth of her loss of connection to her country, culture, family, and parts of herself years after immigration. In 2004–2007, Kohuri was a young therapist working in a public middle school in Brooklyn. She was working with a group of fourth, sixth, and seventh grade immigrant Arab boys who needed help making this transition. In her work with children, this Arab American therapist rediscovered a part of herself she had forgotten. In her efforts to fit into Western standards, she had consciously and unconsciously set aside aspects of her identity and original culture that she believed would not be welcomed or would hinder her attempts to acculturate and fit in. She recounts:

> The three years as a school therapist left me more aware than ever of the pain of mourning a time and space lost forever, yet undying in my mind... Part of the immigrant's psyche, like Peter Pan, lives in a "Neverland," a make-believe imaginary space. There, relatives do not age, his mother still expects him for Sunday lunch, the dog waits for him at the door, and his friends look for him on the weekend. The immigrant relationship to the homeland is stuck to the pre-immigration time, as if time had stopped. The memories and emotional experiences he holds are nowhere to be found.[3]

Kohuri's reflections remind us that even when individuals immigrate under conditions that are neither unstable nor catastrophic, the emotional consequences of leaving one's home country can be profound and disorienting. As a successful clinician, she speaks of the experience of deep mourning and rupture. Despite her professional growth and fulfillment of ambition, her testimony is ripe with loss and pain. Her story is a reminder of the importance of becoming in touch with and staying attuned to the deeper processes at work within.

The more you identify as a forced immigrant, the more you feel your immigration losses. It is useful to have a space like this, one in which you can think through your losses and have them recognized and validated—even if only by a chorus of like-minded immigrants. Having your losses validated and named helps process them. Mourning leaves space for new growth.

Feelings of Duality: Navigating Loss and Possibility

> After so many years away, I began to feel torn—my heart still belongs to my home country, but my mind and daily life are rooted here in the United States. As an only child living alone, I often feel something is missing. At the same time, I know I have built a good life here. No matter where I live, part of me will always be elsewhere.
>
> —Anonymous contributor

By immigrating, we live in duality. We cannot help but compare the life we have with the life we have given up, as well as the life we could have lived if we (or our parents) had not so drastically changed our world. We judge every experience according to two different standards, and when decisions are needed, we have to weigh an extra set of values and consequences.

For good or bad, there is always the tension in immigration between the anticipation of new possibilities and sadness for the multitude of losses. On the one hand, there are exciting opportunities to reinvent oneself professionally, socially, or romantically with stimulation, gratification, and rejuvenation. There is the possibility of having more power, respect, and autonomy, especially as a woman or LGBTQ+ person. On the other hand, there are frustrations, losses, and self-doubt. Often, the hoped-for upward mobility remains just outside of reach, despite achievements. Even in the best-case scenario in which your original culture is appreciated rather than stigmatized and you arrive in your host country with enough financial and cultural capital to get by, you cannot escape mourning and loss. Even when immigration is more of a choice than an unescapable need, there is a lingering question: What has immigration given me and what has it taken away? The answer may change over time.

Salman Akhtar, an Indian American psychoanalyst, describes the sensation of loss in his book *Immigration and Acculturation*. It is, he notes, a multi-faceted loss: the absence of shared life with loved ones, the disappearance of familiar landscapes, and the vanishing of sensory experiences—tastes, smells, sights, and sounds—that once shaped everyday life. Even the animals of one's homeland are missed. Yet, simultaneously, the new environment stimulates the senses in novel and sometimes alluring ways. It is a complex experience. At times you are understimulated and lonely; at other times you are overstimulated as new experiences assault your senses. Especially at the beginning of your journey, there is a continuous expenditure of energy to understand and correct your moves, and there is the sensation of shock and frustration in daily moments of misunderstanding. You often feel a bit off, alienated, or out of harmony, and just when you begin to feel settled and in sync, someone reminds you of your otherness by asking, "Where are you from?"—even if you have been a citizen for years or were born here to immigrant parents.[4]

Immigration is a tiring experience. One has to explain oneself to others to the point of exhaustion. There are the linguistic and cultural losses that make each interaction awkward, without yielding the hoped-for results. Speakers become painfully aware of limitations with the new language and the superficiality of exchanges. They become hesitant, as they cannot assume their message will be understood. It is not surprising that some immigrants become increasingly self-conscious, opting for silence or retreating from people who do not speak their native language. As Liz, an immigrant from Italy, puts it, "I feel like I am experiencing the city though a window. Despite the fact that I have been living in New York for quite a few years and work and family are good, it's as if I cannot find a link with the American people, something is always quite off. It is not just the language; it goes beyond that."

Liz's sentiments are echoed by many of my patients who do not come from stigmatized developing countries and are on their way to creating successful trajectories in the United States. They cannot easily express themselves either in the office or in social interactions. They feel that way despite the possibility of having interesting careers and enjoying an upward mobility that would have been impossible to achieve in their home country; they cannot tailor their conversations appropriately. Their American counterparts—who are fluent and effective speakers—are heard and appreciated, even when they do not offer the most meaningful and thoughtful contributions. The contributions of the newcomer immigrant, even if full of substance, are stymied by an unfamiliar language spoken in an accent that is difficult to understand. Another layer of complication occurs if the immigrant speaker comes from a marginalized group. Their speech does not demand the same attention or respect as that of someone who belongs to a more powerful and imposing social group.

Lele, a patient, who is an Italian temporary resident of modest means, voiced the following complaint at the beginning of his stay: "It can be very isolating when you're not yet fluent in the language. People here rarely slow down or try to include you—you end up sitting quietly, not because you want to, but because you cannot keep up. Where I come from, it would be unthinkable to let a guest feel left out. The whole group would make an effort to help the newcomer feel at ease. Here, you are on your own."

Tom, another immigrant from Italy, expressed the duality he felt in establishing new connections and missing his friends back home:

> Even in the present moments of success and celebration, an underlying sadness intersects with these moments of enthusiasm and growth. I miss my family and friends. I cannot go back, not even for the holidays. I miss very much my friends, those friendships you can call at any time of day and night and you know they are there. But you cannot build these types of friendships here, not even over time, because friendships are different here—or I have not found this type of friendships here yet. Only perhaps one person and he is leaving the country now. It is still a new friendship, so trust cannot be strong. Then there are the difficulties at work, when one wants to communicate the nuances with clients and workers, and it's impossible to express these nuances and get the wanted results in a foreign language.

It is interesting that even those who immigrated to the United States as children may also experience the challenge of not feeling completely understood by Americans. They still must manage the tension between loss and possibilities, between what one has and what one has left behind. For this man whose family emigrated from Brazil, his frustration that he never voluntarily chose to leave was poignant. Having moved to the United States in early childhood, he "passes" as American to others, yet feels torn between two worlds inside. His American friends dismiss his feelings of loss, telling him, "Why do you feel pain about immigration, you are not even from Brazil!" This lack of recognition compounds his internal struggle. His experience is somewhat complicated by the fact that preimmigration memory, while present, is also cut off. The sense of duality for him is particularly tormenting:

> Leaving was never my decision. No one asked if I wanted to go. I had a good life—with extended family around, laughter, and a sense of belonging. I remember feeling safe and known. But after we moved, something shifted. What changed me most was losing my connection to the language I grew up with. Over time, I stopped speaking it fluently, and with that, I lost parts of myself. I could no longer speak easily with my grandparents, and I lost our small rituals that had once shaped my daily life. I lost them twice: once when we left, and again when they passed. I sometimes wonder who I would have become if we had stayed. Not necessarily someone better—but someone different, with a different voice and different roots.

These testimonies may resonate with your experience. Learning that there are other immigrants feeling just like you can help normalize your feelings. If so, take the time to feel and think of your experience. If you tend to feel bad about yourself, about your English proficiency, about your difficulties as you try to be a good person according to two different standards, can you turn down the harsh judgment toward yourself? Can you see how it's not easy for anyone to be proficient and right in two worlds at the same time? Can you give yourself a big hug for trying to overcome all these difficulties? How can you try to bridge the gap and try your best to maintain relationships and be present for your family back home, becoming fully aware that time is passing and there is a geographical distance and that there will be loss?

For therapists: These narratives offer a glimpse into the kinds of silent grief your clients may carry; this grief often needs recognition before it can be released. Consider inviting patients to articulate the daily tension they experience between two cultural standards and explore how this shapes their identity and mood.

Feeling on Hold

> The years before I got the legal papers were the most difficult. Lots of time was spent just to figure out how to survive. That time was the most difficult for me. I don't even know how I did it. I am extremely independent and opinionated and had to cave in and keep quiet. I could not complain or say no, even if I was in the right.
>
> —Ale, a patient

Feeling on hold is a common experience for immigrants. Some delay starting a family due to job insecurity, visa issues, and lack of support, while others, particularly those accompanying a partner who received a job offer or PhD opportunity, put their careers on hold, uncertain about whether they will remain in the country beyond their initial visa period. In such a state of uncertainty, making a big investment to reinvent oneself here may be difficult or unwise.

Florence is an upper middle-class French woman married to a French businessman, who convinced his family to relocate to New York having received a tempting job offer. For her, the two years living in the United States felt like a suspension of her life with no new beginning in sight to her. Like many partners who follow spouses who found work here, she came without a personal purpose, having given up a full life that made sense to her:

> That felt like real life. This feels more like standing on a platform between trains—nothing has arrived, and I am not sure when I'll be moving again. Back there, I also had doubts and tensions, but I felt woven into something larger. I felt more solid, more grounded. Things were clearer. There was a rhythm to follow, like a current that carried me forward. Here, everything feels looser. It is harder to tell who truly sees you, and even friendships have to be penciled into a calendar. I put in a time to meet and then it never happens.

At the expiration of her husband's visa period, Florence's family went back to France.

Many immigrants, especially those who move for a partner's career, may resonate with Florence's experience. When one partner's career advancement precipitates the move, the accompanying partner has to leave behind a full life for the benefit of their partner and family. In this case, the burden of finding one's place in a culture that they did not personally choose can make the entrance into a foreign job market feel impossible. You may have sacrificed your career opportunities in your home country to follow your partner to the United States without having any idea how much time you might have to reinvent yourself here. Your family likely depends on you to facilitate family life in the new environment. This is a tough situation that can produce anxiety, sadness, and lower one's self-esteem. For many, this new arrangement also changes relational power dynamics. With no earning power, identity and self-esteem can suffer. If this is you, address the misalignment and seek the understanding and collaboration of your partner.

As an immigrant in a state of hold, if you do not know just yet if you will permanently stay in the United States or return home, take your time to consider if you have the power to change something, even if it's the smallest step in the direction you want to take. Consider your desires, your motivation, time, and your assets. Consider whether a large investment in yourself, your life, and your career makes sense right now, or whether smaller, more incremental steps are more appropriate for where you are. Consider also skills that are portable, such as internet-based skills or certifications that you can continue to build on wherever you go. These skills not only support your adaptation to the United States but also help create a sense of continuity and opportunity within what may otherwise feel like disruption or interruption.

When you do decide to act, whether with big or small steps, outcomes can vary. You might find that when you eventually leave the country, your efforts resulted in no net gain or even some loss. However, some immigrants are pleasantly surprised by successes, such as building a company they can sell if they repatriate or can continue to grow if they choose to stay permanently. Alternatively, skills and assets that are portable can be taken with you wherever you go. Many of my patients have experienced these "happy events."

When in a state of hold, I generally encourage action, even minimal steps, even if the initial work is far below the social status one held in their country of origin. As immigrants, we need to be flexible because it is often rewarded. For some, this might mean taking a shift serving tables or working at a store like Trader Joe's to gain English skills and familiarity with the new environment. Whatever helps my clients become unstuck is worth considering. Key attributes worth cultivating are flexibility, humility, and a willingness to explore because they often reward the person who is stuck.

Having a partner who spurred the move and earns well puts one in a position in which one does not need to earn an income. This, ironically, has a downside because the push to get out and face the uncomfortable feeling of putting oneself in the game may not be as strong as if someone has kids to feed. If the feeling of being stuck persists and you cannot take any step whatsoever, consider the fact that some of your stuckness may be due to emotional baggage, low self-esteem, and ambivalence. These experiences are common among immigrants, especially when so much is uncertain or beyond your control. Therapy can provide a space to process these emotions, and today more than ever before there are flexible and affordable options.

Therapist readers may observe how even privileged immigrants can feel unmoored when roles and routines are stripped away, an experience that can mimic or mask depressive symptoms.

Feeling Guilt

Salman Akhtar, in *Immigration and Acculturation*, observes: "Children of immigrants often feel the burden of the parentally induced guilt. Often, they grow up hearing their parents say, 'We came to this country so that you can have a better life.'"[5] His words capture the way guilt reverberates across generations, through expectation, dependence, and sacrifice.

This guilt can be further reinforced by the parents who remain behind. It is not unusual for these parents to instill a heavy sense of responsibility in the children who have left. Immigrant parents may, in turn, transfer this guilt to the second generation. For example, their heavy reliance on their children to navigate and understand the new country can hinder the children's natural drive for independence, as the parents need them close by in order to function well. More openly, parents may express to their children that all the sacrifices and suffering they endured during immigration were for the benefit of the children. Jo, an immigrant patient, tells me she found a box of artifacts from the beginning of her immigration journey. When she opened it, she was caught off guard. Opening the old box of mementos flooded her with feelings. Jo suddenly realized she was becoming an "intermediate" immigrant.

The five years spent in the new country corresponded to years she had lived away from her family. Though she was lucky enough to visit home once a year for Christmas, she started to wonder how many more Christmases she would be able to enjoy with her parents. Would these ten days a year be enough to fill the void if her parents were to pass away? Was her career important enough to justify the sacrifice of not being closer to them? As she lives her full life in NYC, her parents are not frozen in time. She suddenly realized, at an emotional level, that they continued to age and become more vulnerable and needy. She realized she had just opened an immigrant's Pandora's Box. All the mementos of the many benchmarks she had achieved in the United States were staring at her from the box, but a lot was also missing. What emerged was the realization that time is ticking—in both her world and theirs.

Finding the box gave me a sense of vertigo, as if I was dwelling inside a tower that all of a sudden had mushroomed fast and tall; so tall I could not look down without a feeling of vertigo. All of a sudden, I realized I have been living in the U.S. for five years. I did not realize how much time had passed. So many things have happened in my country, I feel like an outsider there. My friends there have husbands and children and I barely know their names. My parents have a hard time grasping what I do for a living and how I live. I do not know the music and the new trends. I lack the pop references. My friends say I am politically correct and "American;" they make fun of me. We have less and less to talk about. I understand that one cannot have everything, but it pains me that I don't have friends for the long run. I thought that my college friends would have been here for me forever. I am in a new phase of rupture. The values I hold dear are starting to be different than when I left. I see my parents getting old and wonder, Will I go back to take care of them at some point? I feel bad. I am making the choice to spend my time far away from them. One does not realize that years pass; it gives me a feeling of guilt. It brings up the question of what to do with time. This question would not be so urgent if I had not moved. Time and space would not be so wrought with guilt, loss, and longing.

Lin, whose brother died while she was in the United States, told me she feels guilty about having missed so much of her life with him, about missing the funeral, about not having been there to participate in his care, and preparing for the mourning ceremony.

I feel like a sister standing on one shore, calling out for my brother across an ocean that doesn't echo back. It's different for the family that is there. They are busy taking care of things. I would have wanted to be there in this important moment. I feel guilty for living the loss from afar and not supporting them with my love and care and not doing the actual work of helping with all of this. I feel I am copping out.

In psychoanalysis, guilt is the feeling we experience when we believe we have done something wrong. It refers to our actions: what we have done or failed to do. For example, I might feel guilty for lying to a friend because I believe honesty is an important value. Guilt can be helpful because it encourages us to make things right, like apologizing or changing our behavior. Guilt signals the possibility of still being a good person who has done something wrong and needs to make amends.[6]

Shame, on the other hand, is deeper. It's the feeling that there is something wrong in us; that we are not "normal." While guilt is about what we have done, shame is about who we are. For example, instead of feeling guilty for lying, I might feel ashamed because I think being dishonest is who I am: I am a bad person. Shame can be much more harmful because it makes us feel unworthy, inadequate beyond what is acceptable as humans (indeed only humans experience shame). Summing up: Guilt is "I did something bad." Shame is "I am bad." Understanding the difference is important because while guilt can motivate us to improve, shame often leaves us stuck because if we are intrinsically bad we are unchangeable, we can only hide the defect; it can damage our sense of self-worth and hinder our self-development. For therapists, this is often a crucial moment to help patients reframe shame into manageable guilt: something that invites repair, not self-condemnation.

Therapists may observe how cultural expectations of filial responsibility compound clients' emotional struggles and create internal conflict about "home." In countries where children are expected to take care of their aging parents, such as India, Latin America and Italy, leaving one's family and familial responsibilities is riddled with guilt.[7]

In speaking of phases of immigration, Salman Akhtar describes a phase of reparation, where guilt emerges when the immigrant feels he repudiated his motherland. This feeling engenders creative reparative gestures, like sharing knowledge and resources and building infrastructure to better the motherland.[8]

As Salman Akhtar notes,[9] immigrants from former colonies or economically disadvantaged countries may experience guilt when their achievements in the host country surpass those of their compatriots—either those who remained behind or those struggling within the diaspora. While these feelings of guilt are unhealthy, they are understandable.[10] They stem from deeply ingrained, unconscious expectations and social hierarchies established during colonial times, which were designed to keep subordinated people in a lower status. Many are made to feel inferior, unintelligent, and incapable of recognizing or confronting their exploitation. This mindset is pervasive, and even the most independent individuals can begin to feel inferior, unable to break through the structural barriers society has imposed on them, once these limiting messages are internalized.[11]

Akhtar writes:

> For immigrants from African and Asian countries, the guilt of doing better than the "folks back home" can be compounded by intrapsychic resistances to achievement and success. Such resistances are often related to decades, if not centuries, of colonial devaluation of dark-skinned people.[12]

Takeaway Exercise

Reflect on these questions and write your responses in a journal:

1   As you acquaint yourself with your new world, what are the lessons you learned back home that you want to keep in your current daily life?
2   What legacy of artifacts (e.g., music, pictures, recipes, wisdom, values, words, and sayings) do you want to highlight and potentially share with others?

3   Consider making a list of your gains and losses, such as this assessment from one of my survey respondents:

> What I LOST: Health insurance; the possibility to continue my education at accessible costs; all the privileges that a socialist country offers; seeing my family & friends from Italy; living in my beautiful country full of art and beauty; living in Europe.
>
> What I GAINED: Being part of a huge, marvelous artist community (all fields), studying/working with the best artists and teachers; living in the incredible city that is New York City; being with my incredible friends who are my second family.
>
> —Anonymous contributor

4   For those important relationships that you want to keep alive despite the distance, think of ways in which you can be present and ways to purposely keep the fire on.

Whether you are an immigrant or a therapist walking alongside one, these reflections offer a moment to pause, honor what has been lost, and begin to name what is still unfolding. Naming loss does not erase it, but it does allow it to be seen, and sometimes, that is where healing begins. As you move forward, carry with you the knowledge that these questions do not need quick answers. It is the act of staying with them that matters.

Therapists may consider using these prompts in session to help clients externalize their grief and better articulate their immigration-related experiences.

Notes

1 Lama Zuhair Khouri, "The Immigrant's Neverland," *Contemporary Psychoanalysis* 48, no. 2 (2012): 213–214, doi:10.1080/00107530.2012.10746499, 213.
2 Khouri, 113–137.
3 Khouri, 215.
4 Salman Akhtar, *Immigration and Acculturation: Mourning, Adaptation, and the Next Generation* (Lanham, MD: Jason Aronson, 2011), 180.
5 Akhtar, *Immigration and Acculturation*, 173.
6 June P. Tangney, Rowland S. Miller, Laura Flicker and Deborah H. Barlow, "Are Shame, Guilt and Embarrassment Distinct Emotions?" *Journal of Personality and Social Psychology*, 70 (1996), 1257.
7 Akhtar, *Immigration and Acculturation*, 172.
8 Akhtar, 16.
9 Akhtar, 46.
10 Akhtar, 47.
11 Akhtar, 47.
12 Akhtar, 46.

References

Akhtar, Salman. 2011. *Immigration and Acculturation: Mourning, Adaptation, and the Next Generation*. Lanham, MD: Jason Aronson.

Khouri, Lama Zuhair. 2012. "The Immigrant's Neverland." *Contemporary Psychoanalysis* 48 (2): 213–237. doi:10.1080/00107530.2012.10746499.

Tangney, J. P., R. S. Miller, L. Flicker, & D. H. Barlow. 1996. "Are Shame, Guilt and Embarrassment Distinct Emotions?", *Journal of Personality and Social Psychology*, 70 (6): 1256–1269. doi:10.1037/0022-3514.70.6.1256.

3 Finding Yourself Between Cultures

> I often feel nostalgic for where I grew up—for its beauty, the local accents, the spontaneity, and the freedom to travel on a whim. But visiting is hard. My life now feels so different from the lives of those who stayed. I used to think of home as a place full of friends and memories, but most of those friends have moved away. When I go back, I realize I am missing something that no longer exists.
>
> —Anonymous contributor

Somewhere in Between

> My immigration was challenging because I felt I was between two worlds and two sets of expectations. Finding myself in this split culture has been a long and ongoing battle.
>
> —Anonymous contributor

The journey of mourning losses associated with immigration is a lifelong process, coloring each stage of life. Finding oneself in this process, moreover, is rarely linear. It unfolds within moments of disconnection, across shifting landscapes of belonging, and through the resilience required to hold onto more than one world at once. To find ourselves, we must understand the place that we find ourselves in.

As an immigrant, you may feel a constant sense of missing something. This something may feel just out of reach—like you are endlessly running on a treadmill to identify it. For therapists, tuning into this vague but persistent feeling of displacement can reveal hidden grief or longing, even in otherwise high-functioning individuals.

While some losses are inevitable and can only be mourned, others can be managed with the help of new communication technologies that have brought the world closer together. However, despite the ways we can extend our reach due to technology, people still feel the loss of their place of origin. Years pass, and the streets, shops, people, conversations, and connections with old friends are no longer the same. There is the city of our early memories, whose streets we walk in our minds in our absentminded moments, the city that we search for on Google Maps, Facebook, and Instagram, and the one that appears in our nighttime dreams.

DOI: 10.4324/9781003648703-5

There is also the place that we find when we go back to visit. People have all sorts of reactions when they return to their home country. Some feel that their homeland has drastically changed and that they have lost all connections to it. Others find the place unchanged and stuck in time—out of sync with the person they have become. A patient reflected on her experience of the people in her home country as follows:

> I saw my old friends, and they were old also. We are all old. I feel like I just woke up from a coma. You know when people wake up and find the world changed. The world carried on, and I just found out.

For others, their place of origin holds the power of a myth—memories filled with beauty and warmth. All negativity is denied. But when they visit their home country, they discover a different reality.

For people coming from regions that have experienced significant upheaval and crisis, such as Venezuela, where, as of 2024, nearly 8 million refugees are displaced globally (according to UNHCR),[1] and where democratic breakdown, violence, food shortages, and disarray in services prevail, their country of origin must be mourned. The preimmigration country does not exist anymore, and it is often impossible to simply take up with the life or experiences within that country one had before migration. Although memories remain, they feel disconnected from a homeland that has been profoundly transformed.

Due to the losses involved with migration, some people choose to cut ties with one of their homes to focus on living fully in the other. Others, like a ping pong ball, bounce between the two countries in an attempt to be both "here and there" simultaneously, as though this balance could ever be fully achieved. Many feel, at least at times, "neither here nor there."

Two similarly titled documentaries about immigration explore this feeling of not belonging. It's telling that all three of us—myself and the filmmakers—chose similar phrases to define the immigrant experience. The first film, titled *Neither Here Nor There*, directed by Ema Ryan Yamazaki,[2] explores the lives of Third Culture Kids, children who grow up immersed in multiple cultures. The second, *Caught Between Two Worlds* by Iranian American filmmaker Persheng Vaziri,[3] focuses on the Iranian American immigration experience. I sense that, for these filmmakers, exploring the felt sense of being neither here nor there was also a way of working through their own feelings of internal division. Similarly, this book has been a personal attempt for me to process my own sense of split. In addition, the writing and work of psychoanalyst Lama Kohuri, as described earlier in Chapter 2, reflect her efforts to navigate her personal feelings of being divided between worlds.[4]

The question all these experiences raise is this: How can you feel at home—truly yourself? One approach is to honor both, deciding what parts of each home you want to preserve, what parts you want to transform, and what parts you wish to blend and integrate. Transcending the feeling of being split is a deeply creative endeavor. Another way to work through this split is by connecting with others—whether clients, coworkers, or friends— who also experience this tension, especially other immigrants. In such environments, the split can be more easily acknowledged and explored, and people can support each other in navigating the complexity of their identities.

As we move forward, I will continue to explore the themes of duality and belonging introduced in a section of the previous chapter, Feelings of Duality: Navigating Loss and Possibility. I have highlighted the challenges of existing between two places, never fully belonging to one or the other. Yet, with these difficulties come a certain richness. Having two worlds to draw from offers unique perspectives—an aspect we will delve into in greater depth. While you may feel the tension of being split between them and the extra time it takes to feel somewhat in sync, I encourage you to lean into your experience. Make a conscious effort to stay true to where you are, even when the world around you devalues or invalidates aspects of your identity and belonging. Embrace all parts of yourself and your connections to both places and pass this wisdom on to your children.

Five Attitudes to Help Immigrants Manage Their Feelings

Moving to a new country means leaving behind family and friends, familiar places, personal possessions, and a sense of safety. It means having to learn, often as an adult, everything, from new ways of relating to the use of new utensils. It causes a rupture in one's experience of space and time. It can be disorienting. It creates a feeling of shame for not knowing and not being skilled. It is nearly impossible to avoid experiencing trauma.

According to Salman Akhtar, *repudiation, return, replication, reunion,* and *reparation* are strategies that a person uses to manage the immigrant experience.[5] Reunion is defined as the excessive love and attachment to the motherland. The motherland is idealized. Memories and nostalgia prevail. Replication refers to the tendency to reproduce old habits and objects in the new country, sometimes with ritualistic precision, as if to recreate the old in the new environment. Reparation includes mechanisms fueled by guilt and love in which the immigrant makes reparation for having abandoned the motherland. Reparation spurs creativity and acts of generosity.

In the beginning of this process, newcomers may want to protect themselves from the pain of mourning by holding onto the belief that nothing has changed despite the immigration. They may think that the immigration is temporary or they may not even fully recognize the true reality and impact of immigration. This becomes a psychological strategy of refusing to accept the loss.[6]

Giorgio, the husband of one of my Italian patients, was living in the United States exactly as if he were still in Italy. As much as he could, he refused to speak English and tried to avoid interacting with the local population. When in mixed groups, he insisted on speaking Italian, unabashedly cutting some people off from the conversation. He insisted on eating only Italian cuisine and lived as if the environment around him had not changed.

On the opposite side of the spectrum are immigrants who too quickly divest themselves of their original identity and attachments, in an attempt to fully Americanize. They may adopt a stance of counterphobic assimilation, appearing brave to mask an underlying fear. While this strategy may look courageous, it can carry psychological risks.

Another common way of managing feelings about immigration is to develop an immoderate phantasy of return. People may devalue the local population, refuse to make an effort to enjoy daily life, and wait for positive experiences to start once they return to the motherland. Although this strategy has a psychological purpose that may be useful in the moment, it can become unhelpful, even all-consuming. When the focus on the imagined future takes the place of an investment in the present, the phantasy of the good times in the motherland deprives the immigrant of a good foothold in the present.

Often, the return remains a fantasy. And when it does happen, it rarely unfolds as imagined. Maruja Torres[7] coined the phrase *the wound of return* to describe this experience: The immigrant cannot pick up where they left off. The old country has changed—and so have they. Instead of reunion, return can feel like a second immigration. Some find themselves missing the country they once hoped to leave behind.

Cultural grief, a term often overlooked, captures the slow ache of losing not only a place but the rituals, scents, sounds, and language that once defined belonging. It is the longing for a grandmother's cooking, the comfort of one's native tongue, the unspoken ease of being among one's own. For many immigrants, this grief remains unnamed and misunderstood.

If you are a therapist, consider how these psychological strategies may present in your clients—not necessarily as pathology, but as efforts to cope and preserve identity. Gently exploring the function of each strategy can help individuals assess whether it is still serving them. In the context of cultural grief, attuning to subtler losses, often expressed through metaphor, food, or ritual, can allow clients to feel more deeply seen.

To understand an immigrant's current struggles and future hopes, it is essential to consider the whole arc: premigration life, departure, travel, and the complex adaptations that follow. Traumatic events, such as a dangerous journey, a harsh premigration environment, or detention while seeking asylum, can leave deep marks: PTSD, anxiety, diminished vitality, low self-worth, and fractured relationships. What was endured and what was dreamed of continues to echo in the present. These wounds may resurface unexpectedly, especially in old age, during transitions, or in moments of emotional rupture.

Reflection as Integration: Questions to Deepen Insight

Keeping in mind how losses may show up, as obstacles to living fully or as the sense that something vital is being left behind, work on establishing meaningful connections, reinforce your self-esteem, and work at integrating the different aspects of your life and bring your attention and care to how you are experiencing your ongoing phases of immigration. Take a moment, breathe, and remember—you are not alone in this experience.

For therapists working with newcomers, remember that early phases often involve profound disorientation. Your empathy and curiosity can serve as a stabilizing force, offering not only tools, but a relational anchor. Do not underestimate the value of naming the split—the sense of being divided between two worlds—even briefly.

If you are about to embark on your journey, consider this book a preparatory reading and a safeguard from feeling unmoored. Take this writing as the equivalent of the cough drops and anti-pain medication that you brought with you to the United States from your own country, just in case, even if you are in good health. If you are at the beginning of your journey, expect to experience a lot of stress. Do not be surprised if you find yourself hiding painful feelings in the depths of your heart. However, it is important to keep in mind that most immigrants report that, with time, many problems resolve, and they are able to master the challenges. There is hope. No matter how hard it may be right now, keep in mind that you are on a journey. These journeys are neither simple nor straightforward; they are often complicated. It is a journey into your heart and the very depths of what makes you you. And, there will be growth.

"Neither here nor there" is not only an individual issue. It is also an intergenerational issue. A patient recently verbalized his concerns about raising his children in the United States. He experienced growing ambivalence about the values of his host country and was startled by the unexpected ideas his children picked up in kindergarten:

> I am concerned that immigration is depriving my children of the values of my homeland, and that despite all my efforts, I am raising "American" children. By the time my grandchildren are born, their connection with my homeland will be completely lost.

He had immigrated to North America by choice and was initially more focused on what he would gain from the process. He felt fully Italian and had no sense that by living here he would be tainted by the many aspects of the American culture that he did not appreciate. But his progeny being born and bred in the United States brought this issue to his attention. He became alarmed about what might be lost; about his inability to pass his values on to his children—who are from here while he is from there. Because repatriation was not an option, he felt a sense of responsibility to increase his efforts to foster a positive sense of history, values, and traditions, as opposed to the homogenization he perceived coming from the school environment.

Italian American journalist Stefano Vaccara, who spoke at a conference on wellbeing and immigration held at the Italian Consulate in New York, shared that he willingly took the "fork" of becoming also American only after becoming a father. Embracing an American identity, he explained, became a necessity if he wanted to fully participate in the life of his American born children.[8]

As an immigrant, you face pressures from both sides: to conform to local standards from one side and to keep your original ways from the other. These pressures affect you and your interactions, both consciously and unconsciously. And because life moves so quickly, and we are all so busy, it's not always easy to take the necessary time to pause and reflect on the influences, gifts, successes, losses, and obstacles we encounter in our journey—the things that inform our values and give shape to who we are becoming. Much can be gained when you take stock of your situation, including your history and the overarching social dynamics that affect you. With this knowledge, you will be able to focus better on your trajectory, understand your feelings and difficulties, improve your relationships, and define your goals.

For therapists, intergenerational conflict may surface in nuanced ways—through guilt, fear of loss, or a desperate push to preserve heritage. Naming this tension can create space for intentional choices and reduce unconscious friction between generations. Recognizing this complexity, both for yourself and those you support, can deepen empathy, reframe expectations, and renew your sense of direction.

Takeaway Exercise

Take a moment each day to focus on yourself and meditate on one of these questions. Journaling would be best:

- If, in your immigration journey, you can discern periods or phases that are distinctively different, what are those?
- How do you manage the duality of belonging in your body and mind, in your home, and with the people near to you and far away?
- What are your values, and how are they evolving?
- Thinking back to the influence of your family and ancestors, what are the sociocultural and economic forces that affected you and/or your family's move?
- How and why did your immigration process start, and how has the world around you influenced, sustained, and complicated your journey?
- Where are you headed now?
- What's the next step, with regard to your immigration journey?
- What are the influences that helped shape your journey?
- Who are the mentors—people, religious figures, or books—that helped shape your journey?
- Who else could mentor you now?
- What else is important to ask yourself now that you have not yet asked?

As you sit with all this—losses mourned and strengths reclaimed—remember that you are not alone. This journey of "neither here nor there" is also a journey of becoming. These questions are offered as companions along the way.

Family Separations

A more dramatic situation often unfolds when one or both parents migrate to the United States to work and send money back home, as commonly occurs in the Caribbean and Latin America, laying the groundwork to eventually bring their children over. By the time the children arrive, however, both parents and children may have idealized the long-awaited reunion and find themselves unprepared for its emotional complexity. Children may harbor resentment about having been left behind and miss their caretakers, while parents—exhausted by demanding work schedules—struggle to be present. These reunions are often marked by tension, emotional distance, and unmet expectations, making adaptation especially difficult for the children. In some cases, the challenges are so great that the children are ultimately sent back to their countries of origin.[9] Notably, the length of separation does not always predict distress; what matters more is the emotional quality of relationships before, during, and after migration. When the separation is framed as temporary and meaningful—undertaken for the good of the family—and when children are supported by emotionally available caretakers and remain psychologically connected to the absent parent, they often show remarkable resilience. But when grief, ambivalence, or silence surrounds the separation, children are more likely to feel abandoned. For therapists, these findings serve as a reminder: Reunification is not a simple return, but a deeply symbolic and relational turning point—one that must be navigated with care, intention, and support.[10]

Children show remarkable resilience, especially when well supported, even if after enduring multiple traumatic experiences. However, when family separation is caused by forced removal rather than a shared family decision centered on the future wellbeing of the family, it is far more likely—if not certain—to have harmful effects.[11]

Takeaway Exercise: Forced Separation and Reunion Sharing (With a Therapist or Facilitator)

If your family was separated by force—whether by war, detention, deportation, or the economic demands of migration—your pain is real, and so are your strengths. This reflection invites you to name what was lost, what still hurts, and what can be reclaimed. It is not about erasing what happened, but about acknowledging it with care and witnessing your own survival. What was taken from you without your consent? What emotions did you carry through the separation and the reunion? Who showed up for you emotionally—if anyone—during that time? If the separation was never fully addressed or acknowledged, what would you want someone to say to you now? What message do you want to give to yourself today, knowing what you have lived through?

Optional: Write a short letter to your younger self who lived through that separation. Say what was never said or what needed to be heard.

Takeaway Exercise: Stitching the Pieces of the Journey Together: A Family Collage (With the Help of a Therapist or Facilitator)

This activity is designed for immigrant families, including children and adults of all ages—especially those who have experienced family separation, reunion, or transition. It offers a creative way to process memories, honor experiences, and reconnect across generations. However, it is best to do this with a therapist who can determine if the family is ready and safe to do this exercise, and the therapist can monitor participants' reactions along the way.

Materials Needed: A large sheet of paper or fabric for base; old photographs, scraps of magazines; photocopies of documents, drawings, maps, stamps, ticket stubs; scissors, glue, colored pencils, markers.

Create Together: Each family member takes time to recall a personal moment connected to their migration story: What was left behind; hopes or fears about the journey; a cherished object or sound; a moment of connection or loss.

Express yourself and as a family with art: Everyone contributes something to the collage. You can display it, save it, or dispose it either in a body of water (if not polluting) or by putting it in the ground or burning it; taking all necessary safety precautions and under supervision of adults.

Therapist Note: In clinical work, it is essential to validate that not all separations are chosen, and not all reunions bring relief. Therapists should be attentive to the ambiguity, grief, and injustice that accompany such experiences. Encouraging clients to narrate their separation stories—with control over pacing and language—can be a powerful step toward integration. It is particularly relevant to explore the attachment dynamics of the family members.

When trauma is expressed visually and collectively, it becomes more manageable. The exercise above encourages storytelling, strengthens bonds, and honors the full expression of the migration experience—loss, joy, confusion, pride. It teaches that nothing is fixed: we can rebuild, repurpose, and redefine what has shaped us.

For families with histories of separation or trauma, however, the process may evoke intense emotions or painful memories. In such cases, it is essential that a therapist or trained facilitator be present to guide the experience, hold space for ambivalence, and help prevent retraumatization.

As therapists, by facilitating and witnessing this process, we open a window into family dynamics and intergenerational memory. It is not only an act of expression, but one of healing—inviting families to recover together.

Notes

1 UNHCR, "Venezuela Situation," *UNHCR Operational Data Portal*, https://data.unhcr.org/en/situations/vensit.
2 *Neither Here Nor There*, directed by Ema Ryan Yamazaki (2015).
3 *Caught Between Two Worlds*, directed by Persheng Vaziri (2002).
4 Lama Zuhair Khouri, "The Immigrant's Neverland," *Contemporary Psychoanalysis* 48, no. 2 (2012): doi:10.1080/00107530.2012.10746499.
5 Khouri, 12–34.
6 Salman Akhtar, *Immigration and Acculturation: Mourning, Adaptation, and the Next Generation* (Lanham, MD: Jason Aronson, 2011), 12.
7 Maruja Torres, *Mientras Vivimos* (Barcelona: Planeta, 2000), 112.
8 *Cultura e Benessere Beyond Borders: Exploring the Strengths and Struggles of First Generation Italian Immigrants' Well-Being.* This conference was organized by Leide Porcu, PhD for Comites NY and took place in November 2024.
9 For a discussion about the Caribbean context please see Martha Bragin and M. Pierrepointe, "Complex Attachments: A Discussion of the Nature of Attachment in Families Where the Global Economy Has Necessitated Migration to the North," *Journal of Infant, Child, and Adolescent Psychotherapy* 3, no. 1 (2004): 41–46, doi:10.1080/15289160409348773.
10 This summary draws on Suárez-Orozco, Todorova, and Louie's (2002) study of immigrant family separation and reunification, which highlights how children's emotional responses depend more on the quality of relationships and communication than on the length of separation. See Carola Suárez-Orozco, Irina Todorova, and Josephine Louie, "Making Up for Lost Time: The Experience of Separation and Reunification Among Immigrant Families," *Family Process* 41, no 4 (2002): 625–643.
11 See also Laura C. Wood, who describes the severe psychological effects of forced family separation on refugee children. Laura C. N. Wood, "Impact of Punitive Immigration Policies, Parent–Child Separation and Child Detention on the Mental Health and Development of Children," *BMJ Paediatrics Open* 2, no. 1 (2018): e000338, doi:10.1136/bmjpo-2018-000338, 1–6.

References

Akhtar, Salman. 2011. *Immigration and Acculturation: Mourning, Adaptation, and the Next Generation*. Lanham, MD: Jason Aronson.
Bragin, Martha, and M. Pierrepointe. 2004. "Complex Attachments: A Discussion of the Nature of Attachment in Families Where the Global Economy Has Necessitated Migration to the North." *Journal of Infant, Child, and Adolescent Psychotherapy* 3 (1): 41–46. doi:10.1080/15289160409348773.
Suárez-Orozco, Carola, Irina Todorova, and Josephine Louie. 2002. "Making Up for Lost Time: The Experience of Separation and Reunification Among Immigrant Families." *Family Process* 41 (4): 625–643. doi:10.1111/j.1545-5300.2002.00625.x.
Torres, Maruja. 2000. *Mientras Vivimos*. Barcelona: Planeta.
UNHCR. 2025. "Venezuela Situation." UNHCR Operational Data Portal. https://data.unhcr.org/en/situations/vensit.
Vaziri, Persheng, dir. 2002. *Caught Between Two Worlds*. Documentary.
Wood, Laura C. N. 2018. "Impact of Punitive Immigration Policies, Parent-Child Separation and Child Detention on the Mental Health and Development of Children." *BMJ Paediatrics Open* 2 (1): e000338. doi:10.1136/bmjpo-2018-000338.
Yamazaki, Ema Ryan, dir. 2015. *Neither Here Nor There*. Documentary.

Part II

Integrating and Adapting

At this point in my life, I see living in the United States as a positive experience. I find myself able to connect with both immigrants and Americans. I have always loved culture, and now that I am older, I can better appreciate the opportunities this country offers—opportunities that were harder to access in the place I came from. Over time, I have found more people who share my values. It feels like a place where growth is possible.

When I go back to visit my home country, I sometimes feel out of sync. Many of my old friends seem to hold views that feel outdated to me, especially when it comes to gender roles. Here in the U.S., there is more room for women to speak openly and be taken seriously. But back home, I still hear casual sexist remarks, and I am surprised that many women seem to accept them without question.

—Anonymous contributor (Western Europe)

4 The Immigrant Paradox

Sometimes the First Generation Thrives More Than Their Children and U.S.-Born Peers

A Therapist's Guide to Understanding the Complexities of Adaptation

Understanding the Immigrant Paradox

Research highlights that some groups of immigrants arrive in the United States with better overall physical and mental health than the general population.[1] This is referred to as the *immigrant paradox.* [2] However, this phenomenon is not universal and varies across different populations, influenced by factors such as region of origin, socioeconomic status, racialization, and generational change. This pattern runs counter to research showing immigrants as more vulnerable to deleterious health effects that stem from acculturation and trauma.[3] However, the advantages some immigrants show tend to erode over time. Second-generation immigrants in particular face systemic challenges and adopt less beneficial aspects of American society, and this may have consequences to their mental health. While first-generation immigrants may experience cultural dislocation, their retention of traditional practices often serves as a buffer—one that tends to diminish in the second generation. Second-generation immigrants, however, frequently grapple with the loss of these protective factors, compounded by experiences of marginalization and racism.[4] This trend is particularly observed among some Latino and Asian immigrant groups, although it is not universal and may depend on legal status, race, and premigration conditions.[5]

Carola and Marcelo Arredondo Orozco's research[6] offers valuable insights into these dynamics. Their study found that second-generation Mexican students in the United States often exhibit diminished academic motivation and achievement compared to their peers in Mexico. These students' disengagement frequently stems from systemic inequities, such as limited professional opportunities, despite their qualifications. This can lead to disillusionment and behaviors mirroring those of their American peers, including reduced respect for authority and a decrease in academic rigor.

Using interviews and projective tests, the authors compared achievement rates among three groups of students: 1) students living and studying in areas

DOI: 10.4324/9781003648703-7

of Mexico experiencing high emigration rates, 2) recent U.S. Mexican immigrants, and 3) children of U.S. immigrants, or second-generation U.S. immigrants. Their research shows that while the Mexican students had high achievement rates, were committed to school and homework, and wanted to achieve, make money, and take care of their families, the longer the Mexican immigrants were in the United States, the less they cared about school performance and achievement. The more the immigrants settled, the more they had an increasingly bad attitude toward school, became disrespectful to their teachers, and were lax in their work, similar to their White peers. It was as if, over time, the negative attitudes of the local populations had rubbed off on them. As the authors point out, Latino kids were justifiably disillusioned about school. Statistics show that Latino Americans with the same college level as their White counterparts fare differently than White Americans in their professional life and have lower earnings.

These data allow us to understand in a deeper way the forces at work within immigrant communities. They also counteract the public rhetoric and stereotypes that portray immigrants in a negative way, especially when contrasted with "the American way," which is regularly touted as the ideal that immigrants should emulate wholesale. They also highlight the importance of maintaining some of their original healthy habits, culture, and community, of nurturing a sense of pride in their children, helping them navigate local challenges and hold onto valued aspects of their heritage. Although the host country provides many opportunities, it can also take things away. Knowledge of the immigrant paradox provides clients with an anchor to hold onto when they feel diminished by local negative biases. It is helpful to consider that immigrants, despite the common feeling of never being enough, have much to offer professionally and culturally.

For clinicians and community workers, it's crucial to be aware of these dynamics and validate immigrants' experiences while helping clients maintain a connection to the strengths and cultural values of their heritage. The research on the immigrant paradox provides insights into the complex health dynamics immigrants may experience. This understanding encourages the implementation of proactive health monitoring and culturally sensitive interventions to address the unique challenges immigrants face, such as language barriers, cultural differences, and limited access to healthcare services.

The concept of the healthy immigrant paradox underscores the health-promoting values and traditions within immigrants' cultures of origin, reminding individuals of the aspects worth retaining and offering professionals a deeper appreciation of these strengths. However, it's important to note that there is no consensus among researchers regarding its universality. Some studies have even indicated that what appears to be an immigrant advantage may actually be a result of methodological flaws. For instance, research in Canada has revealed that older racialized immigrants are underdiagnosed for mental illnesses, suggesting they may not be as healthy as previously believed.[7]

Moreover, the immigrant paradox does not operate in a vacuum. Its expression varies significantly across racialized groups, especially for immigrants of African descent.

The Elevated "Black" Immigrant

Immigrants of African descent face unique challenges and opportunities within the U.S. racial hierarchy. As researcher Christina Greer has found, Afro-Caribbean and African immigrants, unlike African Americans, often emphasize their foreign identities to navigate systemic racism.[8] As she maintains:

> The "forever foreigner" concept that is so readily attached to Asian Americans is manifested differently for African and Afro-Caribbeans, who actively attempt to remain foreign. Junn and Masuoka (2008) argue that the "untrustworthy perpetual outsider" status of Asian Americans serves as a glass ceiling preventing full social integration for Asian Americans. However, for Afro-Caribbeans and Africans, their desire to remain an outsider or foreigner actually precipitates a stronger sense of inclusion into American society, especially by White Americans and economically privileged groups.[9]

This strategy can offer a path to upward mobility—though second-generation immigrants often grow disillusioned as the realities of systemic inequities emerge.

As Nina Jablonski[10] explains, U.S. society is "color obsessed." Even if scientifically untrue, racial hierarchical classifications based on color are a common way of seeing people, which are not only used by commoners but are also still used in medical and scientific systems (e.g., "Black" and "Caucasian" are used regularly in surveys and medical data collection).

The critique of using the term "Black" as an ethnicity in the United States must be understood within the broader context of extensive U.S. literature that uses "Black" and "White" as practical and widely accepted terms to denote socially constructed racial identities. While these categories are recognized as socially and historically constructed rather than biological absolutes, they remain essential for understanding social dynamics, inequalities, and group identities. Greer also acknowledges that descriptive representation—sharing racial, ethnic, or gender characteristics—can foster feelings of solidarity, familiarity, and self-esteem within groups, notably Blacks.[11] Thus, despite the problematic origins of racial categories, the concept of "Blackness" in the United States continues to serve as a significant and meaningful social identity, one that unites diverse groups belonging to the African diaspora (e.g., African Americans, Caribbean Black communities, African immigrants, and other Afro-descendants) while also reflecting internal differences and struggles.

While the socially constructed nature and practical utility of racial categories is widely acknowledged, for the purposes of this discussion it is important to recognize how they are imposed on the dark-skinned immigrants upon arrival to the United States. Once here, they are often, consciously or unconsciously, seen, categorized, and judged according to local schemes, stereotypes, and hierarchies of value.

Dark-skinned people who immigrate to the United States often resist these negative stereotypes by continuing to emphasize their country of origin in their self-presentation, even long after immigration, as a way of defining their identity. In contrast, light-skinned people, after being a long time in the country, do not feel the desperate need to maintain their link to the country of origin for self-definition and to maintain self-value and respect.

In her study of New York City's workers of the Social Service Employee Union (SSEU) Local 371, Greer made valuable observations in this regard.[12] According to Greer, racial classification in the United States has moved over time from White versus non-White to Black versus non-Black, Black being the least valuable social position in society. In her research, she divided the population in her study into roughly three groups: African Americans, Afro-Caribbeans (mostly second-generation) and African immigrants (first-generation). She explored how Black immigrants from Africa and the Caribbean who come to the United States face two distinctive problematic frames that define them: the immigrant versus native binary; and the Black versus non-Black binary. Black immigrants, by the symbolic power of sheer color, no matter where they come from or who they are, are socially lumped and pegged as "Black" alongside the local dark-skinned populations, regardless of their country of origin or individual identity. In the United States, skin color becomes the most salient marker of group membership. However, interestingly, Greer maintains, as non-Americans, they can escape the negative stereotypes reserved to African Americans and can possibly be "elevated" by White Americans to the special status of "good Blacks," that is, dark-skinned immigrants who are hard-working and smarter (meaning, unlike the African American population).

Greer talks of the stratagem of the *forever foreigner*, which, for Black immigrants, is a favorable route to upward mobility.[13] However, she found that among dark-skinned immigrants, the belief in the American Dream fades over time. Second-generation Afro-Caribbeans were the most disillusioned, while new African immigrants hold onto the American Dream, perhaps because many of them cannot return to their home country, whereas first-generation Afro-Caribbean people, if unsuccessful, can resort to returning home and have another chance of realizing their dream.

One of my light-skinned European patients, who married a dark-skinned man from Tanzania, tells me that all her friends love her very nice, sociable, well-educated, wealthy, and business-wise husband. However, she also tells me with dismay how she is experiencing some racism in the United States, not coming from their friends and colleagues, but rather from the distracted passersby or in situations where her husband is not well known. Unconscious racist/classist assumptions automatically kick in. At large professional and social gatherings, people assume he is not "one of them" but he is there to serve. For instance, despite the fact he was dressed to the nines at a fancy event, people thought he was a server and asked him several times to fetch water or food or handed him their empty glass and dirty napkins.

As is evident from this discussion, racial identities and racial hierarchies are complex. In turn, clients and patients may experience complex feelings of belonging and exclusion, shaped by both their immigrant status and the racialized landscape of American society. For therapists working with immigrants, these insights underscore the importance of exploring the intersection of race, immigration status, and cultural identity in clinical work, in themselves, and in their relationship with their patients.

Intersectionality: A Framework for Understanding Complex Identities

> Intersectionality: The interconnected nature of social categorizations such as race, class, and gender, regarded as creating overlapping and interdependent systems of discrimination or disadvantage.
>
> —The Oxford Dictionary[14]

Kimberlé Crenshaw's concept of intersectionality provides a powerful lens for understanding immigrant experiences. Rather than viewing categories of identities, such as gender, sexuality, nationality, ethnicity, race, age, and ability, in isolation, intersectionality is a way of considering how they intersect and reinforce one another, placing us in positions of relative power, privilege, and oppression, and coming together to shape our experiences. It helps explain why some people face unique challenges because of the way these different aspects of their identity interact with each other. They are forces that are felt but difficult to pinpoint, due to their complexity and often implicit, or unconscious, nature, which makes them hard to resist or challenge. When affected by these forces, we experience situations as our fault; we blame (and are blamed for) a lack of willpower and "laziness." We and others downplay or do not see the categories that converge upon us and help us succeed or not. Working papers and visa difficulties that would already be hard to navigate by anyone can be aggravated by intersectional impediments.

Consider Antonio, a second-generation Bolivian immigrant navigating the corporate world. Despite his professional success, Antonio faces an invisible barrier (both social and internalized) shaped by his ethnicity, working-class background, and second-generation immigrant status. His struggle to find belonging among his elite, predominantly White peers illustrates how intersecting factors create conditions that restrict full inclusion.

Antonio experiences the world in a way that reflects both his success and his roots. Despite his achievements, he has not forgotten his humble origins.

He can easily "adapt" and fit in when attending family celebrations, staying connected to his roots. Antonio is handsome, charismatic, intelligent, and easy to get along with. He is street smart and a reader of people, so he knows how to position himself with people; he is creative, a hard worker, and performs well in teams. He is a combination of an immigrant's mischievousness, characterized by the immigrant way of cutting corners and "making do," and being a "good boy," which he developed in childhood where he learned to anticipate people's needs and wants. His attempt to please, fit in, to feel secure by acquiring both love and safety, is quite often at the expense of his own needs. This type of childhood automatic learning, which was functional back then, is one of the things we are trying to address in therapy, because it is not helpful in many ways in the present. However, it turns out that these skills are somewhat helpful at work.

Over the years, Antonio has successfully moved up the social ladder, making significant progress in his career and earning international recognition within his company, but has now encountered an invisible barrier based on his intersectional identity. His immigrant background continues to shape how others see him and how he feels about himself. Even as he thrives in the corporate world, Antonio still carries the weight of his humble, working-class, blue-collar beginnings. His ethnicity also plays a role, as being of Bolivian descent may expose him to subtle biases or assumptions that affect how he is perceived in professional spaces. On the surface, Antonio's gender and appearance—being a capable and attractive man—might seem like advantages. However, these qualities do not erase the deeper challenges he faces because of his background and identity. The intersections of his second-generation immigrant status, working-class upbringing, and ethnicity create a unique mix of experiences that contribute to his ongoing struggle with impostor syndrome. This stems from growing up without a natural sense of belonging to a social class higher than his family's. Antonio also senses that the leadership at his company sometimes views him through an *alterity lens* and does not offer him the same opportunities of advancement. Alterity means the state of being "other" or different. Despite his success, he sometimes feels like he does not fully belong at the top levels of his company. With every success, another layer of this feeling is revealed. After processing each layer, he is able to take a second look and recognize that what he initially perceived as personal shortcomings or incapacity was, in fact, a distortion rooted in his imposter syndrome.

Over time, Antonio has become more able to accept his success as a genuine reflection of his talent and hard work. However, new achievements reveal new layers of self-doubt, showing that these challenges are both external and internal; they go beyond individual, personal psychology, stemming from the internalization of the social hierarchies and negative classifications present in his environment.

Now that he has almost reached the top of the ladder in his company, he faces a particularly hard roadblock. The C- suite in his company is entirely composed of White heterosexual men, mostly middle aged, from elite families. They have effortless styles, branded narratives, and interests and hobbies that he doesn't share. He has a hard time feeling equal and that he belongs. Indeed, from a socioeconomic viewpoint, he is not equal with them; clearly his parents did not break bread with the parents of these guys. He didn't attend an Ivy League school, like them; he did not go to fancy places for the holidays as a kid. He experiences anxiety and cannot engage with them with naturalness and ease. Antonio spends an unhelpful amount of time ruminating about what wrong thing he did or said, and he dissects his "mistakes." Belonging to this rarefied group would be the next step in his career. However, he has had a hard time finding his C-suite footing, unsure of the contribution he would make or what title would suit him next. His promotion and acceptance as one of this gang are lagging.

Despite his anxieties and self-doubts, because of historical family vicissitudes, he has learned since childhood to shield his emotions. No one notices his anxiety and negative thinking. He is always smiling, charming, contained, and affable. If this way of processing may be unhelpful in other situations (e.g., romantic relationships), the lack of overt emotional expression of his inner turmoil is helpful at work, allowing him to appear unphased even when he feels anxious inside.

More recently, the gap between the Olympian rarefied world of the C-suite and himself is starting to close. Indeed, the more he hangs out with C-suite people, the more he faces his fears. Antonio is also gaining a more realistic experience of them. As he dispels his idealizations and distortions about "who is big and who is small, who has and who has not," his evaluation of this exalted successful elite is changing. He is now realizing that these people are not perfect and do not know everything. The only difference is that they do not care as much about it. They do not obsess about their limitations. He is learning that at some level he is not so different from them. However, unlike him, they have a "natural" trust in the process and their progress. He says:

> I am realizing that everybody, including them, is swimming upstream. Kamala Harris is, my boss John is, his boss James is too. We all are. This is not unique to me. Also, the person across the table, even if they went to an Ivy League, are trying to swim upstream, just like me. So, I need to learn to continue to swim upstream no matter what. I am figuring out that also these people at work, even if they are so intimidating and looking flawless—are normal and are struggling to get upstream too. I just need to remember that, when I feel intimidated and lose focus. The more I get confident and feel I belong to the table, the more I will be in the initial invited list and the more will be able to collaborate on equal terms.

At the same time, the C-Suite seems to be warming up to him, increasingly acknowledging him almost as part of the gang. While Antonio's vulnerabilities and sociocultural barriers are difficult to overcome, his particular background is also his strength; he has a particular way of approaching problems. His current ability to "read a room" and navigate challenging situations is a positive outcome of a difficult childhood, during which he learned to manage family members' needy and erratic behaviors. He is resilient and relentless, having adopted a strong immigrant work ethic from his family, and he is driven by a deep desire for success: he is "hungry for success." Intersectionality helps us see that Antonio's challenges are not only about being an immigrant or coming from a blue-collar family. It is the combination of all these parts of his identity that make his experience more complex, but also more uniquely his own. While initially creating hurdles, these aspects of his background have contributed to his considerable resilience and success.

Moreover, in a similar way that Antonio struggles to find his place in the C-suite, immigrant clinicians frequently face challenges in asserting themselves among their Western colleagues. Their voices and clinical intuitions may not carry the same weight in shaping the field. In some cases, they may even devalue their own insights, feeling hesitant to share their observations with a broader audience. Yet, their unique position, while making them vulnerable, is also a source of strength. Immigrant clinicians, being as "decentered" as their patients, can connect deeply with the immigrant population, speaking their language, understanding their worldviews, and better intuiting the importance of their spiritual practices and beliefs. Comas Diaz,[15] for instance, talks of her difficulties as a Latina with a physical impediment. Yet, her social positioning as an immigrant woman with a history of colonization, oppression, and a slight disability helped her emerge as a powerful voice. Drawing on her unique background, she has helped develop clinical insights and techniques that have shaped the field and deepened connections with her immigrant clients.

Often, immigrants who are privileged, when facing painful immigration roadblocks, do not feel entitled to their pain. They know that many others have it worse. Children of immigrants especially feel this way; they compare their own lives to the harshness of what their parents endured and the living conditions of their relatives who have remained behind.

As therapists, it's important to validate clients' perceptions—to affirm that expressing their distress is not "whining" and that they are entitled to their feelings.

For instance, Diana, a light-skinned professional immigrant from Europe, said:

> Something imperceptible is always eluding me. I live here, but I feel I am looking at New York City from a window. I see the people, I hear their voices, but I cannot connect and be part of the flow. I feel I could do great things, but there is an invisible barrier, and I don't think it is simply a language problem. I don't feel accepted or valued. As a consequence, I am not actualizing as much as I could.

Here, Diana beautifully describes the difficult state of being "neither here nor there"—not properly fitting in, not in sync with the surrounding world, seen as an outsider despite all of her efforts and contributions, and living life more like a spectator than as a natural part of it. Similar comments were made by Liz and Tom from the section Feelings of Duality: Navigating Loss and Possibility in Chapter 2. Also, there is an unspoken structural barrier that pertains to language proficiency. If you do not speak the language well, your contributions, no matter how smart, will likely be othered and devalued.

For therapists, addressing intersectionality means recognizing how these overlapping identities affect clients' mental health and social positioning. Therapists need also to become aware of their own intersectional positioning and maintain a self-reflective stance about their positioning vis-à-vis their patients. Therapists can help clients like Antonio process their feelings of inadequacy, understand where they come from, and develop strategies for self-advocacy and resilience.

Clinical Reflections: Supporting Immigrant Clients

As professionals working with immigrant populations, we must approach their challenges with sensitivity and a deep understanding of the systemic and cultural factors at play, in which we are also implicated. The following reflections may help guide your work:

1 *Validate the Complexity of Experiences:*

- Encourage clients to explore how intersecting identities impact their experiences.
- Normalize feelings of alienation and self-doubt while highlighting their resilience.

2 *Preserve Cultural Strengths:*

- Help clients maintain and adapt cultural practices that serve as protective factors.
- Discuss how these strengths can coexist with their evolving identities.

3 *Address Systemic Barriers:*

- Work with clients to identify systemic challenges, such as workplace discrimination or unequal opportunities.
- Develop actionable strategies to navigate these barriers effectively.

4 *Encourage Self-Reflection:*

- Use exercises like the ones provided below to help clients examine how sociocultural factors shape their lives.

Takeaway Exercise for Readers on this Journey or for Therapists to Give to Patients

As immigrants or children of immigrants, the multiple forces of family history, migration, race, gender, class, and language interact with one another in visible and invisible ways. Reflect on the following questions to deepen your self-awareness:

- Which school and professional possibilities were on the horizon for you growing up?
- Were traditional gender roles salient in your environment growing up?
- What hopes and expectations did people have for you?
- How has the economic status of your family, the race and ethnicity of your family, and your gender affected how you grew up and who you have become today? How do they shape the ways you interact with others and feel about yourself?
- How have socioeconomic, racial, and cultural forces shaped your identity and opportunities?
- What strategies do you use to navigate systemic barriers?
- How do you balance maintaining cultural heritage with adapting to a new environment?
- In what ways do you see concepts like the immigrant paradox or intersectionality playing a role in your life?

Readers: Reflect on aspects of your intersectional identities and how they have shaped your sense of self and journey can help you better understand yourself and reclaim your voice.

Therapists: By integrating these reflective practices into your work, you can support clients in navigating the complexities of immigrant life while celebrating their unique strengths and contributions.

Notes

1 B. Duncan and S. Trejo, *Socioeconomic Integration of U.S. Immigrant Groups over the Long Term: The Second Generation and Beyond* (No. w24394) (Cambridge, MA: National Bureau of Economic Research, 2018).

2 Andrew F. Moore, "The Immigrant Paradox: Protecting Immigrants Through Better Mental Health Care," *Albany Law Review* 81 (2018): 77–120.

3 John W. Berry, "Immigration, Acculturation, and Adaptation," *Applied Psychology: An International Review* 46, no. 1 (1997): 5–34, doi:10.1111/j.1464-0597.1997.tb01087.x.

4 With reference to anti-social behavior, Vaughn et al., report: "Thus far, findings indicate that immigrants are significantly less likely to be antisocial than native-born Americans. This is known as the immigrant paradox, whereby first-generation immigrants display better behavioral outcomes than native-born Americans and more highly acculturated immigrants despite the relative socioeconomic disadvantages and risk factors that immigrants face. ... Based on data from the Pathways to Desistance Study—a longitudinal study of serious youthful

offenders—Piquero et al. (2014) suggested that legal socialization is a significant explanation for the immigrant paradox. In their analyses, first-generation immigrants had more positive views of the law/criminal justice system, had less cynical attitudes about the legal system, and reported greater costs/negative consequences associated with punishment compared to second generation immigrants and native-born youth. Taken together, these results suggest that over time the protective mechanisms among newly arrived immigrants begin to wane."

Michael G. Vaughn, Christopher P. Salas-Wright, and Brandy R. Maynard, "Criminal Epidemiology and the Immigrant Paradox: Intergenerational Discontinuity in Violence and Antisocial Behavior Among Immigrants," *Journal of Criminal Justice* 42, no. 6 (2014): 483–490.

5 For more information on how the immigrant paradox varies across different populations, see:

Kyriakos S. Markides and Jeanne Coreil, "The Health of Hispanics in the Southwestern United States: An Epidemiologic Paradox," *Public Health Reports* 101, no. 3 (1986): 253–265.

Margarita Alegría et al., "Prevalence of Mental Illness in Immigrant and US-Born Latino Groups," *American Journal of Psychiatry* 165, no. 3 (2008): 359–369.

Kate H. Choi, "Reconsidering the 'Immigrant Paradox': An Integrative Review of the Literature on Immigrants' Health Advantage," *Social Science & Medicine* 314 (2022): 115398.

Tod G. Hamilton and Robert A. Hummer, "Immigration and the Health of U.S. Black Adults: Does Country of Origin Matter?" *Social Science & Medicine* 73, no. 10 (2011): 1551–1560.

6 Carola Suárez-Orozco and Marcelo M. Suárez-Orozco, *Transformations: Immigration, Family Life, and Achievement Motivation Among Latino Adolescents* (Stanford: Stanford University Press, 1995).

7 Shen (Lamson) Lin, "Healthy Immigrant Effect or Under-Detection? Examining Undiagnosed and Unrecognized Late-Life Depression for Racialized Immigrants and Nonimmigrants in Canada," *The Journals of Gerontology, Series B: Psychological Sciences and Social Sciences* 79, no. 3 (2024): 1–16.

8 Lin, 26.

9 Christina M. Greer, *Black Ethnics: Race, Immigration, and the Pursuit of the American Dream* (New York: Oxford University Press, 2007), 26.

10 Nina G. Jablonski, "Skin Color and Race," *American Journal of Physical Anthropology* 175 (2021): 437–447, at 442.

11 Christina M. Greer, *Black Ethnics: Race, Immigration, and the Pursuit of the American Dream* (New York: Oxford University Press, 2007), 26.

12 Greer, 28.

13 Greer, 26.

14 Oxford English Dictionary, s.v. "Intersectionality," www.oed.com/dictionary/inter sectionality_n?tl=true.

15 Lillian Comas-Díaz, Barry A. Farber, and John C. Norcross, "Becoming a Multicultural Psychotherapist: The Confluence of Culture, Ethnicity, and Gender," *Journal of Clinical Psychology* 61, no. 8 (2005): 973–981.

References

Alegría, Margarita, Glorisa Canino, Maria J. Shrout, Chih-nan Chen, Sharon L. Monteverde, Michael N. Duan, and Philip K. Liao. 2008. "Prevalence of Mental Illness in Immigrant and US-Born Latino Groups." *American Journal of Psychiatry* 165 (3): 359–369.

Choi, Kate H. 2022. "Reconsidering the 'Immigrant Paradox': An Integrative Review of the Literature on Immigrants' Health Advantage." *Social Science & Medicine* 314: 115398.

Comas-Díaz, Lillian, Barry A. Farber, and John C. Norcross. 2005. "Becoming a Multicultural Psychotherapist: The Confluence of Culture, Ethnicity, and Gender." *Journal of Clinical Psychology* 61 (8): 973–981.

Greer, Christina M. 2013. *Black Ethnics: Race, Immigration, and the Pursuit of the American Dream.* New York: Oxford University Press.

Hamilton, Tod G., and Robert A. Hummer. 2011. "Immigration and the Health of U.S. Black Adults: Does Country of Origin Matter?" *Social Science & Medicine* 73 (10): 1551–1560.

Jablonski, Nina G. 2021. "Skin Color and Race." *American Journal of Physical Anthropology* 175: 437–447.

Lin, Shen (Lamson). 2024. "Healthy Immigrant Effect or Under-Detection? Examining Undiagnosed and Unrecognized Late-Life Depression for Racialized Immigrants and Nonimmigrants in Canada." *The Journals of Gerontology, Series B: Psychological Sciences and Social Sciences* 79 (3): 1–16.

Markides, Kyriakos S., and Jeanne Coreil. 1986. "The Health of Hispanics in the Southwestern United States: An Epidemiologic Paradox." *Public Health Reports* 101 (3): 253–265.

Moore, Andrew F. 2017/2018. "The Immigrant Paradox: Protecting Immigrants Through Better Mental Health Care." *Albany Law Review* 81 (1): 78.

Suárez-Orozco, Carola, and Marcelo M. Suárez-Orozco. 1995. *Transformations: Immigration, Family Life, and Achievement Motivation Among Latino Adolescents.* Stanford, CA: Stanford University Press.

Vaughn, Michael G., Christopher P. Salas-Wright, and Brandy R. Maynard. 2014. "Criminal Epidemiology and the Immigrant Paradox: Intergenerational Discontinuity in Violence and Antisocial Behavior Among Immigrants." *Journal of Criminal Justice* 42 (6): 483–490.

5 Feeling Stuck

A Broken Gear Box of Emotions

I do not remember who said it, but there is a saying that goes something like, "it's through the cracks that the light comes in." That has always stayed with me. I have been broken open in many ways—by loss, by distance, by change—but that is also how I have grown.

—Anonymous contributor

A patient naturally skilled at creating metaphors told me that as an immigrant she feels like she is constantly driving a car with a broken gear box. To those of you who are immigrants, this image may resonate. And to therapists, take note: Metaphors like this often carry emotional truths that can unlock deeper layers of your client's experience.

The metaphor of driving a car with a broken gearbox is a powerful one. It represents the struggle to move forward, despite feeling like something essential is out of alignment. No matter how hard you push, things don't run smoothly, and that creates frustration, exhaustion, and emotional wear. Many immigrants can relate to this, feeling as though they are navigating life with parts of themselves still stuck in the past or in a place that no longer exists as they remember it. They are driving a wreck without the money to repair it in a world that requires they race against mint race cars. But like the quote above from an anonymous contributor, this process of struggle and heartache can also lead to growth. The difficulties immigrants face are not merely obstacles: They are opportunities for transformation. They challenge us to reconsider who we are beyond the labels and attachments we once had. In time, this painful breaking can help open us to new possibilities, new strengths, and a deeper sense of self that transcends a single place or culture.

Feeling Overwhelmed and Disorganized

Feeling overwhelmed by sadness and anxiety can lead to a feeling of paralysis. Worry can compromise concentration and organization. These afflictions are sometimes the result of a diagnosable psychological condition or cognitive impairment requiring professional attention, but this is not

DOI: 10.4324/9781003648703-8

always the case. Often, for immigrants and their children, such struggles are not signs of pathology but of complexity. They are part of the adaptive process.

Therapists must be mindful that organizational habits are culturally acquired. A client's "disorganization" may stem less from pathology than from a culturally influenced response to stress or a different way of prioritizing life.

As an immigrant, a child of immigrants, or a temporary resident, these indispositions are a common way of being, engendered by layers of complexity in your life. For example:

1   You wrestle with the difficulties of speaking a new language or navigating different languages at home and at work; you may not have learned the local customs and organizational techniques that are expected from you in your new country.
2   You are grappling with the subtler disruptions of your habitual and unconscious ways of being, which are so automatic that you are not even aware of them until they don't work anymore, and you find yourself out of sync.
3   You may have been given an overview about the local "best practices" at your orientation at work or school, which may contradict the best practices you learned in your home country.
4   You may have heard other immigrants complain about local ways, or locals complain about your way of doing things, often dubbing them "the wrong way," leaving you uncertain as to who is correct.
5   You learn the new ways by trial and error, making lots of mistakes and feeling shocked, frustrated, tired, and surprised.
6   You may feel temporarily sad, overwhelmed, and disorganized because it is hard to adjust to your environment.

Wrestling with Time, Priorities, Scheduling, and Relativity

Starting graduate school at Columbia University in New York City was a shocking experience for me. I did not learn organizational skills from my dad, who was highly organized in his work. Instead, I took after my mom, as I spent most of my time with her. As an illustration of her organizational habits, she often didn't know when my grammar school would restart after the summer until the last minute. She would anxiously ask my dad, who would eventually call the school to find out. I remember worrying about missing the first day of school and not knowing whether I would attend in the morning or evening, as there were two shifts at my school.

On a few occasions, I showed up to class wearing slippers because preparing for school was so riddled with anxiety and confusion. Still, I managed to always arrive on time, complete my homework well, and hand it in on time, so it was not all bad. I had the time to study and succeed. There was no pressure or rigid schedule outside of school. I just had to be on time and meet my deadlines.

The real issues arose when I had to deal with the outside world. With my mom, any interaction with the outside world was filled with uncertainty. Even doctor's appointments were loosely kept in memory or written on scraps of paper that were easily lost. To call the doctor, we'd first have to find the slip of paper with his number. However, on the bright side, this experience made me comfortable with uncertainty as an adult.

My story is an idiosyncratic story that does not speak necessarily of the typical way time is conceived in Italy. It may not even be helpful to talk about a "typical Italian way," for there is variation and intersectionalities in Italy (and also in the United States). But it may be worth saying that, in the United States—a country whose hegemonic view is the one expressed in the Protestant ethics and the exigencies of industrialization—time is linear and well measured to increase productivity. Punctuality is important, and time becomes a quantity and a value that should not be wasted. Obviously, there are people who resist this view. Even therapists like me propose a revision when this view is so extreme that it becomes counterproductive; we will then invite the patient to reconsider their sense of urgency, priorities, their attempt to overcontrol themselves and others, and their emphasis on "doing" over "being." Such focus on the future, productivity, and success when pushed to an extreme creates stress at the cost of missing out on a lot of important dimensions in life.

In contrast, time in Italy tends to be more open-ended, centered around quality moments and human connection. Much is still done with world-renowned craftsmanship and precision, which takes time. There is a strong focus on the present, as well as on history and tradition. Some may see this as idealized or outdated—Italy as bound to an agricultural and a religious calendar—but despite globalization and pressures toward efficiency, many communities continue to value taking time and prioritizing family and community. The U.S. model is both emulated and criticized.

This contrast is especially marked in southern Italy and Sardinia, where time is often shaped by cyclical rhythms, religious seasons, and communal life rather than by economic demand. Productivity and commerce are important but often woven into seasonal and touristic rhythms that reflect local values. These are broad generalizations that risk reifying reductive North–South stereotypes, because even in small Sardinian towns there is great variation. In my own family, for example, my father—always in a hurry—was a successful, punctual businessman, while my mother, though she valued punctuality, was guided by different priorities and a looser rhythm.

Northern Italy, by contrast, is more industrialized and globally integrated, often mirroring the fast-paced, time-is-money culture of the U.S. and parts of continental Europe. There, tight schedules, urgency, and a future-oriented mindset are more prominent—and it is also where resources tend to be concentrated.

In anthropology, there has been a shift in the theorization of time—from a generalized East-West dichotomy,[1] to a more nuanced perspective that recognizes both cultural particularities and the globalizing forces of modern life.[2] While aware of this shift, I still find value in the mid-20th-century views of thinkers like Edward T. Hall, whose insights often resonate with the lived experience of immigrants and may now be considered common knowledge.[3]

Edward T. Hall observed, based on informants' perceptions, that mainstream Americans tend to be more preoccupied with tight scheduling and the cramming of multiple activities into limited time than Europeans, including even northern Europeans. In contrast, Europeans appear less pressed for time and are more likely to leave unstructured space in their schedules. Hall summarized the reflections of several of his European informants with the remark: "In Europe, human relationships are important, whereas in the United States, the schedule is important."[4] Edward T. Hall distinguishes between *monochronic* and *polychronic* time. In monochronic cultures, such as that of the United States, time is perceived as linear, segmented, and tightly scheduled: one thing at a time, in a set order. In many cultures, especially in parts of Latin America, the Mediterranean, the Middle East, and parts of Asia and Africa, time is experienced more fluidly. In these polychronic cultures, multiple activities often occur simultaneously, and relationships take precedence over strict schedules. Immigrants who are accustomed to this relational orientation to time may be perceived as disorganized or intrusive in more schedule-bound environments. (It is also worth noting that within the United States, many women—particularly mothers—must navigate polychronic time, coordinating multiple roles and responsibilities at once.) These mismatches in temporal expectations often lead to misinterpretations and unfair judgments in school, work, or therapeutic settings.

By the time I arrived at Columbia for graduate school, I had made some improvements in managing time, punctuality, appointments, and organization compared to my grammar school days—but not that much. Growing up in Italy, I had been taught to focus deeply on each project, taking whatever time was needed to do it well. At the University of Cagliari, finishing a project quickly was likely to evoke more suspicion than praise, as it was often seen as a sign of superficiality. Courses moved at a slower pace, with fewer daily demands.

In my graduate school at Columbia, I suddenly had to fit a tremendous amount of work in an hour, and to do so, I had to learn to be organized, work quickly, and avoid reading every assignment in detail, letting go of my old habits of precision and curiosity. I learned to eat at my desk and sleep very little and only when needed. I cut out almost all social life for years. I embraced it without question. I learned new practices and a new vocabulary: *multitasking, shortcutting, skipping, skimming,* and *prioritizing.* I was faced with a schedule of weekly assignments that could not be completed with my Italian standards and my language skills. I had to put those standards aside and learn the value of the timely delivery of work that was "good enough" or "passing for good enough." To meet looming deadlines, I had to stop looking for all the layers of meaning. As an immigrant with intermediate English, I was lucky if I was able to grasp the manifest meaning of my assignments.

The Socratic method encourages open dialogue and critical thinking by inviting participants to explore ideas through thoughtful questioning. Rather than repeating the content of books and offering commentary—as I was accustomed to doing in my Italian university—I was now expected to question and critique authorities, scholars, and experts, even if I had only read limited, decontextualized excerpts. While this was often confusing (how could one have the authority to speak and criticize without deep knowledge?), I also experienced a new kind of freedom. It felt like a liberating permission to speak off the cuff, without shame—an invitation to think aloud, even imperfectly. The encouragement to speak freely, little by little, to hone an argument in dialogue, helped me develop my own voice.

People from cultures that do not parcel their time and tasks in the ways that have been ingrained in North Americans since kindergarten as the *gold standard* often find themselves at a disadvantage. They may wear a mask of competency and nonchalance. Unable to adjust, however, confusion and loss generate gradual feelings of incompetency that become increasingly paralyzing. When you tell people back home how difficult it is, you feel invalidated by their responses: "You are lucky," "Don't complain," "Other people in Venezuela (or whatever country) are truly struggling!" In the great scheme of things, you believe that you have no right to feel bad. After all, you are able to live in a safe country, have opportunities, and are not struggling for survival. Then, ironically, guilt and shame converge to further obstruct your ability to integrate into the new culture.

The incongruity, however, is that those who come from countries with a more open-ended sense of time can become even more inflexible than North Americans once they embrace punctuality and master tight scheduling. Although they initially struggle with the new standards, they tend to be intolerant of people from their home country for what they now perceive as a poor use of time, lack of productivity, and stagnation. They have indeed drunk the Kool-Aid. Similar to people that stop drinking or smoking and then become extremely intolerant of people who have not made that lifestyle change, new people who have embraced the American lifestyle can become intolerant of the traits that they used to have. Perhaps a strong rejection of their own ways and habits helps them maintain the new position. In some cases, there could also be an *identification with the aggressor* quality to the stance. That is, the pain and humiliation they experienced from being made to feel wrong have led them to adopt the perspective of those who once criticized them. They now repeat the same dynamic with other immigrants, their parents, people from their own countries or other targeted communities, but from a position of self-righteousness.

Even though an immigrant may feel bad and unprepared for not mastering time the way Americans prefer, these American practices do not represent a universal standard of perfection. They are simply one standard, the local standard. Your old ways have value as well, but they may not work as well *here* and *now*. When we feel deflated, incompetent, or not good enough, the problem in part is that we are interpreting our difference and difficulty with local expectations in a catastrophic way of all-or-nothing. We immigrants forget all the good things we know and do: our successes, values, and our potential. We do not consider the time it takes to adapt to a new setting and align with a new rhythm. I am not encouraging complacency. On the contrary, your old ways may have value. But if they don't work as well here, you need to reassess your values and practices to be able to function well. You still need to find ways to succeed. This requires compromise, stretching, and growth.

Therapists: Consider also how cultural expectations around time and productivity shape your clients' sense of competence. This is where validation and reframing can be powerful tools—helping clients see their efforts not as deficits, but as adaptation in progress.

Immigrant readers: Struggles with "efficiency" may not reflect disorganization but could rather represent a deep cultural mismatch with unfamiliar systems. Naming this gently can reduce shame and support adaptation. This book provides a number of tools to help you track your time, manage your schedule, and focus on and finish your tasks. My hope is that by expanding your know-how, you will be able to increasingly function better in complex situations.

Takeaway Exercise

Reflect on the ways your culture of origin organizes practices and creates a hierarchy of values. What strategies do you think could support you in sustaining your worth and allowing you to still be effective? Answer the following questions:

1   How do my homegrown ideas and practices complement or complicate my life, work, and rhythms in the United States? Are they in conflict or in sync with the values and practices I am expected to embrace in my U.S. context?
2   Which worldviews and practices are important to me? Which ones promote my growth here in the United States?
3   How do I want to negotiate my position with regard to the important people in my life and the values and practices I have embraced all my life? How do I want to negotiate new values? Am I willing to turn the dimmer switch down on practices that do not work as well here?
4   Am I okay with shifting my identity and practices, depending on the context? Or does that feel like a loss of integrity, a devaluation, or an unacceptable submission?

Even if your gears are still grinding, you are not stalled; you are evolving. As you wrestle with competing values and evolving identities, remember: integration is not perfection, it is movement, adaptation, and discovery.

Notes

1 See Edward T. Hall, *The Dance of Life: The Other Dimension of Time* (New York: Anchor Press, 1983) and *The Hidden Dimension* (New York: Anchor Books, 1966).
2 Muhammad A. Z. Mughal, "The Western and Non-Western Dichotomization of Time in Anthropology," *International Journal of Anthropology and Ethnology* 7, no. 7 (2023), all the essay is relevant, particularly page 6–11.
3 See Hall, *The Hidden Dimension*, 131–132 and 173–174.
4 Hall, 132.

References

Hall, Edward T. 1966. *The Hidden Dimension*. New York: Anchor Books.
Mughal, Muhammad A. Z. 2023. "The Western and Non-Western Dichotomization of Time in Anthropology." *International Journal of Anthropology and Ethnology* 7: 7.

6 Common Stressors in Immigrant Life

> I try to be hopeful, but there are days I feel like my future belongs to someone else.
>
> —Anonymous

Financial Stress

Phrases like "The American Dream," "The Land of Opportunity," or "Making it in America" may still resonate for some, but for many, these ideals remain entirely out of reach. Some immigrants continue to strive and keep fresh the myth of the American Dream while their reality, with their hard-working families living modestly and in poverty, does not live up to the dream. One notable immigrant, the writer Ocean Vuong, poignantly reflected on the idea of social progress, upward mobility, and personal worth, as follows:

> American life, as I saw it, growing up as an immigrant in this country, didn't work like that. My aunt works at FEDEX for almost 40 years. My brother works at Dick's Sporting Goods for 15 years. The people who I love—they worked the same jobs, they drive the same car, they live in the same homes for 20, 30 years. Some of them don't get raises. Some of them don't move up. And yet, their lives are not worthless.

A common source of stress for immigrants is the lack of financial stability tied to immigration status. A second-generation Latino patient, Antonio, who is financially well off, was about to schedule a first meeting with a financial advisor. But he was anxious. Raised in a household with little financial planning and no formal budgeting, he now felt the weight of breaking old patterns and setting a new precedent for the next generation. In our session, he shared the following:

> I grew up in a family where there was an aluminum foil wrapper in the freezer, next to the butter. It contained a stash of cash. Each month, my father would divide the money—what we would need to live on and what we would send to the family back home. It was like that for a lot of

DOI: 10.4324/9781003648703-9

families. It was day to day, and it was total chaos. Now I know my father is the first to break the cycle of depending on the children in the family. He is still working hard because he wants to put money aside for the grandchildren. I did not grow up in a family that taught me about finances or budgeting. I see my nieces and nephews are not learning these things either; no one is providing them with sound teaching about saving for the future and good financial literacy.

Antonio's story reflects how even financially stable immigrants may carry the emotional weight of past instability and the pressure to ensure a better future for the next generation. Other immigrants or temporary residents may not have experienced poverty directly, but their legal or visa status creates present-day uncertainty, making it difficult to engage in long-term planning, invest in careers, or feel stable. They may feel as if their life is on hold. Some of them, even after they receive their green card, still feel hesitant to leave their job. After years of stagnation, they have become timid, have lost a sense of direction, their self-esteem has plummeted, and they have lost their spirit.

This is what happened to Maria, a Peruvian woman working as a psychotherapist in a low fee clinic. She was lured to the United States by a job contract. The charisma of New York City and the possibility of earning a good wage for the same work she was accustomed to in her home country made immigration attractive. Once she arrived, however, she soon realized that her salary, although high compared to her earnings in Peru, barely covered her survival needs in New York City. She worked long hours and had no time to take care of herself or take steps for career advancement. Her options were either to return to Peru and start over or endure her current situation in New York City. She felt stressed, ashamed, and depressed, which diminished her prospect for future success.

If you are managing your money well, but make little money, living paycheck to paycheck, you probably feel overwhelmed and anxious. You live in a foreign country that does not offer any basic safety net. Most likely you are experiencing anxiety. Your anxiety may represent a realistic well-founded fear. Financial security is fundamental for psychological wellbeing.

Ana, a 1.5-generation Latina, accumulated what seemed like insurmountable debt in school. She finished college and is finishing a master's while working long full-time hours for a non-profit, plus additional evening, night, and weekend hours, which do not count as overtime. Each month, she pays her rent, her monthly student loans, and her credit card bill. Although she had a full scholarship in college, she still needed to rely on a credit card to cover living expenses and help her family. After paying her bills, Ana is left with $200 to $300 each month for transportation and living expenses in New York City. She constantly worries about balancing her budget and how to plan for a better future, including starting a family. These financial concerns consume much of the energy and time she could otherwise invest in career advancement, social justice volunteer work, rest, and self-care.

Therapists: Be alert to the hidden toll of student debt and economic precarity, especially in first- and 1.5-generation clients. What looks like overworking or lack of boundaries may reflect a collectivistic cultural viewpoint; that is, survival logic, not pathology.

My current client population, although they rarely have periods of extreme hardships, are nevertheless affected by the residue of a difficult childhood or transgenerational experiences of indigence or financial incompetence. Shame may prevent immigrants from speaking up, even when they are financially literate or well educated. In clinical practice, it is not uncommon to see clients who, despite having the education and intellectual tools to manage their finances, struggle silently with debt, budgeting, or asking for support. Cultural narratives about pride, self-reliance, and sacrifice, which are especially common in immigrant communities, can create an internalized belief that one should "figure it out alone" and "one should not have dug themselves into a financial black hole." Speaking up about financial stress may be perceived not only as a personal failure, but as a stain on the family's reputation or legacy of hard work. This is particularly true for those who are the first in their family to succeed academically or professionally; they may feel a strong obligation to appear competent and independent at all costs. Therapists should be attentive to this dynamic. Avoidance of talking about finances may not be due to lack of knowledge or irresponsibility but to an internal conflict between needing support and wanting to preserve dignity, belonging, or familial loyalty. Gentle, non-judgmental inquiry, and psychoeducation about the impact of stress on decision-making, can help open up this conversation.

Often the families of immigrants and second-generation individuals never taught them how to manage money, leaving them without financial literacy. As a result, they are unlikely to seek professional advice, as it's not something they were exposed to or feel comfortable with. Often raised in environments of chaos and scarcity, they lack a culture of using financial tools. Consequently, they continue to live in the emergency mode they learned as children, with no financial plan for their daily lives or future. Even those who are financially well off tend to save or invest less than they could, missing opportunities to build a secure nest; and some, unfortunately, embrace the U.S. credit culture, either out of financial need or a lack of understanding of the long-term costs and consequences.

Sometimes our financial problems originate as a result of difficulties we have in managing feelings and as a maladaptive coping response to a poor sense of one's value. Buying gives us a rush of positive emotions and helps keep feelings of sadness, loneliness, and inadequacy at bay. In the United States, where there is an abundance of goods, we often buy things we don't need in an attempt to manage our self-presentation, emotions, and relationships. The ubiquity of advertisements and immediacy of social media apps have the potential to trigger feelings of inadequacy, of not dressing well enough, or of not having the right body, lifestyle, or of being marginalized from groups who have greater wealth and buying power. These feelings can instigate a desire to shop more to compensate.

Other times, financial problems are worsened by codependency or by culturally sanctioned financial obligations to others. It's important to distinguish between the two. In many families and cultures, members are expected to look after one another, no matter the circumstances. This might involve supporting a depressed or substance-abusing spouse or parent who refuses to seek help or continuously financing a sibling or child who is unable to hold a job but expects indefinite support. Others may overwork to sustain a relationship with a partner who takes advantage without contributing.

Some of my clients find themselves in these situations, often without even questioning them, because these financial and emotional burdens are, at least in part, culturally sanctioned. In other words, they have been ingrained from a young age as responsibilities that one simply does not question. Many are conditioned since childhood to adopt a caretaker role. Some people, feeling uprooted and isolated, may fear the consequences of disrupting these obligations. Moreover, these obligations may offer a sense of purpose or self-worth—something you can feel good about fulfilling when so much else feels out of your control. However, if you find yourself feeling particularly upset or exploited by the situation, it could be a sign that you're not fully aligned with these demands, and that a part of you is seeking an exit.

Different cultures address issues of obligation and responsibility differently (and psychological conditions, such as dependency, could also play a role). Now that you are in between cultures, it is even more apparent that values may differ. Since you are in between cultures, you are in the particular position of viewing the situation also from the outside while constructing your idiosyncratic path, choosing aspects of these diverse cultures that you believe are fair and good and that suit you. Pay attention to the way you feel. Take your feelings seriously. If you feel depleted, taken advantage of, or angry, then something has to change. If you recognize that you are carrying too heavy of a burden but are hesitant to bring it up with your loved ones, you need to attend to your feelings and needs, even if it means you fear you may lose their love or will be criticized. Take time to think about how you want to be treated and find ways to speak up about the changes you wish to see in yourself and others. Ask yourself these questions:

1   What is the right balance of cultural values and obligations for me?
2   What is the right balance between generosity with family and friends and self-care, and what is my responsibility to myself and to them?
3   Can I define my boundaries without losing my sense of being a good person and belonging?
4   Can I maintain bonds of love in my life and still be authentic?

Take the time to reflect on your expenses without being too hard on yourself. When financial matters feel overwhelming, it's easy to avoid the problem out of fear that it's too big to solve. This can lead to shame, making it difficult to admit there's an issue. However, the key is to face the numbers and develop a budget and strategy to break free from unhelpful spending habits and debt.

The first step may feel daunting, but it's actually quite simple: Know how much you earn and how much you spend. Write everything down in clear columns. How are you allocating your money? For instance, if you are living on a poor diet for lack of resources and spending all your pension on toys and clothes for your grandkids, you could consider whether you would still feel like a good grandmother if you tweaked your spending a bit. This step not only helps reduce debt but also brings emotional relief. When you understand your finances, you regain control and can create an action plan to move toward financial recovery and address any spending or gambling issues.

Start by tracking your income and expenses, even if it's just for one hour a week. Once you have a clear picture of your finances, you'll feel less out of control. Before making purchases, take a moment to reflect—write down why you want to buy something, how it will impact you, and the short- and long-term consequences. This mindfulness creates a buffer against impulsive spending.

Regularly review your finances, even if you tackle one section at a time. Although it may cause initial anxiety, addressing these issues will reduce your sense of chaos and hopelessness. I recommend seeking support from groups focused on debt resolution, gambling, shopping addiction, or code-pendency. These challenges are often best faced with the help of like-minded people.

Takeaway Exercise

Later in the book, I will discuss how to address unhelpful thoughts and images that may trigger you to spend too much. For now, simply consider the idea that it is possible to choose between when you want to give in to consumerism and when you want to explore other ways to gain comfort or a boost of self-esteem. Summing up, consider also the following:

1   Build a system around money: It is a concrete way of gaining control over your life. You do so by being clear of how much money enters and by writing down everything you spend and realizing the gap between the two. Balancing them is the goal.
2   Take the time to think about how you support others financially. Are you keeping other people afloat for reasons you are aligned with and you feel right about? Or are you enabling bad habits, dependencies, or codependencies? Are you creating more damage than good?
3   Consider how to create boundaries around giving that work for you. Work out a compromise between cultural expectations and your personal views that you find fair.

4   What if you could use the money you usually overspend to pay off your credit cards or put it into a savings account instead? Can you imagine savoring the feeling you would have if you could do that and work toward financial security?

Immigration Paperwork and Work Stress

> Living on a visa has felt like building a life on borrowed ground. I work hard, stay quiet, and swallow frustration—because one wrong move could cost me everything. I have taken pay cuts, hidden my burnout, and watched my voice shrink while my fear grew. The ambition I arrived with got trimmed down to fit someone else's comfort. Still, I stay. Not because it is easy, but because the dream that brought me here still burns. I keep going—not with freedom, but with fire.
>
> —Anonymous contributor

An obvious source of stress for immigrants arises from the challenges of arriving in the United States and the ongoing efforts to obtain and maintain legal status. Over the last few years, immigration to the United States has become a deeply stressful experience, filled with precarity, fear, and bureaucratic humiliation. From my place of relative safety, I can only imagine, or hear secondhand, the devastating realities faced by families attempting to cross the southern border of the US, grappling with ICE, and the uncertainties of immigration. The immigrants and children of immigrants with whom I am more familiar are primarily in the United States legally, but at times their status can become extremely complicated and unpredictable.

If you are an immigrant on a professional or student visa, or in the optional practical training (OPT) phase (i.e., a period when international students on F-1 visas can work in their field of study), you may already know how consuming it can be to secure and maintain your status. This focus limits the energy available for other important aspects of life and career. You may find yourself accepting a job or salary that is far from ideal, simply because it offers a legal pathway. Often, this predicament brings feelings of being stranded, a loss of momentum, and a sense of being in an indefinite limbo. Thoughts, such as "I will be deported," or "My life will be ruined;" can overtake your mind, leading to anxiety and despair. In moments like these, it may help to act against your instinct. When fear clouds your thinking, that is exactly the moment to pause and ask, what is the next best step I can take?

Alberto, a former international student approaching the end of his OPT training, was falling into despair. Though brilliant and highly motivated, he was struggling to find a full-time job. After a barrage of rejections because many employers were reluctant to sponsor a foreign worker due to cost and bureaucracy, he began to lose hope. He simultaneously dreaded the thought of having to go back to his home country, where his professional future was equally uncertain.

This is how he put it, while in the thick of his despair:

> I don't have a clear path. I don't know what to do. I want to be in that stage where I am settled and working but I don't know how to get there. If I don't see a structure, a shape to my days and a projection of my future, then I don't feel comfortable. Now, I don't see a structure; that's why my mind is all over the place. I need stable people around me. I need to know I have a place where I show up at 9:00 am to do my work with tasks that I execute. Then, it does not even matter if I finish at 9:00 pm.

Through a process of counseling, meditation, and employing the tools of cognitive behavioral therapy, Alberto was able to gain a new perspective. Before he was able to take any step in the direction he wanted to go, he needed to calm his nervous system. I prescribed breathing exercises and guided meditations for homework. Also, he needed to avoid catastrophizing, even though losing status and having to return to his country was a very scary realistic possibility. Once he reached a bit of calm and was able to reframe his tunnel vision, he reached out to the International Student Services at his university—a free resource for all international students. You might be aware of services like this too, but when fear and despair take over, even obvious options can become hard to access.

Therapists: Despair can constrict problem-solving and narrow cognitive flexibility. Be mindful that in states of fear, clients may overlook resources that are right in front of them. Gentle prompting can help them regain access to these options.

The student services informed him that the requirements for prolonging his stay were not impossible to meet. Even in the worst-case scenario—if he did not find a job by his visa expiration date—he could fulfill immigration requirements by volunteering with certain eligible companies. This would allow him to maintain legal status while continuing to search for paid employment.

While that was news of incredible relief, another problem remained: How could he support himself in New York City while volunteering? This was a big problem for sure, but not insurmountable in New York City, where the informal job market is quite strong. Nevertheless, as it turned out, he didn't need to serve tables. He was offered a job by a company in his field. It was not a full-time job with the prospect of a green card just yet, but it was a contract with a large company, one that could possibly sponsor him in the future. And this work experience would look great on his resume, increasing his chances of eventually finding a job that would sponsor his green card.

Like Alberto, many immigrants face significant obstacles as they try to establish themselves professionally in the United States. The uncertainty around securing work and maintaining status can lead to feelings of despair and self-doubt. If you relate to Alberto's story, know that you are not alone. Many immigrants face professional limbo and emotional burnout as they try to stay afloat.

Clelia, an Italian entrepreneur who successfully created a small oasis of stability in the food distribution industry, also encountered her own frustrations despite her success. The hard and stressful work of establishing the family business over the years bore fruits financially. But it also took a toll, physically and psychologically, on both her and her husband. They felt emptied out. The nature of the job, which needed constant alertness and single-minded focus to stay afloat in a competitive and unpredictable market, was exhausting and all-consuming, particularly for immigrants, who did not know the local rules very well, lacked a powerful network and could not access standard sources of credit. As Clelia confided:

> The sacrifices you have to make as an immigrant entrepreneur are greater than if you are a citizen and have lived in the United States for a long time. If you start your business when you get here, you have to face many obstacles in addition to the normal risks and difficulties of any entrepreneur: You don't know the market; you don't know the system; people work very differently, and you need to juggle many languages and cultural contexts. You cannot count on lifelong friendships and PR for your development and expansion. No one gives you financial credit, and you have to wait many years before you can access any decent line of credit. You cannot trust that your know-how from your country will work here. I'm not excited anymore. I changed a lot during the last years, and I don't like some of the changes. The people we meet through work are not sophisticated or curious. I feel alone and intellectually stagnant; I feel like I lost many good things about myself. There should be more to life than this! But I cannot quit. I wish I could reinvent myself. My company is my security but also my prison. Reinventing myself in the US is not easy; my degree is worth nothing here. My papers, my immigration status, is linked to my work. I need to find new strength to break these chains and change my life again.

Therapists: Pay attention to how identity loss can emerge even in stories of external success. Listen for language that signals internal dissonance, especially when clients downplay their accomplishments or question whether their life reflects who they truly are.

The immigrant experience is filled with uncertainty, even for skilled individuals. To stay afloat and grow, one must maintain a clear focus and steady mind, learn to move quickly and strategically, and manage the anxieties and sadness that this uncertainty brings, both the objective challenges and the ones our sensitive minds tend to magnify. Mindfulness and meditation can be helpful tools. Simply sitting, walking, or shaking, bringing your attention to your breath or different parts of your body, or performing grounding exercises like feeling your feet on the ground can provide relief. You can also try the "Tree Meditation," which is available on my website (www.leideporcu.com), or use the short "Set Your Intention" meditation, described in Chapter 22, to focus your energy.

In the second step you analyze the situation and your thoughts. De-escalating unhelpful, black-and-white, or catastrophic thinking through a Thought Record or the Nine-Lens Reflective Tool (also explained in later chapters) can help bring balance to your perspective. Once you're centered and thinking more clearly, the third step is to create a plan comprised of small steps toward solving the problem and achieving your desired outcome. The key is to cultivate a resilient mindset that is positive, flexible, hopeful, yet vigilant. This attitude allows you to move forward, even if it means starting over multiple times.

A practical and fundamental step in resolving your immigration issues is consulting an immigration lawyer, and it's often beneficial to have at least two or three consultations with different lawyers. Many lawyers offer a free first consultation, and this is worth doing even if you already have access to a lawyer through your job. Keep in mind that in-house lawyers are paid by the company, so their primary client is the company, not you. By consulting multiple lawyers, you can either confirm the same path or gain multiple perspectives, which may help you make a more informed decision.

Whether you are navigating this process yourself, or accompanying someone who is, remember that immigration is not only a legal journey, but also a psychological one.

I learned this through personal experience. During a free consultation, a lawyer recommended a clinic where I could potentially work and secure the necessary papers. This lawyer was helpful in many ways, but later, when I was hired, they filed my paperwork in a way that caused repeated audits, delaying my green card process. After seeking another consultation, a different lawyer identified the mistake causing the audits. I switched lawyers, and the new application process went smoothly.

You may feel hopeless about securing legal status, but a lawyer can often find a path forward—and sometimes the involvement of a clinician can make a difference as well. For example, did you know that asylum seekers who submit an affidavit, along with their application, which includes an evaluation from a mental health professional or doctor, have a higher success rate? According to a study by Lustig et al. between 2000 and 2004, asylum applications supported by an affidavit from Physicians for Human Rights (PHR) had an 89% success rate, compared to a national average of 37.5% for cases without such evaluations.[1] The difference is remarkable. Furthermore, paid affidavits are no more successful than pro bono ones; love and care, combined with professionalism and objectivity, go a long way.[2]

Did you also know that filing your application in a state with fewer cases for your visa type can speed up the process? Or that unaccompanied undocumented minors have a strong path to legal papers, provided they apply before turning 21? These are just a few tips I've learned from friends, clients, and lawyers. However, as I finish writing this book in 2025, I am fully aware that the immigration process is changing daily and perhaps for a few years it will be hard to have a clear path. Among the few good things I have recently learned is that regardless of immigration status, if you are victim of a crime and you have witnesses to prove it, or, if you are exploited or you get injured at work or if the employer withholds pay, even if you are in deportation proceedings, you may be entitled to a U visa.[3] However, you need to report to the police and collaborate with the investigation. Some immigrants, out of ignorance, pride, or fear, may not take advantage of these possibilities. Also, it is important to be aware of the fact that your presence in court, when you are mandated to appear, may not be necessary if your lawyer is able to schedule an online appearance for you.[4] When you do not need to be in person with your court appointment, you may have one less chance to run into ICE on your path. Always consult an immigration lawyer and double-check what options are available and applicable to your situation.

Takeaway Exercise

Take a moment to reflect on the emotional and practical demands of maintaining legal status in the US, and consider the following questions:

1   How has my immigration status affected my stress levels or sense of stability?
2   What compromises, either personal, professional, or emotional, have I made (or am I making) to remain in this country?
3   If I am currently navigating immigration uncertainty, what could help me stay grounded and motivated, even when the future feels unclear?
4   Can I consult with a trusted expert, such as an immigration lawyer or advocate, to help clarify my options and next steps?

Your Personal History

I've been here so long that there's no clear line between before and after. Migration didn't just move me across countries—it broke the frame entirely. I stopped trying to fit into someone else's idea of who I should be. I am not American. I am not just from where I came. I walk a path that doesn't follow the map. The violence against people like me—over there and over here— made it clear: some doors will never fully open. But I don't need permission to believe in something bigger than borders. Even as I carry my history, I claim a wider world.

—Anonymous contributor

Immigration will be more challenging if you have not adequately learned how to manage your emotions and set reasonable expectations. Take charge of a situation by exploring what you bring to it. For example, notice patterns in your behavior and ways of thinking that make your life difficult and the people around you miserable. Do you have the same grievances over and over about people and work, no matter in which country you live? Do people complain about you in similar ways? As hard as it may be to accept or admit, it is quite possible that you are part of the problem. The good news is that you can change your behavior much more easily than you can change other people or the immigration law. You can uncover the issues that cause your discomfort and then make helpful changes.

Takeaway Exercise

Tease apart, as much as it is possible, from the situation you are immersed in, with all its limitations, frustrations, and multiple determinations, the baggage you bring to the table. Humbly take in other people's feedback and ask them to point out both your strengths and those aspects of you that hold you back, are annoying to others, and that you may not be seeing. Ask them to speak from a position of love and objectivity and to refrain, for a moment, from responding from a position of self-interest. Ask them for specific examples that provide evidence to their feedback. Then try to see your original perspective in light of theirs.

Developing a Toolkit

> I was the first. The only one. No trail to follow, no hand to hold. I've had to carve out every step on my own. And maybe that's the strength—I don't wait for a blueprint. I build as I go. I'm still here because I'm relentless.
>
> —Anonymous contributor

Feeling overwhelmed is to be expected given the changes you have experienced as you live between two or more countries. While it is natural to feel unsettled, you still have to make the best of your situation. Make space for your inevitable mistakes and moments of dissonance. Let yourself keep going, even when things feel messy and unclear. As you integrate into a new culture and learn how that culture operates, you'll need to be a little less self-centered and more comfortable with not always feeling on top of things or competent about yourself. Soften your pursuit of perfection. Give yourself more room to observe how things work. Can you accept that perhaps for some time you will not be fully part of the flow? (As if anyone ever is!) Or that you may not meet your own internal standards of competence? Acceptance is not defeat. It is a foundation for growth.

As you learn to operate in different environments and acquire flexibility, patience, tolerance, and cultural competence, you are in fact building a toolkit for graceful integration. As an outsider, you're forced to think outside of the box. You may be confused now, lacking the subtleties and the subtexts of a new language or culture, but over time, you will be increasingly able to operate at a higher level of complexity. You're learning to work under stress, and you know how to operate in emergency situations. You know how to juggle and keep moving forward at the same time. You know how to switch gears and stay afloat. These are hard-earned skills that will increase your capacity to address increasingly complex situations. Reflect on these issues and zoom into where you need to grow and prepare.

Consider a relativist approach, which recognizes the values of the host country, as well as those of your original education and culture, then proceed strategically. The dominant population with power establishes the norms of a culture and naturally assigns greater value to practices that give them an advantage. As a newcomer, it's incumbent upon you to become fluent in these practices, while holding onto the values and practices that were passed on to you by your culture of origin. In other words, integration is the goal. Do not engage with American culture in a way that devalues your original culture and knowhow. This attitude weakens you. Most likely, your cultural values, practices, and knowledge will eventually serve as an advantage, if you stay in the game. The people who succeed in the long run are the ones who do not give up. When mistakes are made, humbly reassess and continue. Progress is like learning to walk: one step at a time.

Takeaway Exercise

1   Take some of the pressure off: Acknowledge how difficult your situation may be, due to cultural differences, power dynamics, immigration paperwork, or financial instability.
2   Think of ways in which you might find your own balance between your needs and responsibilities and the ones of your loved ones.
3   Be self-reflective, compassionate, and proactive about your responsibilities, shortcomings, and limits.
4   Craft in your mind an image of a successful and fulfilling future. Visualize it in detail, and notice how it makes you feel. Return to this image often.

Notes

1   Stuart L. Lustig, Sarah Kureshi, Kevin L. Delucchi, Vincent Iacopino, and Samantha C. Morse, "Asylum Grant Rates Following Medical Evaluations of Maltreatment Among Political Asylum Applicants in the United States," *Journal of Immigrant and Minority Health* 10, no. 1 (2008): 7–15, doi:10.1007/s10903-007-9056-8, 14, 11.
2   Lustig et al., 10–11. Also, asylum seekers who were represented by pro bono legal advocates were more likely to be granted asylum than those who were charged for legal representation (Pearson chi square = 8.4, p = 0.01).
3   The U visa, or U Nonimmigrant Status, is a form of immigration protection in the United States for people who have been victims of certain serious crimes. To qualify, a person must have suffered significant physical or emotional harm and must be willing to help the police or other authorities investigate or prosecute the crime. Interview with Immigration Layer Saverio Lo Monaco, July 6, 2025.
4   Interview with Immigration Layer Saverio Lo Monaco, July 6, 2025.

References

Appadurai, Arjun. 2013. *The Future as Cultural Fact: Essays on the Global Condition*. London: Verso.

Lustig, Stuart L., Sarah Kureshi, Kevin L. Delucchi, Vincent Iacopino, and Samantha C. Morse. 2008. "Asylum Grant Rates Following Medical Evaluations of Maltreatment Among Political Asylum Applicants in the United States." *Journal of Immigrant and Minority Health* 10 (1): 7–15. doi:10.1007/s10903-007-9056-8.

Vuong, Ocean. 2025. "*The Oprah Podcast, Featuring Ocean Vuong.*" Recorded May 13, at Starbucks. YouTube. www.youtube.com/watch?v=CghReJZYQ2k.

Part III

Finding Your Voice

Sometimes it feels like I'm talking underwater. People don't really hear me, or they only get part of what I mean. I have to explain things that others don't even think about. It's like I'm always trying to catch up, just to be noticed. But I keep speaking up, even when it's hard, because I want to be seen and understood.

—Anonymous contributor

7 Finding Your Voice Across Cultures

Cultural alienation and identity negotiation are key themes in the lives of immigrants and their second-generation progeny, often beginning with intergenerational tensions. In this regard, author of *The Other Americans*, Laila Lalami, says:

> My parents put me in a French school, so I grew up speaking a language that my grandmother, who was illiterate, did not speak... Within three generations, ... forces like education that are positive but also other forces like colonial influences can create a sense of cultural alienation within a family.[1]

Laila Lalami explains that this disconnect extended to her father as well. Within three generations, her family experienced the gulf produced by education, colonial influence, and differing frames of reference, showing how mobility can fracture cultural bonds within immigrant families.[2]

Immigrant readers: Have you experienced similar ruptures, as what Laila Lalami describes, within your family caused by education, mobility, or language?

For psychologists, social workers, and professionals working with immigrant populations: These conflicts offer critical insights into how individuals navigate the pressures of belonging to multiple cultural systems. This chapter examines how immigrants reconcile the competing voices of family, heritage, and societal expectations, alongside the internalized pressures they impose upon themselves.

By exploring real-world cases, theoretical concepts, and practical applications, this chapter provides a framework for understanding and addressing these conflicts. It emphasizes how professional support can empower immigrants to find balance and cultivate resilience while respecting their unique cultural contexts. Immigrant patients may find it beneficial to extend their self-reflective work beyond the therapy room. The takeaway exercises offer an opportunity to continue their exploration independently and at no cost.

DOI: 10.4324/9781003648703-11

Navigating Conflicting Voices

Immigrants live at the intersection of multiple cultural demands, often feeling pulled in different directions. These demands include the following:

1   *Home culture pressures:* Family and heritage impose expectations, such as adhering to traditional values or fulfilling familial obligations. For some, this includes the pressure to succeed while upholding cultural norms.
2   *Host culture expectations:* Immigrants encounter societal pressures to assimilate and adopt the dominant culture's language and values, which may conflict with their cultural identity.
3   *Internalized standards:* Self-imposed expectations often stem from guilt, perfectionism, or a desire to prove one's worth in the new environment.
4   *Intergenerational conflicts:* Anika, a second-generation Asian American patient, describes the tension between her and her mother as follows:

> In part, my mom feels proud: she raised an independent and successful young woman; a good kid. In part, she feels judged: I am still unmarried. We have this thing in our community where everybody is curious about other people. People do not only wonder but also ask why I am not married and why she has not done "the right thing," whatever it takes to get me married. She feels the pressure to come up with an excuse. Sometimes specific thoughts from our culture come into her head, and she puts me under a lot of pressure.

These intergenerational dynamics illustrate the emotional toll of living between two worlds. Anika's narrative reflects how cultural values shape familial expectations and personal identity.

Therapists: You can help clients explore these conflicting voices through reflective exercises, helping them clarify their priorities and values. Also, it might be useful to consider your own reactions when your client brings up tension with their family over cultural values—what is your first emotional or cognitive response? Reflecting on your own reactions can deepen your understanding of how you perceive the situation.

The Language of "Should"

Immigrant readers: Do you hear internal voices that drive you relentlessly to succeed? Or punish you for not doing enough? The "language of should" often emerges in therapy as a source of emotional distress. It is rooted in cultural, familial, or societal expectations and manifests as harsh self-criticism.

Case Study: Tom

Tom, a European professional, wrestles with self-imposed perfectionism:

> I am afraid of becoming complacent. If I do not push myself to the limit, I fear I will not be able to make it. I did good work, and I am proud of that. But I had no time to make steps toward looking for a new job. When I realize that I get off track that way, I get worried that I should do more. I am not going anywhere. I am stagnating. I am wasting time. I am failing.

Tom's narrative reflects the emotional cost of unrealistic *shoulds*. These pressures often lead to a downward spiral of negative thoughts, a concept well-documented in CBT.

Immigrant readers: What happens in your body when you pause and challenge your inner critic?

Therapists: Consider how might your own cultural values about achievement shape your response to perfectionism in your clients?

Takeaway Exercise for Patients

Notice how often you use "should" in your language and to what extent your internal narrative or self-talk underscores what you are not and how you should be. Answer these questions:

1 Do your "shoulds" help you improve your mood and effectiveness, or do they mostly make you feel empty and wrong, bog you down, and stifle your enthusiasm?
2 Could it be that to self-motivate and function at your peers' level, you push yourself too far?
3 Are you striving for perfection?
4 Whose harsh voices are you listening to internally?
5 Are the voices echoes of disapproving and perfectionist parents?
6 Are the voices the pressures of a society that tries to force you into a positive or negative stereotype or to reject and marginalize you, as discussed in Chapter 4, for instance, when dark-skinned immigrants are frequently perceived through a racial lens.

Clinical Application

CBT techniques can help clients like Tom reframe shoulds into constructive goals. For instance: "I should always succeed" can become "I value doing my best while balancing rest and growth."

Assertiveness and Boundary Setting

Immigrants often struggle with assertiveness, particularly when transitioning from collectivist cultures, which emphasize familial obligations, to individualist cultures that prioritize personal boundaries. This tension can result in feelings of guilt, isolation, or frustration.

Case Study: Isabella

Isabella, a young Guatemalan immigrant, describes her life as being prematurely aged by her responsibilities: "I am a 40-year-old woman trapped in a 20-year-old body!" Balancing work, school, and family obligations left her physically and emotionally drained. Her story highlights the necessity of teaching assertiveness skills as a form of self-care.

Therapeutic Implication

Role-playing exercises can help clients practice setting boundaries while respecting cultural values. Discussions about the balance between independence and interdependence can empower clients to find their own path.

Takeaway Exercise for Patients

Ask yourself the following questions:

1   How do I fit in and how do I want to fit in?
2   How much do I value independence and interdependence?
3   How do I want to conceive and express respect, equality, and authority?
4   What are my needs and what are the needs of others?
5   What do I want to honor, and what do I want to resist—and how can I do that, given societal possibilities and limitations?

Therapists and immigrants alike: Consider how integration is not just social or political—it is also internal, intimate, and unfolding. It can occur along a gradient: from refusal and isolation, to the integration of multiple cultural identities, to full integration. It is an ongoing process shaped by individual choices, available opportunities, power dynamics, and the level of acceptance within the cultures involved.

Conclusion

The cacophony of competing voices that immigrants experience is a reflection of their unique and multifaceted identities. By integrating psychological tools with cultural awareness, professionals can help clients transform this cacophony into a symphony of voices—a harmonious balance of heritage, self-expression, and societal integration.

Notes

1 Laila Lalami, *The Other Americans (Live Presentation), in NBF Presents: Borders of Belonging.* YouTube, posted by National Book Foundation, March 25, 2021, www.youtube.com/watch?v=G_m_p0PM7rA.
2 Lalami.

References

Lalami, Laila. 2019. *The Other Americans*. New York: Pantheon Books.
Lalami, Laila. 2021. The Other Americans: Live: "NBF Presents: Borders of Belonging."March 25. *YouTube*. www.youtube.com/watch?v=G_m_p0PM7rA.

8   Between Obligation and Longing

Navigating Needs, Desires, and Expectations Across Cultures

> I came to the U.S. as a child, hoping for a better future. After high school, I could not afford college and began working to support my family. When a loved one became ill, I gave up my studies to help. Years later, I realized I still wanted a career—to uplift my life and others'. I am now proud to be enrolled in college.
>
> —Anonymous contributor

Negotiating our desires, our sense of right and wrong, obligations, politeness, and respect is a common predicament that is full of trepidation. Often, others' needs trump our own. Coming from cultures where people are taught to unquestioningly defer to elders and to families, it is complicated to refuse authority figures both in personal relationships and at work. Yet, this dynamic can be upsetting. Some of my patients voice their resentment of relationships that are not mutual, feeling that too much is expected of them. They feel overwhelmed and pressured but also stuck because they don't know how to change a dynamic that entails not only meaning, love, and value but also frustration and invalidation. They feel they do not meet the expectations of their families or fit into the roles required of them.

Here are two examples. The older relatives of a young Latina patient who works hard to meet the demands of school and work expect her to make long weekly visits that greatly interfere with her limited time to tend to many other personal obligations. If she skips a week, she gets scolded. If she complies, she doesn't have enough time to finish her assignments, which feeds her frustration and anxiousness. She feels that her family cannot acknowledge the time constraints of her schedule or how overwhelmed she feels.

The family of a second-generation Latino patient expects the hard-working and already overwhelmed child to provide continuous financial resources and services. Even though he willingly and generously provides these resources with love and pride, he is still resentful, especially because, in his opinion, the family does not manage the money well, squandering resources.

Many young immigrants that I see as patients are ambitious and capable. They struggle to put themselves through school and secure good jobs. Because as immigrants, they feel that it is more difficult for them to succeed,

DOI: 10.4324/9781003648703-12

they are willing to work doubly hard while also attempting to negotiate a complex landscape in which they are constantly deciding which micro-aggressions to address and which to ignore. They go home exhausted only to take up with family obligations well into the night. If they are hetero-sexual, pressures to find a suitable partner and settle into marriage and parenthood loom largely. For instance, Isabella, a hard-working, respon-sible, articulate young woman from Guatemala, always perfectly poised and tastefully dressed despite limited means, spoke candidly about the complexity of her life. At just 20 years old, the emotional burdens she car-ries and the responsibilities she shoulders have aged her beyond her years. Her body remains young, but her mind feels decades older. "Some days I feel like a turtle living in a squirrel body!" she quips, with a wry sense of humor that underscores the paradox of her experience. The lightness and spontaneity typical of someone her age have been overshadowed by the demands of work and family. Her metaphor captures, with both poignancy and irony, how the weight of responsibility has prematurely aged her, despite her impeccable appearance.

My young patients are determined to make it, despite the difficulties they face. Often, as we also saw in Chapters 6 and 7, many clients, especially young women, are highly self-aware, capable, and committed to both self-care and family care. Often, they hold full-time jobs in modest or low-paying sectors, such as childcare or administrative assistance, while also working toward a university degree that promises a better life. Several are women, who have many family responsibilities. Yet, they believe in self-care (after all, they chose to be in therapy) and appear to be more self-aware and better functioning than other members of their families. How-ever in spite of their healthy choices, family obligations often outweigh personal needs, leading to guilt and resentment when asserting boundaries. Because of familial pressures in their lives, they feel inefficient, over-whelmed, conflicted about putting others first, and guilty for taking care of themselves. Assertiveness may be culturally discouraged, which leaves them vulnerable to burnout and a sense of being "on the edge" all the time, causing them to be irritable and angry.

Therapists: When a client's sense of duty begins to erode their sense of self, how do you help them recognize this? What cultural logics are at play, and how might you validate their loyalty while supporting boundary setting? When clients are caught between interdependence and autonomy, between sacrifice and self-expression, your role may include helping them reframe loyalty not as silent endurance, but as something that coexists with honesty, limits, and self-care. Can you invite them to imagine a form of love that includes the freedom to say no?

It is important for therapists to reflect on their own cultural assumptions when it comes to working with these types of dilemmas. What assumptions are you bringing to the room about autonomy, success, independence, or what constitutes growth? Theories and practices of Western psychotherapy are not neutral; they are embedded in specific cultural narratives that may not align with your client's values and lived realities. There is no way of thinking or acting entirely outside these frameworks, but we can remain aware of them. This awareness invites us to de-center ourselves, and instead listen openly and carefully. Where does your client want to go? What tensions are they navigating? Can you support them modulating the tension between cultural logics without prematurely imposing a standard of development that may feel right to you but is not necessarily ideal for them? Therapy, at its best, makes space for clients to build their own multicultural journeys, on their own terms, in their own time.

When they come to me for help, I see their predicament, stranded as they are between cultures. Their culture of origin is more patriarchal and family and community oriented. It often demands that they sacrifice time and be the financial support for the family. Their work and school environments require much of their attention and energy, as well as considerable financial expenditures so that they fit in with the lifestyles of other students and colleagues. These demands may be further intensified by unresolved psychological struggles, stemming from experiences of emotional neglect in childhood. In these cases, parents may have been frequently absent due to working multiple jobs during critical developmental stages when a sense of security and safety was being formed. American mainstream culture, at least as an ideal, places a great deal of value on self-development and self-care. However, it does not offer equal opportunities for people to pursue it.

It is important that you tease out the different cultural demands that are pressuring you, and find your way. You may need to forgo some of the valuable but overbearing aspects of each culture. If you can tolerate some of the guilt and shame that your choices induce, you may be able to find some freedom and authenticity as you adjust your relationships to reflect your evolving values rather than imposed expectations. At the same time, proceed slowly because you do not want to alienate yourself altogether from your family or your diverse social groups. It is not easy to juggle all these different factors, but there is often some room to maneuver in order to find a comfortable spot for yourself in the world.

These tensions can feel paralyzing, yet they often mark the beginning of a deeper personal reckoning. As immigrants begin to navigate these conflicting roles, many come to a pivotal question: Who do I want to become? The journey toward integration is not just about balancing others' needs, it is also about naming one's own. This movement from compliance to conscious choice is neither quick nor easy, but it's a mark of self-actualization. As we saw in Chapter 6, when survival mode becomes the norm, it is difficult to recognize when change is possible. And in Chapter 7, we explored how integration requires learning to hear—and harmonize—competing internal voices. The following vignette captures this moment of emerging clarity.

My patient, Maya, seeks to sort out who she is vis-à-vis her birth and chosen countries and her family. As a second-generation Latina, she is pegged disapprovingly as "American" by her more traditional and less wealthy relatives:

> "You are an American now. You talk rude to us," my family says to me. But I am not rude. I cannot stand how they sugarcoat things, where I come from. They gossip and smile. I am not like that. I will tell them to their face and why. But is that because I am American? I do not think that is the case. Americans are stereotypically famous for not telling you stuff to your face and being all pleasing and agreeing, while in reality they don't feel that way and keep it for themselves. I think it is more that I am becoming my own person and part of it is therapy too. I am figuring out who I want to be and how I want to treat and be treated. I also have the money to be independent now, so I can tell it as it is.

These are not easy balances to strike. But with time, reflection, and support, you may find ways to honor your cultural roots while also growing into your most authentic self.

Takeaway Exercise for Immigrant Readers

Your reaction to the tensions you are experiencing between honoring others and honoring yourself is not problematic—it is a sign that you are growing into a more complex identity. Take some time to reflect on the voices that shape your choices. Ask yourself:

1   What are the core needs and desires that I tend to silence or postpone?
2   When I feel guilty or selfish for asserting a boundary, whose voice do I hear in my mind?
3   Are there moments when saying "no" might actually deepen—not weaken—my relationships?
4   What compromises do I make to belong, and which ones feel too costly?
5   If I could imagine a self that honors both my cultural heritage and my evolving identity, what would that look like in my daily life?

If you feel torn, remember: You are not choosing between two worlds—you are building a third space that belongs to you.

Takeaway Exercise for Therapists

Before offering an intervention, consider this:

1   What assumptions am I making about what this client *should* want?
2   Am I interpreting their hesitation, loyalty, or self-sacrifice as pathology, when it might be relational wisdom within their culture?

3   What cultural scripts about autonomy, boundaries, or individuation am I unconsciously bringing into the room?
4   Can I slow down enough to ask: *What kind of balance is this client trying to create?*
5   How might I make space for ambivalence, for loyalty alongside self-assertion, without prematurely resolving it?

Try this: For your next session with a culturally diverse client, challenge yourself to *wait one more turn* before suggesting a solution. Use that space to deepen your inquiry. Instead of guiding the client toward resolution, ask, "If we don't rush to fix this, what else might we learn from sitting with the conflict?"

9   What Languages Reveal and Hide

In the excerpt below, Elena Ferrante refers to the language dynamics of her characters as they find their way in life, straddling the "emotionally robust" Neapolitan learned in childhood and the "fragile" Italian of their adult life; dialect, as she says, feels like an eruption, in the text:

> Dialect… at moments of crisis imposes itself, moves into the standard language, emerges in all its harshness. In other words, when, in my books, Italian succumbs and takes on dialectal cadences, it's a sign that, in the language as well, past and present are getting anxiously, painfully confused…[1]

This moving between languages will resonate with you, as you speak different languages in different contexts and, depending on the situation and language used, your experience and your emotional temperature may differ. You may have one language for deeper feelings and another for prosaic communication; one that feels more protective and another that creates distance; a language for work and business and a language for home.[2]

Noticing your language patterns is an entry point to exploring your feelings and those of other people, especially if they speak multiple languages. While your emotions and experiences may translate seamlessly in every language you speak, for many immigrants, experiences and emotions can be properly contained in one language and not in another.

Language and power are intimately related. Language structures the meanings that we live by. It can express inclusion and exclusion and subvert existing structures. For example, the growing body of discourses on #MeToo and #BlackLivesMatter creates awareness, mobilizes action, and helps people recognize and conceptualize behaviors and change beliefs and entitlements. Recent attacks on language, in particular the language of diversity, are politically motivated. These attacks aim to undermine social progress by trying to erase the language used to affirm and expand the rights of individuals and marginalized groups.

A specific word, accent, or symbol, in an otherwise seemingly neutral communication, can evoke larger structures of power, and activate hierarchies and

DOI: 10.4324/9781003648703-13

power dynamics that may put down, displace, or erase us. In these situations, we may experience confusion or a sense of disorientation as to what specifically is occurring, but we know that it is painful to encounter—it feels like a sting.

And as we try to manipulate, peg, insult, and persuade one another, in constructive or aggressive ways, we are not only shaped by language, but may also be the ones invoking its transformative power. For example, it is quite rare, but it still happens, that an Italian client or new acquaintance calls me *Sardignola*, a deprecating word for Sardinian. Or, they linger on my surname with a knowing playful smile; Porcu is not a noble name; it means *pig* in Sardinian and has the same root in all Romance languages. By adding a mocking Sardinian accent, staggering syllables, which is somewhat stigmatized in Italy, a northern Italian patient is invoking Sardinia's subalternity to the mainland (and therefore, more crucially, my inferior position vis-à-vis their own). For some Italian patients, it can be an uncomfortable experience to come to my office to seek my help. The use of language as just described is an attempt to rebalance the power differential, to take again the upper hand and quell and project their shame onto me.

Takeaway Exercise

Take a moment to reflect on these questions:

1   When I speak any particular language, how do I feel?
2   When I switch languages in the middle of my speech, what makes me switch?
3   How do I feel when I speak or when people speak to me in a particular language?
4   How does that affect my behavior and their behavior?
5   How does that affect the power dynamics between us?
6   When someone switches language when speaking with me, what do I feel has just happened?
7   You can go further and explore: What kinds of larger structures, hierarchies and ideologies, have been summoned, by changing language? And now that I see this level of language/power organization, how do I bring this up or use it to reassert my place and my power?

Microaggressions and Microinterventions

Merriam-Webster defines *microaggression* as "a comment or action that subtly and often unconsciously or unintentionally expresses a prejudiced attitude toward a member of a marginalized group (such as a racial minority)."[3] As the term microaggression has become more widespread, people are increasingly recognizing them when they occur, rather than unconsciously accepting them. They are also becoming more vocal in denouncing them. A common microaggression reported among my patient population is, for instance: "Yes, you are American, but where are you Really from?" Generally, the seeker is relentless until the not Anglo-looking person reveals the origin of parents or grandparents who had come to the US before them.

Another example affecting immigrant patients is when they are excluded from conversations that directly concern them. For instance, a doctor or authority figure may only address the husband, ignoring the wife even if she attempts to speak. Similarly, elderly immigrant parents may be spoken to through their children, as if they lack the capacity to communicate themselves (even when they speak the language!). These situations can be both frustrating and alienating, reinforcing a sense of invisibility.

Microaggressions can also be well-intentioned. Consider an immigrant professional who is praised for speaking such good English, as if proficiency in the language is unexpected. Moreover, a comment like, "You're surprisingly dedicated for someone from there," might sound like a compliment on the surface, but underneath it suggests that people from my background are not usually seen as competent or hardworking.

Experiencing microaggressions is frustrating and alienating, and over time, they can erode one's self-esteem and sense of belonging. Responding to them can also be exhausting, so it's important to assess when to respond and when to let it go. After receiving a microaggression, take a moment to check in with yourself: Do you have the emotional energy to engage, or is it better to move on? If you choose to respond, do so calmly and strategically, using what Sue et al.[4] describe as a *microintervention*. Microinterventions disarm and dismantle microaggressions, preventing the harm that comes from silence, while promoting self-respect and self-worth.

Sue et al. outline four major goals for microinterventions: (a) make the invisible visible, (b) disarm the microaggression, (c) educate the perpetrator, and (d) seek external support or reinforcement.[5] Deciding how to respond should be weighed carefully. Whether you choose to confront the situation, let it go, or seek help, it's essential to be prepared, both for yourself and for your children. Recognizing and addressing these biases is crucial to maintaining psychological wellbeing.

Specific tactics to employ and examples of how they are executed are listed below. I quote and paraphrase liberally from Sue et al.[6] Consider these efforts as first steps toward building your own self-defense and self-affirming vocabulary:

- Develop the capacity to see the hidden toxic message. You may feel it in your body. It may sound like a joke or a compliment, but if you feel uncomfortable, trust your instinct.
- Name the offense for what it is: "This comment is racist."[7]
- Name your experience: "Ouch! What you just said hurts."[8]
- Bring to light the implied toxic message. For instance, if you are a second-generation immigrant whose skin color pegs you as "other," you

might be told, "Your English is so good!" You can highlight the implication with this reply: "Thank you. I hope so. I was born here."[9]

- Challenge the stereotype: "No need to follow me around the shop. I am Black but I am not a thief."[10]
- Broaden and dilute the stereotype: "Yes, some immigrants may be lazy, but so are many Americans."[11]
- Ask the attacker to elaborate, so as to openly express the bias: "What do you mean?" or "Do you realize what you just said?"[12]
- Restate the bias openly in your response: "You're telling me that you're not going to consider Jamal for the manager position because White coworkers aren't ready for a Black boss."[13]
- Redirect and mimic the perpetrator. For instance, in response to the implied toxic message above, you might say: "Thank you, your English is good too."[14]

You can also set a boundary by walking away, while shaking your head. Another option, if appropriate, is to remind the speaker of a workplace's code of conduct. You might also express your disagreement and ask the speaker for a behavior change. Ultimately, you might appeal to the enlightened part of the microaggressor and promote empathy and commonalities. Remind them of their values and differentiate between "good intent" and "harmful impact:" "I know you meant it as a joke [intent], but it really offended Aisha [impact]."[15]

The work of Sue et al. is important because it not only brings attention to the widespread use of microaggressions, but it also offers good examples of microinterventions that are helpful templates to use if you want to find ways to raise awareness, make the invisible visible, fight back, and break the silence.[16] I particularly like a jujitsu style intervention: repeating back the offensive words of the offender out loud slowly while looking at them calmly and letting their words hang in the air and fill the room with their own toxicity. This is an effortless way to disarm someone. Of course, always be mindful that some people are deranged. If they look belligerent, at least for now, walk away.

Language Compartments

> I have the feeling that talking in German I shall have to remember something I want to forget.
>
> —A patient quoted by the psychoanalyst Ralph Greenson[17]

Some emotions and experiences are recalled only in the language in which you were operating at the time an event occurred. In the case of trauma, often the experience can only be accessed in the language used at the time in which the trauma occurred. Our minds keep us functioning by sealing off toxic experiences in forgotten spaces, such as in a particular language. Rose

Mary Pérez Foster, in her 1996 paper, "The Bilingual Self: Duets in Two Voices,"[18] talks of the treatment of a middle-aged Cuban American who escaped Cuba with her family when she was six years old. Her early life was marked by loss and neglect. To psychologically save herself, she embraced her new country and its language. She was "adopted" by her teachers and perfected her English. These choices offered her possibilities of identification, adaptation, and reinvention. As an adult, English was her everyday language of ease and efficacy. Spanish remained the language of sorrow, rage, and the language in which her trauma was encapsulated. Thus, on the one hand, the English code became developmentally the second symbolic medium through which she conducted particular relational experiences and came to evolve complex, creative, and adaptive functions in her self-development. On the other hand, English allowed her to ward off and efficiently encapsulate, as might any well-articulated characterological defense, the anguish of her early psychic life. The actual loss of her father and the psychic loss of her mother and motherland were primary objects of trauma that she unconsciously encoded into her original language. Some traumas are not able to be articulated at all. However, access to them can happen in another language. Perhaps the memories were encoded in the other language.

Language Battles

> The most common English word spoken in the nail salon was "sorry." It was the one refrain for what it meant to work in the service of beauty. Again and again, I watched as manicurists, bowed over a hand or foot of a client, some young as seven, say, "I'm sorry. I'm sorry. I'm so, so sorry," when they had done nothing wrong. I have seen workers, you included [mother], apologize dozens of times throughout a forty-five-minute manicure, hoping to gain warm traction that would lead to the ultimate goal, a tip—only to say sorry anyway when none was given.
>
> —Ocean Vuong, *On Earth We're Briefly Gorgeous*[19]

Language is a battleground. One of my Latino patients tells me that even when she is speaking English (admittedly with a strong Spanish accent), she has been scolded with a sentence like: "We speak English here!" Other patients feel silenced by their inability to speak proper standard English. They speak in a tentative soft apologetic way. And yet, as shown in the quote above, an immigrant in a subordinate position can still find a way of exploiting the dominant language to their advantage, like turning a rhetorical self-subordinating apology into covert financial coercion.

A person with a lot of social and economic power could use non-standard English in a grammatically incorrect way, and yet their speech would still be effective. The burden to understand is on the receiver. In the best-case scenario, their non-standard pronunciation may even be deemed charming. If you, as an individual or as a people group, do not have that sort of power, you may not be listened to even if your English is sublime. Language doesn't happen in a vacuum. Therefore, if you lack power, it would be perfectly understandable if you are hesitant and self-conscious to speak freely. But do not give into your fear and embarrassment. You will improve only by actively speaking. Speak slowly and be mindful of your enunciation, so you can be more easily understood, and repeat, if necessary. You may encounter a narcissist here and there who understands you very well but pretends not to. In such scenarios, the fight is not worth the effort. If someone makes fun of your English, keep your cool and let them know that you speak more than one language. Ask them if they'd fancy code-switching to one of your other languages? Or would they like to try pronouncing the word in your language?

One of the problems with putdowns, invalidations, and shame-inducing comments is that if you make them, eventually they get back to you. Thus, the negative cycle repeats. If you do not want to live in a toxic environment, do your part in not passing on the hurt by shaming the people more vulnerable than yourself. Instead, cultivate a more inclusive, compassionate, and mutually beneficial way of relating.

A very successful second-generation dark-skinned young woman, Sue, tells me how she "puts on her chunky boots" before going to work every day, to protect, ground, and charge herself. She creates an image in her mind in which she is putting on her armor and entering the battlefield, ready for a fight. She wonders about what stupid words from older White men she will hear on that day: whether she will be called "honey," "sweetie," or "you remind me of my daughter." She wonders if the new client will treat her as an equal or linger to start the meeting, asking when the big boss will join them (all of the above are microaggressions). It does not naturally occur to him that the boss is the young dark-skinned second-generation woman sitting in front of him, at the head of the table. Obviously, to be a young dark-skinned woman in an old or middle-aged White male field, she must possess superior skills. And still, she is underestimated. With her invisible armor on, she moves through the room with quiet strength, outperforming every man who once doubted her.

A Latina patient motivates herself similarly, as she struggles during the last stretch of graduate school finals, while juggling full-time work, relationship losses, and earlier traumas that still burden her. She does not have the luxury to sit and read, take it all in, read some more, reflect, rest, and write. This is how she does it:

> I am talking to myself as if I am in a UFC fight. The Ultimate Fighter Challenge is a boxing and martial art sport; it's real and deadly and lots of immigrants participate in it. I like to watch it and root for my people, when I can. It is in three rounds of five minutes each. I keep on telling myself, at finals, as if I were my trainer: "You went through the first round, which was classes. You got beat. You got in some punches; you

received some punches. You were puffy and got your Vaseline, but you were good." Then the beginning of finals week, which was second round, I made improvements, I fought back, but at the end I got beat and it was bad. The third round is now, the end of the semester. It is almost done! It's hard, I am exhausted, I can't take it. But it is as if the trainer is talking to the fighter, trying to make me understand I only have five minutes left. The coach inside me repeats: "I am going to get hit; it's going to hurt, but after these five minutes the fight is over. The end is in sight. It is a fight to survive. If you win, good, or you will figure it out: I got some good punches, and it is not win or lose. I am not gonna get the A+, but I'm still gonna pass. Or if I don't pass, I will take the semester again. This fight is terrible, but it's not gonna knock me out. Because I have been in previous fights that have been worse, and I have not tapped the ref. So why tap now.

Takeaway Exercise

Despite modest language proficiency and other socioeconomic factors that may put you at a disadvantage, think strategically about the following questions:

1   How can you use language to give you a leg up in the conversation; alternatively, if nothing else can be achieved, how can you highlight the power imbalance?
2   How can you motivate yourself to enter the ring, keep your cool, and, perhaps, find ways to make your opponent take you seriously?

Therapist Note: Navigating Language Boundaries and Responsibilities

Therapists: As explored throughout this chapter, language is never neutral. It carries cultural, emotional, and political weight. It shapes memory, identity, power—and the therapeutic alliance itself. When working with bilingual or multilingual clients, we must ask: How does language frame the emotional field of the session? What parts of a client's experience might be lost or revealed depending on the language used?

When therapist and client share a mother tongue, something particular can emerge—a sense of closeness, shared belonging, or emotional resonance. It can evoke nostalgia, comfort, or even a powerful recognition: "You understand me like no one else can." But it can also stir ambivalence, perhaps annoyance, discomfort, or the desire to distance from a past identity one has worked hard to shed. As therapists, we must remain attentive to these layered reactions, in ourselves as well as in our clients. What feels like connection may also carry residue. It may produce a false twinship and in any case it needs to be analyzed. Let us notice, feel, and gently interrogate our responses, without assuming that sameness equals safety.

Some memories, especially traumatic ones, may remain encapsulated in the language of origin and only be accessible through it. Others may emerge more readily in a second or third language, which can serve as a buffer or coping mechanism. For clients who migrated young or intentionally distanced themselves from early trauma, the new language often becomes a tool of forward movement—a means to regulate emotion, reconstruct selfhood, and adapt.

Allowing a client to speak freely in their native language can support emotional processing. However, if you do not understand that language, it is best not to encourage this without proper support. Some in the field suggest inviting clients to speak and then translate afterward—but this poses significant clinical risk. If you cannot track what is being said in real time, you may miss subtle signs of emotional escalation, dissociation, or even decompensation—leaving the client unsupported at a critical moment.

When interpretation is needed, aim for the following:

- *Trained and neutral:* Interpreters should understand confidentiality and maintain therapeutic neutrality.
- *Culturally attuned:* Ideally, they are familiar with the client's cultural and linguistic context.
- *Collaborative:* Build in time for briefings before and after sessions to ensure alignment on tone, content, and possible miscommunications.
- *Triadic structure:* Whenever possible, ensure visual access among all three participants (therapist, client, interpreter), especially for nonverbal cues.
- *Expand time:* Sessions will take longer. Plan accordingly, allowing time for interpretation as well as pre- and post-session debriefs.

Avoid using:

- family members or children as interpreters
- community members unless they are explicitly vetted by the client and professionally trained.

Although language brokering is common among immigrant families, it can place a heavy emotional burden on children and compromise the safety and confidentiality of the session. That said, research on language brokering is nuanced. While some studies emphasize stress and role confusion, others find positive outcomes, such as enhanced family cohesion, social intelligence, resilience, and verbal acuity.[20] Anecdotally, many of my patients and students who served as language brokers in childhood have grown into adults with remarkable articulation and interpersonal skill. Like most migration-related experiences, the outcomes depend on context, meaning, and support.

Do not ask bilingual colleagues to interpret unless this is part of their paid role. Even if they are willing, such requests place undue pressure on them, blur professional boundaries, and contribute to invisible labor. Advocate for appropriate compensation and role clarity.

Having an interpreter may change the feeling in the room. It may raise anxiety, disrupt intimacy, or create polarization. However, when the therapist and interpreter have clearly defined roles—and time to debrief—an interpreter can be very helpful, especially if they bring insight into cultural aspects the therapist may not be aware of.[21]

When using an interpreter, depending on the topic or culture, it may be important to match gender or religion, and to assess whether someone from the same community would help or hinder the therapy. Ideally, you will have choices and can discuss these with your patient.

Be attentive to language nuance and idiomatic meaning. For example, a Latino client using the expression *"Me voy a matar!"* (literally, "I'm going to kill myself") may not require an emergency psychiatric response. It may be an idiom of distress rather than a suicidal threat.

Be aware of structural barriers non-native English speakers face. Not only in session, but in navigating intake forms, untranslated materials, websites, or interactions with front desk staff. These linguistic barriers compound the daily systemic challenges clients already face.

When interpreter resources are limited, be creative. Reach out to local schools, non-profits, advocacy groups, and university departments that may have shared language-access resources or interpreters-in-training. Plan ahead for critical sessions. Include interpreter access in grant proposals or clinic budgets. When needed, consider referring out to a provider fluent in the client's primary language.

Above all, treat a client's ability to speak in their most comfortable language not as a luxury but as a basic right. That right may be fragile, overlooked, or systematically denied, but in the therapy room, it can be protected. Language access is part of the client's dignity, their safety, and their full participation in care.

Also remember that language is not only verbal. In many cultures, especially among elders, psychological distress is expressed somatically. Pay close attention to posture, breath, facial expression, pacing, tone, and culturally shaped idioms of distress. Sometimes what cannot be said can still be heard and seen—if we learn how to listen differently.

Familiarize yourself with the *DSM-5-TR*'s section on *cultural concepts of distress*,[22] especially the idioms of distress, cultural syndromes, and explanatory models. The list is not exhaustive, but it offers a helpful framework for interpreting unfamiliar presentations without prematurely pathologizing. Engaging with these frameworks encourages us to meet clients where they are—not where our training tells us they should be.

This section offers only a brief introduction. For additional readings and resources, visit www.leideporcu.com. Language work requires clinical humility, cultural curiosity, and a commitment to equity. In my own practice, I've found that the deepest therapeutic breakthroughs sometimes come through the least expected words—or silences.

Notes

1 Elena Ferrante, "We Don't Have to Fear Change, What Is Other Shouldn't Frighten Us," *The Guardian*, August 29, 2020.
2 Freud reported a joke about this topic which, despite its unacknowledged mis-ogyny and sadism, expresses well how—in this case during labor—multiple lan-guages may emerge. It is also a cautionary tale about how *not* to be like this doctor when we do therapy: it is a reminder of the importance of listening atten-tively and being fully present. The joke illustrates the layered and regressive nature of language use during states of distress, such as labor. In the story, a doctor playing cards with a husband during the wife's labor dismisses the woman's cries in French ("Ah, mon Dieu, que je souffre!"), and then in German ("Mein Gott, mein Gott, what terrible pains!"), insisting the time has not come. Only when the woman cries out in raw, pre-verbal sounds ("Aa-ee, aa-ee!") does he jump up and say, "Now it's time." Freud uses the joke to demonstrate how pain strips away layers of socialization and reveals something primal—what he calls "primitive nature." It also suggests that attunement to subtle linguistic shifts may carry diagnostic and relational importance. Freud, *Jokes and Their Relation to the Unconscious*, Standard Edition, Vol. 8, 81.
3 Merriam-Webster, "Microaggression," www.merriam-webster.com/dictionary/microaggression
4 Derald Wing Sue, Alisia G. T. Alim, David P. Rivera, and Christina M. Nadal, *Microintervention Strategies: What You Can Do to Disarm and Dismantle Indivi-dual and Systemic Racism and Bias* (Hoboken, NJ: Wiley, 2021), XIV.
5 Sue et al., 3.
6 Sue et al.
7 Sue et al., 94, 129.
8 Sue et al., 132.
9 Sue et al., 99.
10 Sue et al., 94.
11 Sue et al., 97.
12 Sue et al., 98.
13 Sue et al., 98.
14 Sue et al., 99.
15 Sue et al., 108.
16 Sue et al., 93–94.
17 This quote is taken from the paper "The Mother Tongue and the Mother" by Ralph Greenson. Ralph Greenson, "The Mother Tongue and the Mother," *Inter-national Journal of Psychoanalysis* 31 (1950): 18–23.
18 Pérez Foster, RoseMarie, "The Bilingual Self: Duet in Two Voices," *Psycho-analytic Dialogues* 6, no. 1 (1996): 99–121.
19 Ocean Vuong, *On Earth We're Briefly Gorgeous* (New York: Penguin Press, 2019), 91.
20 Lisa M. Dorner, Marjorie Faulstich Orellana, and Christine P. Li-Grining, "*I Helped My Mom, and It Helped Me*: Translating the 'Bilingual Advantage' for Language Brokering Youth." *Journal of Adolescent Research* 22, no. 2 (2007): 204–227.

21 Shadin Atiyeh, Mina Attia, and Julie Beckmann, "Interpreter-Mediated Psychotherapy with Refugees," *Journal of Counseling Research and Practice* 8, no. 1 (2023): Article 9, doi:10.56731/2688-3996.1057.
22 American Psychiatric Association, *Diagnostic and Statistical Manual of Mental Disorders*, 5th ed., Text Revision (DSM-5-TR) (Washington, DC: APA, 2022).

References

American Psychiatric Association. 2022. *Diagnostic and Statistical Manual of Mental Disorders*, 5th ed., Text Revision (DSM-5-TR). Washington, DC: American Psychiatric Association.

Atiyeh, Shadin, Mina Attia, and Julie Beckmann. 2023. "Interpreter-Mediated Psychotherapy with Refugees." *Journal of Counseling Research and Practice* 8 (1): Article 9. doi:10.56731/2688-3996.1057.

Dorner, Lisa M., Marjorie Faulstich Orellana, and Christine P. Li-Grining. "I Helped My Mom, and It Helped Me: Translating the 'Bilingual Advantage' for Language Brokering Youth." *Journal of Adolescent Research* 22 (2): 204–227.

Ferrante, Elena. 2020. "We Don't Have to Fear Change, What Is Other Shouldn't Frighten Us." *The Guardian*, August 29.

Foster, RoseMarie Pérez. "The Bilingual Self: Duet in Two Voices." *Psychoanalytic Dialogues* 6 (1): 99–121.

Freud, Sigmund. 1960. *Jokes and Their Relation to the Unconscious*. Standard Edition, Vol. 8. London: Hogarth Press.

Greenson, Ralph. 1950. "The Mother Tongue and the Mother." *International Journal of Psychoanalysis* 31: 18–23.

Merriam-Webster. "Microaggression." Merriam-Webster.com. www.merriam-webster.com/dictionary/microaggression.

Sue, Derald Wing, Alisia G. T. Alim, David P. Rivera, and Christina M. Nadal. 2021. *Microintervention Strategies: What You Can Do to Disarm and Dismantle Individual and Systemic Racism and Bias*. Hoboken, NJ: Wiley.

Vuong, Ocean. 2019. *On Earth We're Briefly Gorgeous*. New York: Penguin Press.

10 A Few Pointers for Communication

In the beginning, just the idea of applying for work made me panic. I did not think anyone would hire someone who spoke like me. Then I found a place where speaking my language was a strength, not a flaw. That gave me a start. Still, to this day, the words I dread the most are: "What do you mean?" They stop me cold. Not because I do not have something to say, but because I worry they are not hearing me—just my accent.

—Anonymous contributor

Many elements shape the way we communicate, and some of them are not always apparent to us. We learn how to communicate from our families and from all the cultures to which we belong. We have our innate predispositions and abilities, the emotional weight of our history, and the web of socioeconomic dynamics from which we operate, shaping our style of communication. Our interlocutors also speak and listen from their own complex multilayered positions. It can be hard to understand one another and get along. Take the example of Diego, a friend of mine who often gets into misunderstandings in his relationships, with friends, at school, and even at work. Diego passionately thinks and speaks with strong emotions. His emotions, though, are often misinterpreted in the United States as anger, which puts people off. He becomes frustrated because well-meaning educated people who talk about "diversity" and "cultural relativity" are the ones asking him to tone it down and accusing him of being belligerent. He maintains, instead, he is only passionate and wants to respectfully get his point across while remaining authentic in his delivery. He maintains he shouldn't have to transform his delivery into what he sees as the mainstream White way of separating emotion from content. He wants to remain Latino and be able to speak in White spaces, which ideally are grounded in mutual respect for cultural diversity. He recently shared the following: "I am not angry. They don't understand that *diversity* is not an abstract word. My way of talking is not based on anger. I communicate with commitment and passion. I am not angry. But if I am not soft- spoken like they expect me to be here, they mistake my tone as disrespectful and angry."

DOI: 10.4324/9781003648703-14

Therapists and educators: Consider how Diego's story—and the communication strategies that follow—might inform your work with immigrant clients or students, especially when misunderstandings arise around tone, assertiveness, or emotional expression.

When we are stuck in a disagreement in a well-meaning exchange, when both parties want to understand one another and get along, it can be helpful to stay very close to the facts, or, better stated, describe what we perceive is going on and exchange points of view until we reach a mutual understanding. By expanding a common mental framework with all the layered cultural and historical contributions that shape each person's point of view and that inform our emotional reactions and behaviors, we can better understand the reactions we have to one another, and gain mutual understanding and empathy.

It is also essential to work on ourselves and increase our emotional awareness without being cluttered by unmanageable feelings and blinding defenses. It is equally imperative for us to stretch our cultural limits and understand there are other ways of communicating, and we need to honor and respect them.

It is important to bear in mind that when our ways do not work it takes courage to recognize that and seek other ways, rather than becoming headstrong. Learning how to speak clearly and using the best words to convey your meaning is important. I am not only referring to grammar and accent; I am thinking about the use of the rhetoric of persuasion for promoting peaceful relationships, for defusing anger, for gaining the floor, and for making the world a comfortable place for all to inhabit through our words (despite the structural constraints that limit the magnitude of what we can achieve).

The following guidelines are some of the points I share with my patients, many of which draw from the work of renowned therapists like Harville Hendrix and Sue Johnson, as well as relationship researcher John Gottman.[1] I have found these strategies particularly helpful for immigrants who are confronted with extra layers of complexity in communication. Give them a try if you are running into misunderstandings or difficulties in your workplace, friendships, or intimate and familial relationships:

- *Limit negativity:* Ideally, when something is not working, rather than complaining or expressing anger, try instead a simple request to change things.
- *Create a memory bank:* Journal, take pictures, or create a memento chest (or at least a memory bank) of all the good moments and things that are working in your relationships. Memorialize these moments with a family member, your partner, or a friend; talk about them, and express gratitude. You are creating the positive basis on which the relationship is being built, and you need this memory bank to withstand the low points in your relationships.
- *Practice the 5:1 ratio:* According to the researcher John Gottman, for a marriage to go well, the magic ratio should be five positive comments to

every negative one. Limit the blaming and nagging. Cultivate the qualities of compassion, forgiveness, gratitude, acceptance, appreciation, and humor to train yourself to focus on the positive.

- *Choose your battles:* Use "I" language: "I feel this way when you do this." Then request a behavior change. Avoid phrasing, such as "Why do you" and "You are always/never doing." You want the other person to be receptive and willing to consider what you need, rather than to become defensive and angry.

- *Balance appreciation with requests:* Although it may feel trite and insincere to many people, there are good reasons to recognize what is actually working before pointing out what is wrong and asking for a behavioral change. This helps to establish a safe environment in which things are mostly working. Then, the perception is that the relationship is not in danger and the other person is not only bad. It also helps the recipient to feel safe rather than attacked, making collaboration more likely.

- *Be specific:* Give concrete examples of the offending behavior and not generalizations. The more you zero in on what about the behavior is offensive and the more you are specific about what you need, the better the outcome. It is on you to ask for what you need.

- *Ask for what you need:* People cannot read your mind.

- Do not jump into conclusions or mind read: Avoid jumping to conclusions about what others are thinking.

- *Recognize limits:* Remember that you cannot change people. You can request a change of behavior, but you cannot expect an overall makeover, even if that is what makes sense to you.

- *Give notice before hard conversations:* If you want to talk to someone about something that upsets you, give them a heads up, so that they do not feel ambushed and have the time to get into the right frame of mind to listen.

- *Hold regular check-ins*: Introduce a weekly check-in with your partner, roommates, coworkers, or colleagues so that frustration does not accumulate.

- *Listen fully before responding:* When people tell you their complaints, give them the space to talk. Do not interrupt them with "Yes, but" or "You did the same yesterday." That leads nowhere. Give them the experience of being listened to and await your turn to speak. The main goal is to listen.

- *Keep complaints short:* When you express a complaint, keep it short and sweet. Also, only address one complaint at a time, as the listener needs to digest what you are saying and then report back to you, to make sure they understand. If a person is flooded with complaints, they may feel deflated, misunderstood, and frustrated. It becomes hard for them to absorb all that you are saying. At some point in the conversation, they may check out.

- *Reflect and clarify:* When you are on the receiving end of a complaint, once the person is done speaking, give them back their message: "What

I heard you saying is..." Then ask, "Is there more?" When reporting the message back, use the same words you heard, without adding irony or a tone, or rolling your eyes, which would defeat the purpose of honestly listening and putting oneself in the other person's shoes. The goal is to become a sounding board for the other person. Look each other in the eyes and really be present. This does not mean submission or invalidation of your point of view. Listening and repeating does not mean that you are giving up your point of view. You are letting them know that you heard them and are interested in knowing more about how they see things. If they feel heard, they can relax and eventually hear you when it's your turn.

- *Speak your truth after listening:* After the person has been fully heard, speak your truth, and share your feelings. It will then be the other person's turn to return the favor to you by listening and repeating. This type of communication may feel clunky at first but increases the chances of listening to one another with respect and empathy.
- *Let go of being "right":* Don't react based on your assumptions. Give people the benefit of the doubt and the space to explain why they think and act a certain way. Consider how and why it makes sense for them to do what they do given their history and background. We all speak from different positions and may have different points of view (POVs). We need to let go of the idea that we are right and hold the only truth. Opening a safe space in which you can unpack all the overarching layers that contribute to your POV helps depolarize conflict.
- *Describe observed behavior:* Ask people what's up by pointing to what you see: for example, "You are looking at your phone and you have been yawning as I am talking to you. What is going on?"
- *Use a code word:* If things get too hot, have a code word (e.g., "Fire!") that you say to alert the other person that the conversation is getting out of hand, and you need to take a time out. (A time out is not an abandonment. It actually preserves the relationship.)
- *Practice rupture and repair:* Don't be afraid to speak up if something feels off. Sometimes people don't speak because they are afraid of ruptures. They keep things inside and then move further and further away and disengage or explode at some point. In therapy, we have the concept of "rupture and repair," or forgiveness and reconciliation, which comes originally from infant observation studies. When all goes well, mother and child engage in a harmony of gazes and cooing sounds. The mother is attentive to her child's needs, meeting them, and giving words to the baby's needs and feelings. However, from time to time, there is a gap in the tracking. When there is a rupture, the repair that follows brings growth and understanding. Similar experiences happen in grownup relationships. Through ruptures and repairs we transcend the moment of disharmony and increase our capacity to withstand and accept each other's differences and engage as separate persons in mutual support.

- *Beth's example:* If you are not too angry, address the issue on the spot by saying something like: "What just happened?" This can help both of you pause, rewind, and reflect. For example, Beth, a young woman struggling with low self-esteem and depression, had a rare moment in which she was motivated to care for herself by taking an action that would have positive effects on both her self-esteem and depressive symptoms. When she shared this rare moment of motivation with her mother, "It's a beautiful day, I think I'll go out for a walk," her mother's response was, "It's going to rain and your jacket doesn't fit because you've gained so much weight." Rather than withdrawing or reacting with anger, Beth applied what she had learned in therapy. She calmly replied, "Mom, look what just happened. I told you I was going out for a walk, and you responded by saying it will rain and that I've gained weight. That makes me feel deflated and sad. It makes me not want to share things with you. What I need instead is for you to be my cheerleader—someone who can see the positive and share in my small victories." This brief, clear statement included an invitation to reflect, an expression of feelings, the impact of the behavior, and a simple request for change, offering the possibility of repair rather than rupture.

- *Apologize when needed:* If you hurt someone, apologize. It is not shameful to do so, and it strengthens the relationship.

- *Forgive when you are ready:* If you are not ready to forgive, don't. It is a relief to forgive, and it frees you, but you can only do it when you are ready.

- *Improve your language skills:* Even if your trade is not strictly related to language or writing, make perfecting your language a priority. Speaking well is something that doesn't cost anything to improve. You can read and listen to people who speak well and emulate them. It benefits your career, communication, and helps you get what you want.

- *Improve your pronunciation:* Listen to one of your favorite English voices and record yourself repeating their phrases. Then listen to yourself and compare (without judgment). This can be done in just a few minutes a day.

- *Make space for boundaries:* In your vocabulary there should be plenty of space for "No," "Stop," and "I disagree." The language that is necessary to setting boundaries goes hand in hand with your work developing a growing sense of self. Learn to recognize your discomfort and honor it. Learn to set your boundaries and express them firmly. If people minimize or invalidate your feelings and trespass your clearly stated boundaries, you are in the wrong company.

- *Build an arsenal of "interruption shields:"* As Neelu Kaur, the author of *Be Your Own Cheerleader*, calls them, these phrases help regain the floor.[2] Practice them out loud so that you have them ready when you need to make a point and have your voice be heard. When interrupted, silenced, or ignored, find an opening to re/enter the flow of the conversation by using some of these suggested openings: "I'd like to circle back"; "If I may just complete that thought"; "I'd love to finish my thought before we move on"; "I am excited to hear the next item but I'd like to finish my thought here"; "Please allow me to finish"; "May I interject here?"; "Hold on, I need to jump in here"; "One thing we are missing is..."

- *Learn how to "turn the spotlight:"* Kasia Urbaniak, an expert on power dynamics and the body, teaches this technique for moments when you freeze under unwanted attention. Instead of responding and defending yourself, redirect focus by asking a question. It can be curious, clarifying, or even playfully nonsensical.[3]

- *Acknowledge kinkiness:* Communication is not limited to spoken words. Our bodies, gestures, silences, and even our desires speak— sometimes more clearly than language ever could. Sexuality, in particular, is a form of communication that is deeply shaped by culture, history, and personal experience. The "scripts" we follow in intimate settings are not only shaped by our needs and preferences but also by the cultural messages we have absorbed about what is acceptable, healthy, or moral.

The Language of Desire: Communicating Through Fantasy and Play

As Esther Perel notes in *Mating in Captivity*, American therapists often work within a particular framework of what constitutes healthy sexuality—one that may appear "vanilla," restrained, and bounded by ideals of equality and control.[4] Other forms of sexuality are considered marginal and struggle to be accepted. While this model may offer safety and clarity and reflects the achievements of control over their bodies women have attained over time, it can also leave little room for fantasy, transgression, or erotic play. A too rigid idea of what sexuality should look like may also stifle women in their ability to shamelessly ask for whatever they desire. Perel makes a distinction between the everyday relationship and the erotic, maintaining that sexual play does not necessarily undermine the ongoing quest for women's liberation. In many cases, people feel ashamed of their desires when those desires seem at odds with mainstream or feminist ideals—especially when power dynamics enter the bedroom.[5]

But like all languages, erotic expression depends on mutual understanding. As long as there is clear consent and mutual enjoyment between *compos mentis*, equally empowered adults, the erotic can become a language of play, power, and freedom. Take, for instance, the story of a high-achieving American woman who long felt ashamed of her fantasy of being dominated. Her dominant Italian husband understood and respected her desires, and over time, she came to embrace them. What happened in their bedroom did not diminish the fairness or balance in their everyday lives. On the contrary, it reinforced trust, intimacy, and the desire for one another by allowing a fuller, more honest form of communication between them.[6]

Therapists must pay close attention to the cultural and personal "dictionaries" our clients bring into the room. What may appear submissive, unhealthy, or disempowering in one framework may, in another, be an expression of agency and deep mutuality. Just as we are trained to listen closely to a client's choice of words, tone, or silence, we must also learn to listen to the ways their desires speak—especially when shaped by histories of shame or cultural repression.

If shame has muted your ability to communicate your needs or explore your desires, therapy and reflective reading—such as Perel's work—may offer a path toward clarity and freedom. In the end, sexuality is one more way we say who we are, what we long for, and how we wish to be met. It is not separate from language—it *is* a language.

You may have recognized yourself in some of these examples. Whether you are navigating these challenges yourself or supporting others in doing so, every small shift in how we speak and listen creates ripples that change relationships and communities for the better.

For further reading on interpersonal communication, boundary-setting, and emotional regulation, see the Selected Resources section on my website, www.leideporcu.com.

Notes

1 John M. Gottman and Nan Silver, *The Seven Principles for Making Marriage Work* (New York: Crown Publishers, 1999), 26–46; Harville Hendrix, *Getting the Love You Want: A Guide for Couples*, 20th Anniversary ed. (New York: Henry Holt and Company, 2007), esp. 245–283, with a focus on zero negativity (p. 280) and Exercise 8, "The Imago Dialogue," on p. 260; and Sue Johnson, *Hold Me Tight: Seven Conversations for a Lifetime of Love* (New York: Little, Brown Spark, 2008), 63–211, especially the structured "Conversations" and the "Six Steps of Forgiveness."
2 Neelu Kaur, *Be Your Own Cheerleader: An Asian and South Asian Woman's cultural, Psychological and Spiritual Guide to Self Promote at Work* (Post Hill Press, 2023), 41.
3 Kasia Urbaniak *A Woman's Guide to Power Unbound* (Penguin Random House, 2022), 219–234.
4 Kaur, 44–45.
5 Kaur, 57.
6 Kaur, 56.

References

Gottman, J. M., and N. Silver 1999. *The Seven Principles for Making Marriage Work.* New York: Crown Publishers.

Hendrix, Harville. 2007. *Getting the Love You Want: A Guide for Couples.* 20th Anniversary ed. New York: Henry Holt and Company.

Johnson, Sue. 2008. *Hold Me Tight: Seven Conversations for a Lifetime of Love*. New York: Little, Brown Spark.

Kaur, Neelu. 2023. *Be Your Own Cheerleader: An Asian and South Asian Woman's Cultural, Psychological, and Spiritual Guide to Self-Promote at Work*. New York: Post Hill Press.

Perel, E. 2006. *Mating in Captivity: Reconciling the Erotic and the Domestic*. New York: HarperCollins.

Part IV
Teasing Out Feelings and Connecting Body and Mind

11 Identifying and Integrating Emotions as an Immigrant

A Guide for Immigrants and Therapists

Funny you ask if recent events are affecting me. I did not make the connection. I have been completely unmotivated and distracted. I thought I was just lazy and tired. I am so used to compartmentalizing and having my life and work separate, so I can manage, that I tend to forget that the two are not really separate. But it's been a rough week. Come to think of it, a Latino vendor in LA was assaulted. Then there was the video of a Muslim food delivery guy, an older man, who was thrown out of his car by two girls who were trying to hijack his car. It happened in DC. This was not a hate crime, but that video struck me: He laid there on the sidewalk like a piece of meat. He died there. It's happening more and more. I used to take life for granted and maybe that's how it should be. But not anymore.

—Yi, an Asian patient

Labeling

As meditation teacher Sharon Salzberg notes, mindfulness helps us "get better at seeing the difference between what's happening and the stories we tell ourselves about what's happening."[1]

Yi was feeling blah, achy, and unmotivated. Initially, she had not realized how current events were affecting her mental state and emotional energy level. Becoming aware helped her identify her sadness, her guilt over her (relative) privilege, her anger, and her disappointment. As a consequence, she could speak kindly to herself for the way she was feeling, instead of blaming herself for being *lazy*.

As an immigrant, often you will not have the comforts, friendly support, and spiritual guidance you were accustomed to in your home country. However, as you navigate roadblocks and upsets, it is possible that you haven't had time to reflect on how these challenges affect you. Contending with the negative ways immigrants are often treated in your community and in the United States in general can have a physical impact on your body, as was the case with Yi.

Take a moment to consider what is going on inside you and how the outside world may be affecting you. The more you know about your internal life and the characters that live inside your head, the more you can

DOI: 10.4324/9781003648703-16

orchestrate their voices. The more you define and know your emotions, the better you will be able to take care of yourself (for more on internal voices and integration, see Chapter 7: Finding Your Voice Across Cultures).

Once you notice your feelings, the next step is to name them. Names are like boxes or frames; they create order and serve to contain emotions. Names also teach you to observe your emotions, rather than react impulsively to them. When you find yourself experiencing strong feelings, use the proper name for a sensation (e.g., sadness), or a more general label for what you might be doing (e.g., judging). Then take yourself by the hand, so to speak, and talk kindly to yourself to help yourself move to a more objective and balanced state.

The Differences Between Fear, Anxiety, and Depression

Justine, a French patient, came to the United States as a graduate student and is now working as a researcher. She has a hard time presenting at meetings because of her strong accent. Her smooth and flawless French, which made her audience captive in France, is in stark contrast to her awkward English pronunciation and faulty grammar. No one has singled her out for unacceptable performance; she produces quality work, and she is precise and dedicated. However, when she is asked to elaborate at meetings, some of her answers are convoluted and awkward. She has noticed that at her presentations, some of her colleagues appear uninterested and absent-minded. She worries she is below par and that everybody thinks badly of her. Because she expects to be fired, she is considering quitting her job to end her pain and prevent the embarrassment of being fired. She wonders if she made the right decision to leave France. To avoid the feelings of anxiety and humiliations about her perceived incapability, she does her best not to stand out and avoids presentations. She delays starting new projects because she fears exposure and judgment. She procrastinates and feels paralyzed. She has trouble sleeping. When she gives presentations, she feels like a deer in headlights.

Under the sway of her faulty anxiety alarm system, Justine feels she is in great existential danger. Although a presentation is a relatively safe undertaking, her logical brain shuts off while she prepares a flight/freeze response, in an attempt to protect herself (fight, flight, and freeze are typical responses to situations perceived as dangerous). In her private life, Justine avoids speaking English and socializes mostly with her French friends. In this way she protects herself from embarrassment, but she also limits the opportunities that would allow her to practice her English and improve her communication and performance. Her struggle echoes what psychiatrist Mark Epstein has written: "Awakening does not mean a change in difficulty, it means a change in how those difficulties are met."[2] For Justine, the task in therapy was not to eliminate difficulty but to learn to meet it differently—with greater perspective, self-acceptance, and resilience.

Anxiety is a feeling that is disproportionate to the current danger. The feeling that arises in situations of real danger is fear. When our internal alarm system is overly sensitive, instead of protecting us, it hinders us by creating anxiety. Unlike fear, anxiety is an unhelpful and excessively negative reaction, in which the anxious person misinterprets an overall safe situation as dangerous. The subsequent result is to misjudge and minimize one's power or one's odds of success. When we flee from something that is not actually dangerous, we forego an opportunity to grow. When anxious, we cannot rely on the usual resources to think logically, recall from memory, and concentrate. This aligns with how CBT views anxiety—as a distortion of perceived threat.

For instance, as an immigrant, we are more likely to be less competent in social situations and linguistic expression, making it impossible to respond with the same ease and subtlety that we're accustomed to. Additionally, if you are an immigrant of a marginalized population (e.g., race, religion, ethnicity), there is an added complexity to the reasons for feeling uncomfortable in the current environment of hostility and hate. Therefore, you may be vulnerable to feelings of inadequacy and anxiety. However, if there is no danger to your physical wellbeing, then keep in mind that your discomfort is only a feeling. If you can stay with mild (not overwhelming) discomfort rather than flee from it, you'll gradually expand your capacity to tolerate discomfort. In the long term, this strengthens resilience and increases your capacity to withstand uncomfortable situations, fostering growth. Avoidance may provide a momentary illusion of safety, but it ultimately impedes your development.

Do not confuse anxiety with depression. Here is a simple rule of thumb to distinguish the two: You have anxiety when you think that a terrible thing is *about to happen*, and you are too small, too incompetent to withstand it (even if, objectively, this is not the case). You are nervous and afraid because you worry you cannot succeed. You have depression when you feel that the catastrophe *has already happened*. The wind is out of your sails and the energy is sapped out of you. You feel hopeless, you have given up, and there is no prospect and no point to moving forward. If you recognize yourself in this picture, see a specialist. Depression can be lifted with both medication and therapy, and often one can go back to enjoying life. One of the problems when seeking relief from depression is that depression tends to make one feel that everything is pointless, and there is no hope. Therefore, from a depressed individual's perspective, even seeking therapy and medication might seem like worthless pursuits.

Perfectionism and the Immigrant Inner Critic

Eddie came to therapy paralyzed by a feeling of sadness and despair. Eddie is a brilliant researcher who is very dedicated to his work and recently immigrated to the United States to follow his research interests and develop his career. His beginning in the United States was tough. He arrived with the expectation of hitting the ground running, but he encountered an unexpected learning curve. When he fell short ever so slightly in his expectations, he tortured himself relentlessly. He believed he deserved to live only if he were perfect. Short of that, he felt valueless. He longed for a place that could make him feel worthy, appreciated, loved, and seen, all of which was lacking in his life since childhood. He had hoped the United States would embrace him. Now he was disillusioned. While none of his colleagues nor his manager complained about unpardonable errors, Eddie believed (without much evidence) that he was not doing well, and that they were critical of him. His thinking style mirrors what Aaron Beck called automatic negative thoughts, often shaped by early core beliefs.

It took quite a bit of work to change his way of thinking. We systematically analyzed his thoughts and his daily interactions and discussed the ways in which his traumatic childhood history was affecting his present circumstances. He eventually became able to accept a work performance that, to him, felt less than optimal. We also created schedules with time built in for him to engage in pleasurable pursuits. After two years of therapy, his progress was reflected in this statement: "I don't have to be perfect, I just have to be okay. Perfectionism is my enemy when doing good work."

Gradually, Eddie would stay in the negative faulty appraisal space for increasingly shorter times. He began to reframe his thinking with more agility and even learned self-compassion—a word that initially made him cringe.

The Feeling Scale

This Feeling Scale is designed to help you get better at quantifying your feelings. With this scale we are not aiming for scientific precision—an approximation is enough. Simply becoming aware of how your feelings rise and fall can give you valuable information about your internal state, your thoughts, and the situation you are navigating. It also helps you recognize what you might need to feel better and begin to regulate your responses. To create your scale, draw a line with the numbers, as shown in Figure 11.1 (see also Appendix A). The numbers indicate intensity of the feeling. Choose a feeling you want to work on and imagine situations in which you have felt that particular feeling at the maximum (100) and not at all (0). Then choose the midpoint (50) and ultimately the other points. Keep the scale as a reference. You want to learn to gauge your feelings and use the early signals to regulate yourself by thinking or doing what gives you relief and to ask for help if needed. For instance, you want to be aware of your sadness, anger, and anxiety well before it reaches the midpoint. It is easier to attend to it if the number is low.

Feeling Scale

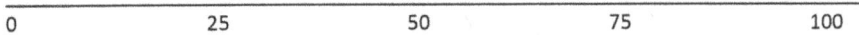

0	25	50	75	100

To get accustomed to assigning a number to your feelings and creating a scale, it's helpful to think about times when you felt 100% and 0% of a particular emotion. What was happening during those moments? Then, consider 50%, followed by 25% and 75%. By progressing this way, you establish reference points that make it easier to gauge the intensity of the feeling you're experiencing in the present moment.

Figure 11.1 Feeling Scale

My former patient Jewang and I created it early in our work together. We began by identifying specific moments that made him feel anxious at the 100 level (maximum anxiety) and at the 0 level (no anxiety). From there, we marked the midpoint (50) and then added intermediate points like 25 or 75. Once your own benchmarks are set (and you can always modify them as you learn to assess your emotions with more precision), it becomes much easier to assess how intensely you are feeling in any moment. You can say, "I feel as anxious as when…" and you can refer to a particular point in your scale or to a point in between, like, 10, let's say.

See Figure 11.2 for an example of how Jewang, a Chinese American patient of mine, assigned numerical values to specific experiences of anxiety, helping him to recognize and track the intensity of his emotional responses.

Note to the Therapist

When working with immigrants who present with high-functioning perfectionism or emotional numbing, be alert to the ways cultural survival strategies may mask distress. Naming this gently—and inviting curiosity about how the body is holding the emotion—can open therapeutic space.

Jewang's Personal Anxiety Scale

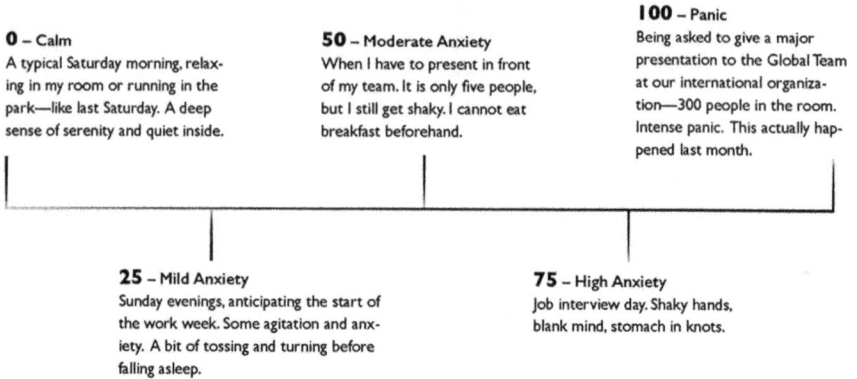

100 – Panic
Being asked to give a major presentation to the Global Team at our international organization—300 people in the room. Intense panic. This actually happened last month.

0 – Calm
A typical Saturday morning, relaxing in my room or running in the park—like last Saturday. A deep sense of serenity and quiet inside.

50 – Moderate Anxiety
When I have to present in front of my team. It is only five people, but I still get shaky. I cannot eat breakfast beforehand.

25 – Mild Anxiety
Sunday evenings, anticipating the start of the work week. Some agitation and anxiety. A bit of tossing and turning before falling asleep.

75 – High Anxiety
Job interview day. Shaky hands, blank mind, stomach in knots.

To get accustomed to assigning a number to your feelings and creating a scale, it's helpful to think about times when you felt 100% and 0% of a particular emotion. What was happening during those moments? Then, consider 50%, followed by 25% and 75%. By progressing this way, you establish reference points that make it easier to gauge the intensity of the feeling you're experiencing in the present moment.

Figure 11.2 Jewang's Feeling Scale

Takeaway Exercise

Pay attention to your language and ask yourself the following questions:

1   Do I talk to myself in a harsh, perfectionistic way?
2   Do I feel lacking, small, and incompetent?
3   Am I aligned with my expectations, or do I often feel disappointed and critical of myself?
4   How is a negative way of relating to myself helpful?
5   How is it unhelpful to me?

Therapists: One useful tool in moments of emotional flooding is to ask clients questions that help clients identify emotions and locate them in the body: "What emotion is loudest right now?" "Can we give it a name and locate where it lives in the body?" The simple act of naming and localizing supports self-regulation and makes the emotion feel more containable.

Naming is not fixing. It is the first step toward reclaiming presence, agency, and care. Whether you are naming emotions for yourself or helping others do so, each act of mindful attention plants a seed for healing.

As we learn to name and feel our emotions more fully, moving beyond numbness or perfectionistic striving, some deeper, more difficult feelings may rise to the surface. For many immigrants, this includes guilt and regret. In the next chapter, we will explore how to face those emotions with honesty, context, and compassion.

Notes

1 Sharon Salzberg, *Real Happiness: The Power of Meditation—A 28-Day Program* (New York: Workman Publishing, 2010), 13.
2 Mark Epstein, *The Trauma of Everyday Life* (New York: Penguin Books, 2013), 74.

References

Epstein, Mark. 2013. *The Trauma of Everyday Life*. New York: Penguin Books.
Salzberg, Sharon. 2010. *Real Happiness: The Power of Meditation—A 28-Day Program*. New York: Workman Publishing.

12 Guilt and Regret and the Emotional Cost of Migration

Not being able to travel while waiting for my immigration papers made me feel like I had turned my back on my family. My grandparents are old and sick, and I carry guilt for not being there with them. I try to stay in touch by phone, but it is not the same. I am still learning to accept the distance and not let the guilt and worry take over.

—Anonymous contributor

What is the difference between guilt and shame? While the distinction between guilt and shame was introduced in an earlier chapter, it is worth revisiting in order to reconsider how these emotions shape our experiences. In therapy we define shame as the crushing feeling that something is fundamentally defective or wrong with oneself. Guilt is more circumscribed: it is the feeling of having done something wrong and experiencing regret. Guilt is based on one's actions, and not on the essence of the person. For both temporary and established immigrants, feelings of guilt and regret are likely to occur.

In this chapter, we examine how guilt and regret appear in the immigrant experience, from familial obligations to identity shifts, and how both immigrants and therapists can learn to hold these complex emotions with compassion and clarity. I will pick up and expand on some of the themes already introduced in Chapter 7: Finding Your Voice Across Cultures.

Immigrant populations experience these feelings for a number of reasons; chief among them is leaving vulnerable relatives behind, in the country of origin, and abdicating equal responsibility for their care. Siblings and other family members may become resentful for being saddled with full responsibility of the family, which only further accentuates these feelings. In these cases, guilt mixes with a tremendous sense of remorse to produce regret. Regret often manifests as sadness over what cannot be undone, such as missed time, missed care. In immigrant families, it may deepen a sense of fragmentation and contribute to intergenerational loss, both emotional and cultural.

These feelings of guilt and regret can also affect relationships with family members nearby. Even if you live in the same city as recently immigrated

DOI: 10.4324/9781003648703-17

relatives, the demands of long work hours may leave you feeling that there's not enough time for family, children, or partners, causing you to miss important moments.

Alicia is a young Latina who, living away from her family and alone in New York City, experienced guilt and resentment toward her extended family, even as she successfully improved her social status. She valued family connections but had little time to nurture these connections. She felt isolated and guilty:

> I grew up in a family where the holidays were spent together with the extended family. Now it's not that easy as we are all spread out. I make an effort to stay in touch. But no matter how much I do, I feel guilty because my efforts are never good enough. My family expects more from me. They don't understand that I am running all day. They think I am a disrespectful rich *gringa*. Maybe I should do more. But I am tired at the end of the day, and I don't want to call them because I'll get frustrated. Instead of a kind word, when I call, I get more scolding. It's all about them. But I am hurting too, and who is offering me help?

In *Culturally Responsive Counseling with Latinas/os*,[1] Arredondo et al. introduce the concept of *familism, la familia*: Family is central, and family members are connected and invested in one another's wellbeing. Relationships are hierarchical, interdependent, and caring. The burden of showing respect, providing services, and offering care falls especially heavy on the younger generations. Second-generation and 1.5-generation immigrants, however, may be more Americanized and not fully ascribe to these values. Their different outlook can produce intergenerational conflicts.

In therapy, Alicia says her family takes a top-down approach, in which they expect her, the younger subordinate, to do much of the work in maintaining the relationship. When she does not do what is expected, the family uses guilt to pressure her into making a bigger effort, no matter what her present circumstances may be. One cousin calls asking her to translate a medical form. Another uncle assumes she will pick up his son from school while she works a double shift. "You're so good at handling things," her brother says, "Could you just fill out Dad's pension paperwork too? It's in English, and you know how to do these things." She wants to say no. She tries. But every time she does, they act hurt—like she's turned her back on her own people. "You're the only one who's educated, who knows the system. What are we supposed to do without you?" So she puts her own needs aside. Again and again. Until the pressure builds in her chest like a silent scream.

Alicia felt guilty and frustrated. She didn't doubt her extended family loved her, but she didn't feel heard or understood. What she wanted from her uncle was validation and empathy.

In addition to familial guilt, many immigrants experience a different kind of guilt associated with "passing," which means blending into mainstream culture. Blending in may be perceived as abandoning their ethnic identity for social or professional success. This feeling often extends beyond family to the broader ethnic community. For instance, a Latino immigrant, now a high-ranking employee at a bank, shared his discomfort with participating in his company's diversity meetings: "I do not belong in these gatherings. In New York, I pass for White and have all the privileges of a White man. I suffer none of the problems that 'my people' experience in this country. Because of my nationality and my Latin name, I am supposed to take part in these events. But it feels odd to me. I may be Latino on paper, but my life is not at all like their lives. Listening to their experiences makes me feel guilty and out of place."

Many people immigrate to the US with high expectations, pumped by media portrayals of success and the good life. However, once here, the realization of how hard life in the US can be sets in. Some feel stranded here and express regrets about having chosen the "wrong" priorities. Some have left behind a country in disarray and cannot entertain a dream of returning. Others (as already pointed out above, in the section "Wrestling with Time, Priorities, Scheduling, and Relativity" in Chapter 5) become part of the mainstream White culture and embrace a middle-class lifestyle, including busy schedules and a reliance on financial and health products. From this perspective, they disdain those in the home country, who have not embraced the same lifestyle, who may be sedentary, with "poor diets," who perhaps still smoke, refuse to go for regular medical checkups, and who are not financially savvy.

Pedro's Full Story

Within the same family, some successful immigrants merge with the White upper-middle class, while other family members struggle and flail. For the more successful, guilt and shame mix with a concern about belonging, as they undergo a process of redefining their identity. Here is my patient Pedro:

> I've been processing guilt and a kind of "shyness" about being so successful. Everyone around me is proud and compliments me. Yes, I worked hard, but I was lucky too. As cousins, as Mexican Americans, we've always had this underdog thing. As a family, we've taken what society says about Mexicans to heart. We've always felt second-class— the ones going uphill.
>
> My cousins especially—when they talk about someone who's successful, it's usually someone from outside the family, not one of us. So I guess that plays a role in how I feel now. Yes, I'm proud of what I've become, but I still want to feel like one of the underdogs, like "one of you guys." It's not that I feel guilty for growing or achieving; it's more

that I don't want to feel separate from where I came from. I don't want to feel like I've outgrown my friends or cousins.

And yet, I'm on this path now—associating with academics, government leaders, finance leaders—and I realize I'm out of touch with the environment I was raised in. There's guilt too: I'm doing well, but I have friends and family who are not. Some of my cousins are still undocumented. I don't know what to do, apart from being present and sending some money. I don't know what to do with the stuff that's happening with this administration.

What makes my eyes weep is the art of my culture. That's where I feel connected. But I'm also losing touch with it, because I'm so hyper-focused on work and surrounded by people who don't make my heart beat. Sometimes at work I feel like I'm Whitewashing myself. I guess I'm still trying to figure out how to be true to where I came from, while living in a world that doesn't always make space for all of who I am.

As a therapist and as an immigrant, I see how hard it is to stay emotionally true to oneself across shifting worlds, especially when love is tinged with difficult feelings, such as guilt, envy, and shame, and closeness becomes harder to hold onto.

Takeaway Exercise

If you feel stuck in a position between differing cultural expectations, stay with your feelings, and ask yourself the following questions. Give yourself the space to change your approach:

1   Why do I say yes?
2   What are my fears, my obligations, and my needs?
3   When you are asked to meet an expectation, think whether a "yes" is good for you in that moment if it's what you want.
4   Think about the consequences of saying "no." If you are not ready to say no yet, try saying: "Let me think about it, I will let you know in one hour" instead of just throwing yourself in it with a "yes." This will buy you some time to sort out your feelings, wants, and fears, and strategize a neutral answer that possibly will not alienate your loved ones.

Note to Therapists About Complex Feelings and Countertransference

For those of us who walk with immigrants in therapeutic roles, these same themes of guilt, loyalty, dislocation, can stir deeply personal reactions. Let us turn inward for a moment. While these forms of guilt live powerfully in the hearts of immigrants, they also stir something in those who work with them. Clinicians, especially those with shared backgrounds or strong political convictions, may find their own sense of helplessness or complicity arising in session.

Guilt and regret in immigrant clients often arise from complex inter-generational dynamics, conflicting cultural values, and perceived abandon-ment or loss. Non-immigrant therapists, especially those in positions of relative privilege, may feel implicated in the pain their patients carry. Feel-ings of guilt, shame, or even envy may surface in response to the patient's story or resilience. These emotional undercurrents deserve close attention, as they may shape the therapeutic alliance and the therapist's capacity to remain attuned.

Similarly, immigrant clients and therapists alike may carry survivor guilt, which is a form of distress that arises from having survived or succeeded when others could not. In recent times, as immigration becomes increasingly criminalized and immigrants are scapegoated in political games, many therapists experience feelings of powerlessness and internal conflict. On the one hand, we know and support many immigrants, celebrating their growth and accomplishments. On the other hand, we witness new policies that threaten to dismantle their progress and security, adding trauma and anxiety to already precarious lives. Many of us also struggle with guilt and a sense of cowardice, knowing firsthand that many of these are good people while feeling unable or unwilling to risk our own safety to defend them. Naming these reactions can help open up space for compassion, reflection, and repair. Not all of us are capable of street protests or bold, public acts of courage. But we can still stretch beyond our comfort zones and contribute in the big and small ways that are within our reach.

Some clinicians may begin to experience what psychiatrist Jonathan Shay[2] has called *moral injury*—a deep emotional wound caused by witnessing or being complicit in actions that violate one's core values or professional ethics. This is not an abstract concern; it is a lived reality for many therapists working on the front lines of immigration and refugee care today.

I witnessed this shift firsthand while teaching "Clinical Practice with Immigrants and Refugees" at CUNY. In 2024, the classroom was filled with hope and energy. By 2025, that optimism had eroded. Students arrived dis-couraged, tired, and overwhelmed. The news cycle had accelerated beyond our curriculum. Tried-and-true readings felt irrelevant in the face of daily policy upheavals. Together, we had to pivot—holding hope for our clients while still being realistic and managing our own sense of helplessness. These therapists did not enter the profession to carry out state mandates; they entered to help. But now, caught within a system undergoing rapid and often regressive transformation, they witness and participate in actions they find ethically untenable.

This is not a bird's-eye view. These clinicians are both maintaining a clinical stance while still being human. They are holding their clients' stor-ies, sometimes crying alongside them, and showing up day after day. And yet, despite their presence and their dedication, they are often helpless. That gap between intention and impact and between ethical commitment and systemic constraint is where moral injury takes root.

Therapists, a question for you: How do you feel when sitting with someone who is, in many ways, less privileged than you—but who may also, at times, hold more social, economic, or symbolic power? Emotions such as guilt, envy, discomfort, admiration, or resentment may arise. Do they influence how you validate or challenge your client?

These reactions can be particularly acute when working with clients from your country of origin or with similar migration stories. When treating patients whose histories echo one's own, there is emotional complexity. Their stories may awaken hidden pockets of unresolved experience: grief over leaving, guilt for having left, or ambivalence toward those who remained. You might find yourself looking forward to or dreading sessions with such clients.

Many therapists write about their countertransference as immigrant therapists and/or as therapists of immigrants. Among them is therapist and writer Lama Zuhair Khouri,[3] who describes how therapists may exile parts of their own immigration history in order to function. These parts are discovered only through their work with others. These dissociated pockets may resurface in the therapy room, often uninvited, demanding acknowledgment. Ghislaine Boulanger offers powerful reflections on countertransference in the context of working with immigrants. As a British therapist practicing in the United States, she notes that many of her patients seek her out specifically because she is an immigrant. Regardless of their own origins, they believe she might better understand the dislocation and complexity of migration. The losses her patients experience are not limited to leaving their countries of origin; they often include the renunciation of parts of the self—abandoned in the effort to belong.

One story stands out: that of her British patient, Patricia. Boulanger was initially ambivalent about taking her on. She worried Patricia might not be as compelling as someone from a more unfamiliar or "exotic" background. Beneath this hesitation, however, lay unresolved feelings about her own identity as a British immigrant in the United States. Yet this therapeutic encounter proved deeply meaningful for both women. It opened a transitional space—a bridge between past and present, and between continents—where the shared experience of being uprooted and rerooted could be explored. In that space, both therapist and patient were able to reflect on and integrate their experiences of living between worlds—experiences that might have been unimaginable to the generation before them.[4]

Becoming reacquainted with these internal exiles is not only a personal task, it is a clinical one—vital to attunement, perspective, and empathy, avoiding overidentifying, judging, or idealizing.

Pause and ask yourself the following questions:

- What part of me feels implicated in this client's story?
- What feelings about leaving, staying, or assimilating are being stirred?
- Is this guilt, or is this grief?

Whether we share our client's background or not, we may find ourselves implicated in their pain—through privilege, proximity, or the political climate we inhabit together. An even more uncomfortable feeling may arise if a patient accuses the therapist of racism or of holding anti-immigrant attitudes. Most well-intentioned therapists I know would be surprised, and perhaps wounded, by such an accusation. However, it is important not to rush to deny these claims with a reflexive "not me," or to dismiss them as mere transference belonging solely to the patient. It may be more fruitful to sit with the discomfort, to pause and wonder what kernel of truth might be present.

There is always a part of ourselves that escapes our awareness and may be perceived by another. Sometimes the other knows something about us that we do not yet know. This is the spirit of the "Radical Openness" stance developed by Anton Hart, who suggests that we do well not to cling too tightly to a fixed sense of identity. Maintaining the possibility that the other perceives something real—however uncomfortable—can be a gift. Coming to know this hidden part of ourselves may not be pleasant, but it can be transformative, both personally and professionally.[5]

Naming these reactions gently within yourself—and, when appropriate, naming the tension in the room—can deepen the therapeutic work. It invites shared humanity while affirming the client's voice and strengths. Guilt may not belong only to your client. Bringing curiosity to your discomfort is part of the healing. It reminds us that in doing this work, we are also working on ourselves—gently, honestly, and alongside those we serve: Hattie Myers says, "If to be human, as Anton Hart says in '*Radical Openness* Part 2,' 'means [to be] largely unconscious of one's thoughts, feelings, perceptions, and tendencies' then what can we do? How can we 'detoxify ourselves and our world' from the things we are largely unaware of? Hart suggests we must 'proceed in dialogue with perpetual humility and uncertainty.'"[6]

Notes

1 Dr. Patricia Arredondo, Dr. Maritza Gallardo-Cooper, Dr. Edward A. Delgado-Romero, and Dr. Angela L. Zapata, *Culturally Responsive Counseling with Latinas/os* (Hoboken, NJ: Wiley, 2014).
2 Jonathan Shay, *Achilles in Vietnam: Combat Trauma and the Undoing of Character* (New York: Scribner, 1994). Tim Hoyt has extended this concept beyond the Vietnam War in: Tim Hoyt, "Moral Injury," *Æther: A Journal of Strategic Airpower & Spacepower* 2, no. 3 (Fall 2023): 60–70, www.jstor.org/stable/10.2307/48743542.
3 Lama Zuhair Khouri, "The Immigrant's Neverland: Commuting from Amman to Brooklyn," *Contemporary Psychoanalysis* 48 (2012): 213–237.
4 Boulanger, Ghislaine, "Lot's Wife, Cary Grant, and the American Dream: Psychoanalysis with Immigrants," *Contemporary Psychoanalysis* 40 (2004): 353–372. doi:10.1080/00107530.2004.10745836.
5 Boulanger, 367–337.
6 Hattie Myers, "Close Up, Part II," *Room: A Sketchbook for Analytic Action* 6, no. 2.1 (2018), 7.

References

Arredondo, Patricia, Maritza Gallardo-Cooper, Edward A. Delgado-Romero, and Angela L. Zapata. 2014. *Culturally Responsive Counseling with Latinas/os*. Hoboken, NJ: Wiley.

Boulanger, Ghislaine. 2004. "Lot's Wife, Cary Grant, and the American Dream: Psychoanalysis with Immigrants." *Contemporary Psychoanalysis* 40 (3): 353–372. doi:10.1080/00107530.2004.10745836.

Hoyt, Tim. 2023. "Moral Injury." *Æther: A Journal of Strategic Airpower & Spacepower* 2 (3): 60–70. www.jstor.org/stable/10.2307/48743542.

Khouri, Lama Zuhair. 2012. "The Immigrant's Neverland: Commuting from Amman to Brooklyn." *Contemporary Psychoanalysis* 48 (2): 213–237. doi:10.1080/00107530.2012.10746499.

Myers, Hattie. 2018. "Close Up, Part II." *Room: A Sketchbook for Analytic Action* 6 (2.1): 7.

Shay, Jonathan. 1994. *Achilles in Vietnam: Combat Trauma and the Undoing of Character*. New York: Scribner.

13 Shame, Success, and the Immigrant Imposter Syndrome

No one in my family and friends ever left home, they are all comfortably set-tled tending their shops. I am the only one that left and now all their eyes are on me, ready to judge. I cannot open up and be myself. They want to hear the amazing Big Apple stories, where all is awesome and big, like a movie. But secretly, I think, they wouldn't mind if I fail and prove that they were right for staying behind. They just don't treat me the same way anymore and don't care how I really feel. So, I am lonely here and I am lonely there too!

—Maria Cecilia, a patient from Latin America

Mariela, a young, successful first-generation Latina, attended a state college, as the first in her family to earn a university degree. After a few professional experiences, she acquired a job with a company that normally hires only graduates from Ivy League schools. As she climbs the ladder, it would seem all is going well for her. Yet, for her, every step was and continues to be a struggle. She lives under the imagined threat that sooner or later she will be discovered as a sham, as someone who does not belong in her position, nor with her employer. Mariela attributes her achievements to *good luck*. And it is partly because of this uncertainty about herself that Mariela has an exces-sive loyalty to her company. In fact, she could earn more money and advance in her career if she were to seek opportunities elsewhere. Her loy-alty betrays her insecurity. In the United States, people change jobs every few years and by doing so they secure better promotions and titles. She stays because she is too insecure within herself to leave a place where she feels accepted and was able to find a minimum of belonging. Because she doesn't feel deserving of her success, she feels fortunate that her employer, perhaps mistakenly she thinks, sees value in her. Consequently, she fears that at any moment he will realize how mediocre she is, and she could be sent tumbling back to the marginal world of her immigrant parents.

Growing up in Queens, New York, with poor but ambitious South Amer-ican parents, Mariela represents the stereotypical American dream of upward mobility, integration, and pride for her family. She has taken on their unspoken mandate to "make it happen." Nevertheless, she feels uneasy. She is overburdened by the pressures of her high-demand job and as a minority

DOI: 10.4324/9781003648703-18

among the New York elite. She also feels she must perform especially well, just to be acknowledged as average. She questions whether her parents' expectations are fair. At times she also doubts whether she is living the life that she wants or the life her parents want for her.

Immigration not only holds promises of fulfillment to dreams of a better life but also can bring with it a unique home-country and family-of-origin shame. Shame is a complex psychological and social experience, but it is an inevitable human experience. It's therefore important to learn how to accept the experience of shame and its resulting pain, so as not to be overcome by it. Accepting the experience of shame means finding space for it instead of resisting, hiding, or escaping from the experience. Parents teach this concept to their children without words, by accepting themselves when they fall short, showing love even when they don't conform to societal expectations. This doesn't mean accepting every flaw unconditionally. Rather, it means striking a thoughtful balance between acceptance and guidance—helping children feel valued while still learning how to be responsible and grow. They teach the child to ease into their mistakes and shortcomings, to be still okay with oneself and to move on, while making amends and positive changes; that is, only if changes and amends are called for. They let the child know, both in the way they behave with each other as parents and the way they approach children, that without doubt and above all, there is still an abundance of love and acceptance for the child; there is still space for self-love.

As adults, we can practice self-compassion before facing others, by embracing ourselves, both physically and emotionally, and offering kind words to ourselves, reflecting very slowly one by one the points below, just as we begin to feel shame or the urge to hide:

> Yes, I made a mistake, or perhaps I wasn't at my best this time. I accept that. But does this mean I'm entirely wrong in everything I am or do? Am I inherently "bad"? Probably not. What are aspects of myself that I am satisfied with? Can I survive this moment? Can I find just enough love for myself to keep going? We are all mixed bags, after all. No matter how ashamed I feel right now—whether it's because I embarrassed myself in public, betrayed someone's trust, revealed a flaw, gave a poor presentation, or had a personal secret exposed—I am more than this moment. People will likely forget, or it will become less significant over time. I have redeeming qualities, as we all do.

Broaden your perspective. As you inhale deeply, let your belly expand and intentionally take up space. Ground yourself in the idea that we are all walking, talking mixed bags: a work-in-progress, complex, and yet full of potential. Even those who judge harshly and contribute to your feelings of shame are no different. They, too, carry their own imperfections. Remember, no matter what you have done or who you are, there is a light inside you. Acknowledge it, and recognize that everyone else is just as multifaceted. We are more than our mistakes, and so are they. When you feel yourself dimin-ished because of your shame (but you are not dealing with toxic or nasty individuals), you can imagine filling the space between you and them and focusing on your shared humanity and on the beauty of authenticity, wher-ever you are on the path of self-development. Imagine love and compassion moving freely like a balm between you. If you are around nasty people, it's okay to leave if you can; it is not copping out. If you have to stay, it's okay to build a protective shield, even if it's not as authentic. Do what you need to do to preserve your self-worth. Imagine wearing your protective shield, a permeable bubble letting the good in and leaving the toxicity out.

In other moments, when you feel at odds and singled out for your non-normative choices but have no desire to conform and are confident in who you are and you are not in danger—despite others judging or wanting otherwise—you might use this type of self-talk:

> I am at peace with myself and my choices. Even if others disapprove or look down on me from their perspective, I choose to breathe and cele-brate my life. I want to feel the life within me, stretch, and expand, reminding myself that I belong here. I embrace the parts of me that others may see as imperfect or flawed, because they are parts of me that I value. I take ownership of these aspects, even if they don't value them. Even if they reduce me to this one part and refuse to see the whole pic-ture, I stand by it. If I feel it's right to stay here, I will. I will occupy this space, being exactly who I am and who I want to be. In time, they will adjust, or their judgment will shift to something else. I will continue to live my life fully and brightly, and eventually, I will find those who accept me as I am.

You can hold your ground till they soften or go focus on something else. You can also decide not to be in their company and find a more suitable group of like-minded people.

I'll give you an example from my life. Despite a few traumatic experiences here and there, I enjoy life like a game. I feel strong and perhaps naively think I can meet almost any challenge as the worst is all behind me. No one can say if this is true or not, life will tell, but it is freeing to think that way. I enjoy what life throws at me. It's like I drink from life experiences and chal-lenges like a thirsty person seeing a faucet in the desert. I love life and what it brings. I have always received praise and perhaps a bit of envy for every-thing I put my energy to. However, after a certain age, being single and without children, I have experienced some judgment and reproach, as if I were not meeting cultural expectations. People openly or in indirect ways have questioned and judged my choices. Attending some larger gatherings, such as marriages and christenings, has been painful, at times. It required me to stretch to be a part of them or decline. I used this kind of self-talk to enjoy being part of the celebrations, despite an occasional shame-inducing comment regarding social expectations not fulfilled or, more bluntly, "What's wrong with you?" This small social reproach can only give me a faint idea of what people in less favorable positionalities may feel. But it is also a good training for the future, toward the inevitable injuries, offenses, and invisibilities that aging brings in this part of the world. So here is the yin/yang in this painful experience. It is nonetheless necessary to prepare for the open and subtle attacks.

In addition to the types of self-talk mentioned above, a powerful antidote to shame is the practice of loving kindness meditation. This meditation involves repeating formal phrases that express love and goodwill, beginning with yourself, then extending to a mentor, someone you love deeply, someone you are indifferent toward, and finally someone with whom you have anger or resentment. It's important, especially when starting, not to choose your greatest adversary. If anger begins to overshadow the feelings of love, gently return your focus to loving kindness for yourself. You finish up your meditation by wishing love to all the world and all sentient beings. By wishing love in words and with intention, one gets used to the idea that developing love is possible, even for the wretched parts of oneself. You can find many versions of this meditation online for free including mine on www.leideporcu.com, YouTube, and the Insight meditation app.

In addition to self-talk and loving kindness meditation, another powerful way to counter shame is to address imposter syndrome, which often accompanies it. Imposter syndrome, characterized by persistent self-doubt and the fear of being exposed as a fraud, is common among high-achieving individuals. This is particularly true for first- and second-generation immigrants, who are often the first in their families to attend college, pursue graduate studies, or enter professional careers. Without a clear precedent or established path to follow, they may feel as though they don't truly belong, which deepens feelings of inadequacy and fuels shame.

Jose, a first-generation Latino professor, suffered from a writing block. Despite academic success, he agonized over his writing. The son of uneducated immigrant parents, he was the first in his family to attend college and earn a doctorate degree. Despite accolades from his students and peers, he believed he had no right to be in academia. He felt like a fraud. As a consequence, the smallest hint of a problem would cause debilitating self-doubt and work paralysis. Many of his American colleagues had a path, curated for them by their families, which provided years of solid education, language competency, and a sense of entitlement and belonging. Jose did not feel he belonged to the circle of effortless academics. He felt like a hybrid; he was no longer working class but not fully middle class, and he was neither American nor Latino. He was anxious and self-critical around academics but not quite at home in his blue-collar family. He would have liked to be proud of his origins, but he could not help feeling shame for some of his immigrant parents' ways, which he also painfully recognized in himself. His solution has been to work hard to create a success story that would erase his and his family's shame and make him feel whole and accepted by others. What an effort it is, though, relying only on relentless work and accomplishments to overcome a transgenerational sense of shame and not belonging.

Reasonably hard work needs to be coupled with self-love and acceptance. Social pressures and unfavorable positionalities need to be recognized. They may have you struggling to switch between the identities that you have to adopt in different situations, including the ones you are beginning to forge for yourself. If you find yourself constantly navigating how you see yourself and how people see you; if you live a life of stage fright; if you struggle juggling the multiple identities that are put on you by yourself or others, the ones you have inherited from your families and cultures, you may feel you're in a pressure cooker. Let's do something to ease the burden. First of all, acknowledge the weight society places on you as an immigrant—as the "Other" and most likely, "less than." When you can, point to the negativity thrown on you. Also, how can you detoxify and reformulate this message, without taking it in at face value?

As you struggle to move ahead, despite the difficulties in your world and in your endless to-do list, it's likely that your focus is too narrow. Take the time to zoom out. This doesn't mean that you are letting go of your striving. If you do not take a moment of rest and recalibrate, you will be floating on an empty tank forever. Remember, you're just taking a moment!

Focus on Emptiness

From your chair where you are sitting, feel yourself there; do a body scan by paying attention to each part of your body, one by one, and letting each one go, starting with your feet and going up (or starting with one foot and up one side and then the other side). Then, imagine zooming out to your room, seeing yourself in it, visualizing piece by piece the four walls and what is in the room. Then zoom out and imagine your building, with you in it; then your neighborhood. As you settle your attention in your neighborhood, gently bring to mind what surrounds you. In your mind's eye, notice the buildings, the cars, the paved roads, the gardens, and whatever is there. Now, let your awareness soften. Begin to set aside all the man-made things. Let the buildings, the roads, the cars fade from your focus. What remains is nature. Stay with it: the trees and leaves, the animals, the small movements of life. Allow yourself to rest here for a few breaths. Then, gradually shift your attention again. Release even the living things, and focus only on the earth itself: the rocks, the wind, the rivers, the mountains. Sense the land and the air. Now, let even this go. Remove your attention from all forms, and rest in the vastness of space. Feel how it is to be unencumbered by noise, tasks, and pressures, floating in space, expansive and free. From this stillness, gently turn your gaze back toward the earth. See it as a whole, from afar. Slowly zoom in: continents, seas, your country, your city, your neighborhood, and at last, your own apartment. Notice what has shifted inside you as you return.[1]

Takeaway Exercise: The Book of Success

To help maintain balance during ebbs and flows of high and low moments, take it upon yourself to highlight your own successes. Consider creating a *Book of Success* (hardcopy or digitized in a private Instagram account), in which you document positive experiences and professional or personal feedback you have received. Ask some of your closest friends what they most admire about you and record their answers in your book. It is very important that you include everything, no matter how minimal you may perceive the value of the achievement. Include acknowledgments of successes, such as thank you notes, printouts of positive emails, letters of acceptance, letters of reference, pictures—mementos of success of any kind. Be fair and realistic, and if necessary, ask for support from a caring friend or partner to help you remain objective. Then, read and reread your book as it grows. Savor it, and let the positive content sink in.

Shame, Identity, and the Work of Reflection: A Note to Therapists

Recent psychoanalytic thinkers, including Boulanger, argue that full assimilation is not only unrealistic but also potentially damaging. Instead, a more sustainable and psychologically healthy approach involves moving consciously between self-states rooted in cultural identities.[2]

This holds particular relevance for immigrant therapists. If you are an immigrant therapist—particularly if you come from a less socially valued part of the world, or if you are a BIPOC (Black, Indigenous, or Person of Color) therapist, you may have experienced shame and othering, even during your clinical training. The Holmes Commission on Racial Equality in Psychoanalysis, established by the American Psychoanalytic Association in 2021, investigated racism and exclusion within the field. It found that not only were institutes and individuals unprepared to engage with race work but that racism emerged even within the Commission itself.[3]

These findings are not meant to indict specific individuals but to underscore a central truth: There is no outside position when it comes to racism, not even in communities committed to anti-racism and healing. Racism will inevitably surface. When it does, we are called not to defend against it, but to stay open to its meaning.

As explored in Chapter 12, Anton Hart's concept of *radical openness* encourages us to acknowledge not only what is conscious and desirable in ourselves, but also the less comfortable parts: those that are hidden, disavowed, or socially conditioned.[4] These include racist or classist assumptions we may carry, especially when we benefit from social privilege. Recognizing these parts does not mean we are "bad people," it means we are human. We must unlearn what we've unconsciously absorbed.

And yet, acknowledging this can provoke shame: the shame of being implicated in something ugly, of realizing we are not who we thought we were. But shame is not something to push aside. It is a powerful signal of inner conflict, and if we attend to it with care, it can become a catalyst for transformation.

As the Holmes Report notes, racism often emerges through enactments[5]— charged moments in the clinical encounter where unconscious dynamics emerge through tone, action, or silence. These enactments are not simply personal slips; they are systemic expressions of how structures live in us. As painful as they may be, they are also opportunities. They allow the work to deepen—if we are willing to stay present.

When you sit with your patients, notice how your multiple identities intersect—not only within yourself, but also in relation to your patient's identities. Together, you are cocreating meaning. Whether you practice psychoanalysis or another modality, transference and countertransference are always present. You are touching your patient's wounds, and they are pressing on yours.

If a charged moment arises—if you or your patient feel discomfort, guilt, resentment, or even shame—pause. Do not rush to apologize or fix it and forget it. If the therapeutic alliance is strong, explore it together. Something important may be trying to emerge.

As therapists, we must become aware of the parts of ourselves we have cut off—not only those we judged unhelpful but those we dismissed as shameful or "inadequate" in the professional world. Instead of editing shame out of our self-concept, we must observe it, understand it, and gently hold it. This process, though painful, allows us to bring more of ourselves into the room; by doing so, we are better able to meet our clients in their full complexity.

Even therapists who immigrated from more socially "favorable" parts of the world may find themselves othered—implicitly placed in a hierarchy where the American White standard is treated as ideal and all others as lesser.

Ghislaine Boulanger,[6] an immigrant psychoanalyst of French English background, recounts several telling exchanges in her adopted country. In one, she runs into her first analyst on the street and mentions having recently published an article on psychoanalysis with immigrants. Her analyst retorted, "Immigrants don't go into psychoanalysis; you're an émigré!"

This exchange feels like a disavowing quip, even if meant benignly. The term *émigré* is imposed on her, suggesting privilege and erasing what she may have had to relinquish from her original cultural identity. There is also an implicit question: Can a privileged immigrant speak authentically about immigration? *Is psychoanalysis a tool that can be used both by immigrants and for immigrants?*

Later in the same day, Boulanger describes another moment of quiet othering: A woman in an elevator remarked something like "You're not from here." Despite "passing" as an émigré, she remains Other. Those who other others are often unaware of its effects, yet the emotional and cultural cost of passing (and not passing) is real.

Many immigrant therapists say that they had to cut off parts of themselves, such as language, customs, and healing traditions, in order to fit in. The shame and grief that led to these choices, and the shame of having made them, often go unspoken. However, these buried parts may reemerge in the therapy room, especially when working with patients whose stories mirror their own.

When working with immigrant clients experiencing shame or imposter syndrome, consider their feelings, their history, as well as the world they inhabit, with its multiple messages, injunctions, and the limitations and barriers it presents. A note for yourself: Can you allow yourself to move beyond the internalized voice of the "clinical training police" and acknowledge not only the intrapsychic, but also the social? Can you bring both into the room—not as a disruption to the clinical frame, but as an enhancement?

Consider the reflections of Lama Zair Khouri[7] describing a group of Arab boys she treated shortly after their arrival in the US. She watched in dismay as the boys shamed a peer for looking "too Arab." Already, they had begun to identify with the aggressor, a defense mechanism in which individuals adopt the values or behaviors of a dominant group in order to gain acceptance or safety. From victims, they became aggressors, projecting their own anxiety and shame onto the classmate who embodied what they had begun to reject in themselves. In that moment, they reenacted the internalized logic of exclusion by turning it against the most visibly different among them. The experience stirred memories of her own early immigration shame: As a young woman, she had felt compelled to distinguish herself from Muslim Arabs by emphasizing her Christian identity. Working with these boys helped her reclaim the very parts of herself she had once disavowed.

Immigrant therapists, like immigrant patients, can experience what W.E.B. Du Bois called *double consciousness*—a state in which a devalued identity coexists with a more socially acceptable one.

> It is a peculiar sensation, this double consciousness, this sense of always looking at one's self through the eyes of others... One ever feels his two-ness,—an American, a Negro; two souls, two thoughts, two unreconciled strivings; two warring ideals in one dark body, whose dogged strength alone keeps it from being torn asunder.[8]

This state of double consciousness may remain hidden until it feels safe to emerge. From the beginning, English South African therapist Azell Hipp[9] tells us, her patient Nell, an Afrikaaner recently immigrated, evoked strong feelings in her. This was tied to the therapist's immigration history and the political divisions in South Africa. Hipp felt shame in the face of Nell's courage. While Hipp had left, Nell had stayed and risked her life to fight apartheid.

Their dynamic eventually broke open when Nell asked a direct question that made Hipp uncomfortable. The therapist, unable to contain her feelings, responded with unexpected bluntness. It hurt Nell, exposing her trauma history—but also allowed the treatment to move forward. The enactment became a doorway to deeper work.

All patients can evoke shame. We can feel our shame and theirs, alongside the shame of social structures that live in us. If we can manage these feelings and sort out how we are implicated in the enactment, it becomes usable, transformative.

As you bring larger dynamics in, let your patient sort out what they want, following them with a light touch "without memory or desire," as Bion[10] used to say. Instead of imposing your received ideas on what constitutes a good life, let them reflect on this question from their complex perspectives and possibilities: What do they want to pursue and what are they willing to give up in the process? Let them make their own strides, with the inevitable losses every step entails. When you get overly enthusiastic about their path, you may be investing too much in your ideas. You need to recalibrate your position.

As a therapist, pause and consider these questions:

- What cultural narratives or meritocratic ideals am I unconsciously reinforcing?
- Do I leave room for the emotional cost of "success" in a new country?
- Am I validating only performance or also witnessing the person beneath it?

Experiences of shame often lead to an over investment in success, but espousing success has its own losses. All needs to be weighed. As you hear your patients' stories and their striving, make sure you leave space to explore the role of shame in their choices. When you hear self-doubt, pause and ask: What would it mean for this client to feel pride? What fears are attached to standing fully in one's achievements? Is shame guiding their perfectionism? Is this painful striving a hidden form of shame disguised as achievement?

In many cultures, mental illness is shrouded in shame, so it is hard to even admit that one is unwell beyond a headache or heartache. In addition, immigrant patients may come from areas ravaged by war or other extreme conditions. They may have experienced rape, trafficking, and all sorts of (at least initially) unnamable annihilating trauma that left them silent and filled with shame. Since in many cultures shame extends beyond the individual to the family and community, they may not be so willing to open up. Make it safe for them; make it felt you are a non-judging person there to help; make sure the interpreters, if there are any, are appropriate. Create a container where it is safe to look at what shame has kept hidden. This also means that you must be at the top of your game and ready to listen and process with them the unspeakable.

Shame and Clinical Training

As Brené Brown observes in *The Gifts of Imperfection*, "Shame hates it when we reach out and tell our story. It hates having words wrapped around it—it can't survive being shared. Shame loves secrecy. The most dangerous thing to do after a shaming experience is hide or bury our story."[11] For immigrants in training, this secret can be compounded by cultural stigma and professional expectations. If you immigrated from a stigmatized or devalued country, recognize that your difficulties are not just personal; they are shaped by unequal socioeconomic structures. You may struggle to build a practice and belong to a professional community that has few people that look and think like you. As long as those ideals you are pursuing feel attainable, you stay motivated. But when the distance becomes too great, negative thoughts creep in. Despite effort, intelligence, and good will, your efforts may still fall short of what is expected or needed to belong. Whether your struggle is psychological, social, or both, you still must care for your wellbeing. It is easy to compare yourself to idealized models, but that comparison may not only be misleading, it could also be damaging. In these moments, give yourself the compassion you offer to your patients. It is hard for you as well.

I want to close with a personal reflection. It took me years to learn how to "pass" as a psychoanalyst. I did not look or act like other analysts. I was too loud, too emotional, too colorfully and scantily dressed. I did not wear "sensible shoes." I was not poised and reflective. With the help of a brilliant supervisor, Debra Schnall, who saw potential in me, I learned. I embraced those shoes, both literally and metaphorically. Over time, I changed. But I am also reclaiming the parts of me I once set aside. The culture of therapy is changing too. There is now more room for difference—for honoring patients' healing traditions and embracing diversity, rather than hiding it.

In "The Immigrant Analyst: A Journey from Double Consciousness to Hybridity,"[12] South African immigrant therapist Glenys Lobban offers powerful illustrations of these tensions. Her earliest experiences of othering began during her school years in the United Kingdom, where classmates viewed her as an oddity and projected primitivist stereotypes onto her. In response, she began telling fantastical and humorous stories—claiming, for example, that in Africa she rode an elephant to town.[13] These performances, laced with concealed wit and subtle resistance, were a response to unconscious microaggressions. They helped her regain a sense of control, turning the tables on those who saw her as inferior.[14]

Later, while attending graduate school in the United States, she encountered a different form of pressure: the implicit expectation to shed her cultural identity and become American and to treat patients in the "American way."[15] She recalls feeling alienated when a supervisor, perhaps in a misguided attempt to bond, made disparaging remarks about a Brazilian patient's spiritual beliefs:

> My program also placed a premium on "Western" values. I had my first lesson about judging and censoring myself when one of my supervisors was scathingly dismissive of my Brazilian patient who believed in spirits,

labeling her as "irrational" and "primitive." I realized that my childhood exposure to spiritualism, ancestors, and astrology would "other" me as "primitive" and was not a safe topic at school.[16]

Throughout her training and personal life, Lobban faced repeated demands to suppress aspects of herself deemed inappropriate or incompatible with dominant norms. Only later, particularly through enactments with patients,[17] did she come to see the psychic cost of this disavowal and split. The pressure to assimilate had required her to sever important dimensions of her identity and split into double consciousness: a public "American self" and a private immigrant self.[18] She eventually developed a more fluid, adaptive identity, following a process of integration and reclamation of the disavowed and disparaged parts.[19]

W.E.B. Du Bois, in writing about "the American Negro," described this process as a "longing to attain self-conscious manhood, to merge his double self into a better and truer self. In this merging he wishes neither of the older selves to be lost."[20] Achieving this integration requires a reckoning with the hidden, disavowed self that is part of that double consciousness and a commitment to being fully present and fully conscious in honoring both selves.

Notes

1 The Emptiness Meditation that inspired the text above comes from: Ajahn Punnadhammo, *Guided Meditation on Emptiness*, May 11, 2013. Available at: https://archive.org/details/GuidedMeditationOnEmptiness20130511.

2 Boulanger, Ghislaine, "Seeing Double, Being Double: Longing, Belonging, Recognition, and Evasion in Psychodynamic Work with Immigrants," in *Immigration in Psychoanalysis: Locating Ourselves*, ed. Julia Beltsiou (London: Routledge, 2016), 53–68, 55.

3 Holmes Commission on Racial Equality in Psychoanalysis, chap. 7, "Enactments," in *Final Report* (American Psychoanalytic Association, 2023), 154–182.

4 Anton Hart, "From Multicultural Competence to Radical Openness: A Psychoanalytic Engagement of Otherness," *The American Psychoanalyst* 51, no. 1 (2017): 12–27, https://apsa.org/wp-content/uploads/apsaa-publications/vol51no1-TOC/html/vol51no1_09.xhtml.

5 Holmes Commission on Racial Equality in Psychoanalysis, "Enactments."

6 Ghislaine Boulanger, "Seeing Double, Being Double: Longing, Belonging, Recognition, and Evasion in Psychodynamic Work with Immigrants," *American Journal of Psychoanalysis* 75, no. 3 (2015), 287.

7 Lama Z. Khouri, "The Immigrant's Neverland: Commuting from Amman to Brooklyn," *Contemporary Psychoanalysis* 48, no. 2 (2012): 213–237, doi:10.1080/00107530.2012.10746499.

8 W.E.B. Du Bois, *The Souls of Black Folk* (Chicago, IL: A.C. McClurg, 1903), 2.

9 Hazel Ipp, "Nell—A Bridge to the Amputated Self: The Impact of Immigration on Continuities and Discontinuities of Self," in *Psychodynamic Perspectives on Working with Immigrant Families*, ed. Geraldine O'Neill (London: Karnac, 2011), 41–58.

10 Wilfred Bion, *Attention and Interpretation: A Scientific Approach to Insight in Psycho-Analysis and Groups* (London: Tavistock, 1970), 41.

11 Brené Brown, *The Gifts of Imperfection: Let Go of Who You Think You're Supposed to Be and Embrace Who You Are* (Center City, MN: Hazelden Publishing, 2010), 13.
12 Lobban, Glenys. 2016. "The Immigrant Analyst: A Journey from Double Consciousness Towards Hybridity," in *Immigration in Psychoanalysis: Locating Ourselves*, ed. Julia Beltsiou (London: Routledge), 69–86.
13 Lobban, 69.
14 Lobban, 70.
15 Lobban, 73.
16 Lobban, 73.
17 Lobban, 76, 79.
18 Lobban, 70.
19 Lobban, 73.
20 W.E.B. Du Bois, *The Souls of Black Folk*, 2.

References

Ajahn Punnadhammo. 2013. "Guided Meditation on Emptiness." May 11. https://archive.org/details/GuidedMeditationOnEmptiness20130511.

Bion, Wilfred. 1970. *Attention and Interpretation: A Scientific Approach to Insight in Psycho-Analysis and Groups*. London: Tavistock.

Boulanger, Ghislaine. 2016. "Seeing Double, Being Double: Longing, Belonging, Recognition, and Evasion in Psychodynamic Work with Immigrants." In *Immigration in Psychoanalysis: Locating Ourselves*, edited by Julia Beltsiou, 53–68. London: Routledge.

Brown, Brené. 2010. *The Gifts of Imperfection: Let Go of Who You Think You're Supposed to Be and Embrace Who You Are*. Center City, MN: Hazelden Publishing.

Du Bois, W. E. B. 1903. *The Souls of Black Folk*. Chicago, IL: A.C. McClurg.

Hart, Anton. "From Multicultural Competence to Radical Openness: A Psychoanalytic Engagement of Otherness." *The American Psychoanalyst* 51 (1): 12–27. https://apsa.org/wp-content/uploads/apsaa-publications/vol51no1-TOC/html/vol51no1_09.xhtml.

Holmes Commission on Racial Equality in Psychoanalysis. 2023. Chapter 7, "Enactments." In *Final Report*, 154–182. Washington, DC: American Psychoanalytic Association. https://apsa.org/wp-content/uploads/2023/06/Holmes-Commission-Final-Report-2023-Report-rv6-19-23.pdf.

Ipp, Hazel. 2011. "Nell—A Bridge to the Amputated Self: The Impact of Immigration on Continuities and Discontinuities of Self." In *Psychodynamic Perspectives on Working with Immigrant Families*, edited by Geraldine O'Neill, 41–58. London: Karnac.

Khouri, Lama Zuhair. 2012. "The Immigrant's Neverland: Commuting from Amman to Brooklyn." *Contemporary Psychoanalysis* 48 (2): 213–237. doi:10.1080/00107530.2012.10746499.

Lobban, Glenys. 2016. "The Immigrant Analyst: A Journey from Double Consciousness Towards Hybridity." In *Immigration in Psychoanalysis: Locating Ourselves*, edited by Julia Beltsiou, 69–85. London: Routledge.

14 Understanding and Releasing Immigrant Anger

Anger is an emotion that develops cognitively, in the space between how things are and how we think they should be. It arises from a sense of injustice. It has a physiological component, often characterized by a release of adrenaline, a flush of heat, muscle tension, sweat, and increased heart rate and blood pressure. The stronger it gets, the more the mind clouds with distortions, such as black-and-white thinking (e.g., "you are all bad and wrong, and I am all good and right") and all-or-nothing thinking ("you always…" or "you never…"). In this state, we lose sight of the details and the shades of gray.

Yet, As Audre Lorde powerfully argued in "The Uses of Anger,"

> Everything can be used / except what is wasteful / (you will need to remember this / when you are accused of destruction).
>
> Every woman has a well-stocked arsenal of anger potentially useful against those oppressions, personal and institutional, which brought that anger into being.[1]

Lorde reminds us that anger is not only a distortion-laden threat but also a resource: a signal of injustice and a potential tool for change.

As many CBT therapists do, I track my patients' anger in increments of 0 to 100, considering 1–30 a state of frustration; 30–60 anger, and 60+ rage. It's important to become aware of the early signs of frustration before the emotion gets the best of us. Hence, the tracking. When we realize we are becoming irritable, it is a good practice to stop and assess what's going on inside and outside.

First, check the physiological components that might be contributing to your anger. Are you hungry, thirsty, tired, or in pain? Are you feeling irritable because you're trying to make positive changes in your life? For example, changes in one's life, even those we intentionally embark on, such as quitting smoking, can affect you both physiologically and psychologically without your realizing it. Address these needs as much as you can. Managing feelings of anger is easier said than done, but we do not do it because it's comfortable or easy but because preserving relationships is important.

DOI: 10.4324/9781003648703-19

When you're in a state of anger, things may have already spiraled out of control, and backtracking becomes much more difficult. Therefore, managing anger early on is crucial, as it can prevent escalation and protect relationships. However, when anger intensifies and reaches a boiling point, the situation becomes even more challenging to navigate—it can become rage. In a state of rage, you might find yourself shouting or even punching a wall—actions that, while not criminal, are unhelpful and damaging to relationships, and often result in shame.

When you feel irritation mounting during an interaction, pay attention to your body: Are your muscles tensing? Has your breathing or body temperature changed? Are you sweating or is your heart racing? These are signs that your anger is intensifying. If you don't manage your emotions and thoughts at this point, you risk losing sight of the conversation's objective and the common ground you share with the other person. Your interlocutor starts to feel like an enemy, and you may find yourself wanting to say something hurtful just to release your discomfort. In the end, however, if you end up doing so, you only harm yourself and the relationship.

Some of us experience anger as if it's an on/off switch. If we move suddenly from a calm state to feeling intensely angry—let's say, at a level of 70—it's likely that we haven't been fully in touch with our emotions leading up to that moment. We did not notice that there was increasing irritation and frustration, because we had become numb. Or we noticed, but decided not to address it. We held in our growing frustration, until at some point, we exploded. Accumulating grievances in this way is not helpful.

Or it could also be that we have a problematic history, perhaps one of trauma, and emotions get suddenly triggered when we are hit with a reminder. If that is the case, therapy is recommended.

Do Not Sit in Anger Alone

Holding anger in silence can be just as corrosive as acting it out. For many, speaking anger aloud may feel shameful, especially if you were taught that anger is dangerous, inappropriate, or unwelcome. But keeping it inside does not make it disappear; it often causes it to harden or erupt later.

Consider joining a group—a safe space for processing emotions, such as an anger management or emotional support group. Exploring anger alongside others, in community and without judgment, is not a sign of failure. It is a sign of care. It means you are willing to understand this powerful emotion and transform it into something more constructive.

It is important to "check in" and "label" the stages of anger with the 0–100 scale and to develop words to describe its layers—for instance, as disappointment, frustration, shame, pain, and anger. Equally important is to create a space of mindfulness; that is, notice what is happening and spend a moment to explore and defuse in order to return to a centered place.

Anger is about a part of us that loudly demands attention; therefore, it can also be well-placed. There are plenty of things in the world that require anger rather than self-complacency or calculated ignorance. When anger is a valid signal that a situation needs to change, but we find ourselves powerless, subordinate, or unheard, the question becomes: How do we channel this well-placed anger?

When it comes to larger situations that demand rightful change and affect more than just a few individuals, I don't have a one-size-fits-all answer, as each scenario is unique. However, I generally stand against violence. In smaller-scale situations, outbursts of anger can damage relationships and harm social and professional lives. While discharging anger onto another person may provide a fleeting sense of relief, it often carries long-term negative consequences. It's crucial to acknowledge and attend to anger so it can soften. Ignoring or disowning this part of ourselves, whether by rushing to settle scores or by blaming and attacking, only escalates the issue further.

Why is it so difficult to manage our anger and express it effectively? For some of us, cultural and family examples have shaped our responses. Perhaps we grew up observing bullies or angry people who were still successful and powerful, and at times, we may have imitated or admired them. Our family, educational systems, and society may not have provided the tools to handle negative emotions or navigate challenging situations. Additionally, our bodies may be flooded with powerful hormones, triggering primitive, uncontrollable reactions. Life often presents us with more complex, offending situations than we are prepared to handle. Furthermore, we each have different levels of comfort when it comes to expressing our own anger and receiving someone else's.

Because anger can be destructive, it is essential to find better ways to argue, lead, and relate. If our outbursts are unproductive and damaging, we must take responsibility for managing them, and it's imperative that we do. Hold space. Calm your body. Clear your mind. Become open to the idea that it would be good to be strategic rather than impulsive or destructive. Keep this idea as a vision and take educational steps to learn to communicate peacefully. Below are exercises to help you identify and work through anger.

Anger Exercises

Water the Positive Seeds

When angry, we revert to primitive thinking and tend to see things in only a duality of "good" and "bad." From this perspective, the most likely response is to blame others. In this frame of mind, we cannot, nor do we want to, see our own contributions to the moment. But, as Thich Nhat Hanh says in his book *Anger, Wisdom for Cooling the Flames*, we all have in us the seeds of both positive and negative emotions.[2] He suggests that we water our seeds selectively. Nurture those seeds of calm, affirming, and kindness in ourselves and those around us. Equally important, demand the same from others.

When angry, embrace your anger as if it were your crying baby who needs consolation. Rather than attacking the offender, step away from the hateful interaction. Do this not out of fear, or to abandon or punish the other, but rather to take care of yourself and to protect the relationship. When angry, regain a modicum of equilibrium. Only then can you address the other person from a balanced position, telling them, for example, that you're angry, because they have hurt you. In moments of pain, before reacting, send loving kindness to yourself, recognize your pain, cradle yourself in loving and warm thoughts, hold and caress your hot head, as if it were the head of your own child.

An Imaginary Dimmer Switch

You may currently have the equivalent of an on/off switch for your emotions. Visualize the possibility of installing a dimmer switch to manage them. Make a daily habit of using this imaginary dimmer switch to help you regulate your feelings and bodily arousal. Check your feelings regularly. When you feel anger and agitation rising, imagine turning the dimmer down a notch. It might also help to picture a relaxing image and take a few slow deep breaths.

Loosen the Grasp on the Outcome

It can be helpful to acknowledge that things should not necessarily be the way you expect. Try to loosen your grasp on the outcome. Do everything you can to make things happen. Do everything you can to explain your point of view and ask for what you need. But then, let go of the outcome. Remember that for the majority of things, there is no rule that says things should go the way we expect. Sickness, aging, death, divorce, and violence are all proof of that. Say to yourself instead, "It would be nice if this or that happens"—and then let it go.

It is also critically important to note that this exercise is appropriate for many situations, except those that are abusive or unjust. In those cases, you need to let go of the relationship and move on. Or, you can unite with others to acquire a critical mass to make a change.

Speak Up

When you feel hurt by those close to you but repeatedly stay silent, you alienate yourself from them and betray your own needs. Being quiet and submissive may be how you were raised, which makes breaking the habit difficult, even if you no longer consciously support a hierarchical mindset. However, by remaining silent, you contribute to the issue. In a loving and cooperative relationship, the other person needs to understand your perspective, but they can't read your mind. By not speaking up, you put yourself in a victim role. It's essential to communicate what works for you and what needs to stop.

Consider whether you may have a psychological dependency, where you need the other person to function emotionally and are willing to tolerate anything to maintain the relationship. This dependency is often mutual, trapping people in unhealthy dynamics. If emotional dependency is keeping you in a toxic situation, consider attending a Codependents Anonymous (CoDA) meeting or reading *Codependent No More* by Melody Beattie to explore whether this resonates with your experience.[3]

If your present silence is based on unresolved past abuse or neglect; if the relationship is between people with gross power inequalities, then that needs to take center stage. A therapist or social worker can help you heal and be free. When the injurious situation comes from social inequities, speaking up and clarifying your position is not always rewarding and thus can be tiresome and frustrating. Speak up when you decide it's right for you. Suggestions on how to speak up are offered in Chapter 10.

Do Not Pass Your Anger Down to the Vulnerable

Not everyone has the privilege to display anger and remain unscathed. One needs to have power to be openly angry. And yet, a full display of anger can also be a symptom of powerlessness or of not having other effective tools to handle the situation. Process your anger so as not to pass it down to others who are vulnerable. Subordinates at work or spouses often become easy targets in these situations, as do children. Don't pass down your anger to your children, which is easy to slip into, especially if, as a child, you were the victim of your parents' anger.

When you respond to an injury, be it physical, psychological, verbal, financial, social, or a combination, address the situation without "annihilating" the other person with your anger. Wait until you can communicate from a place of peace. An internal feeling of peace does not diminish your argument, rights, and reasons. On the contrary, it increases your chances of being heard and receiving reparation. Remember that shaming doesn't help anyone, it works like a boomerang and it's passed on.

Trash Can Visualization

One of my patients felt stuck in a state of anger. Her racing thoughts made her feel like she was "trapped in a smelly bathroom stall at the train station," where she was being poisoned by toxic fumes and waste. She found relief in the following visualization: She visualized a big trash can and imagined throwing—one by one—all her angry thoughts into it. As a thought appeared in her mind, she would imagine lifting the trash can lid and putting the sticky, scary, and explosive thought inside. After a while, she felt lighter and freer. She closed the lid and went out to do something pleasant. This exercise helped her momentarily contain some of her anger, as well as the fear of her explosive anger. She also knew that in a few days, she could come to a session with me, and together we could safely open the can and explore its contents.

Final Pointers on Managing Anger

Some last pointers on managing anger are as follows:

- Speak up before you become too angry.
- Schedule a time to talk about the issue or give a heads up, so that the other person does not feel ambushed, and you have time to calm yourself down.
- Remind yourself and the other person that underneath the current issue, which may be aggravating, there is love and appreciation and a desire to work things out. They will feel safe and more open to you.
- Thich Nhat Hanh suggests that you not only acknowledge your anger to yourself but also let the loved one know with kindness that you are angry with them and are doing your best to manage your anger without putting more wood into the fire: "Darling, I am suffering. I am angry. I want you to know it. I am doing my best." You can also add: "Please help me."[4]
- Use defensiveness-reducing language such as, "I feel this way when you..." rather than "You are always..." or "Why are you..."
- Eliminate entirely negative labeling and injurious speech and ask the other party to rephrase any such language they are using, as it is unacceptable and unhelpful.
- Bring the same awareness to any disrespectful and disparaging body language and reframe it. When you are in listening mode, you should be all ears and bracket momentarily your POV and your unhelpful reactions. Don't think about what to reply at this time. Listening and empathizing with the other does not mean that your POV and emotions are not valid. You are simply trying on their experience.
- Create a plan to de-escalate anger by agreeing that one of the two of you will leave the situation momentarily to preserve the safety in the relationship. You are not abandoning or punishing each other. But, it is important to commit to coming back as soon as a modicum of calm is established to sort things out.
- Create a commonly devised keyword to alert the other person that the situation is getting out of control or that you do not feel safe anymore: "Fire!" "Danger!" or any word works well.
- Take time to speak fully without interruptions, using the format detailed earlier, in Chapter 10, "A Few Pointers for Communication," which opens the layers of understanding and increases empathy.
- Keep in mind that beyond anger, there is hurt, and the other person may be equally hurt. Find a space within yourself and in your communication with the other person to acknowledge that too.

- Establish a weekly "check-in time" with the other person to express what is and what is not working. There will be less chance of bottling up feelings, you will share more of what's in your mind, and you will be better able to take the other into consideration as you proceed.

- Keep in mind that in relationships, winning an argument and being right is not as important as appreciating each other's POV. Being open to listen, eventually, allows the other person (if the partner is good enough) to match you and build an internal space large enough to welcome feelings and needs different and divergent from their own.

- Keep in mind no one should read your mind. Communicate your thoughts, and know that you may also have to repeat yourself. If you find yourself repeating the same remarks to no avail, discuss this issue with the other person and brainstorm as a team on how to address the issue that is so important to you.

- Consider what you are doing and how you might be contributing to the situation. Are you, for instance, disrespecting yourself, putting yourself down, leading someone to disrespect you? Are you being passive aggressive, hiding behind a shroud of goodness while surreptitiously jabbing the other person?

- If the person seems angry to you, but hasn't acknowledged any negative feelings, ask if they feel anger. Describe their tone, words, and posture and ask directly, so that they can come out into the open. Know they may also be okay and may simply have a different communicative style.

- We tend to be on our best behavior with people we barely know but often relax into our mindless and less evolved habits with the people closer to us. Be mindful as to whether you're using loved ones as your trash can for unwanted feelings. Try to remember not to do that and be on alert for your blind spots. Reaffirm your love and respect and express gratitude to your loved ones. Acknowledge and appreciate their manifestations of love. The knowledge of an underlying love and respect, the mutual intention to be mindful of the other, and the unwillingness to cause suffering should be the basis for a workable compromise.

- Consider that different cultures and different families will have different approaches and different levels of tolerance for anger. Make that a part of the conversation.

Guidance for Clinicians

Not everyone has equal freedom to express anger. Women, racialized individuals, and immigrants may find that their anger is dismissed or pathologized more quickly than others'. These dynamics should be considered in both personal work and therapeutic settings.

Cultural relativism does not excuse or justify violence. Practices such as domestic violence, sexual assault, and excessive physical punishment of children—though possibly tolerated or normalized in some countries—are not acceptable and may be illegal in the host country. If a caregiver uses harsh physical discipline, provide psychoeducation about child development and the legal framework, and consult the law. If no one is in immediate danger, seek supervision promptly before taking action.

Clinicians should also be aware that individuals experiencing trauma, PTSD, or high levels of immigration-related stress may be at greater risk of acting out through violence. In some cases, violence is embedded in culturally sanctioned practices that reflect deeply rooted gender hierarchies, such as female genital mutilation. These practices may not be immediately disclosed. By creating a safe, non-judgmental therapeutic space, clinicians may allow patients to explore such experiences and their meanings. When these topics emerge, seek consultation with supervisors and cultural brokers to support respectful, rights-based conversations about alternative ways of belonging, identity, and care.

Notes

1 Audre Lorde, "The Uses of Anger: Women Responding to Racism," *in Sister Outsider: Essays and Speeches* (Freedom, CA: Crossing Press, 1984), 127.
2 Thich Nhat Hanh, *Anger: Wisdom for Cooling the Flames* (New York: Riverhead Books, 2001), 76.
3 Melody Beattie, *Codependent No More: How to Stop Controlling Others and Start Caring for Yourself* (Center City, MN: Hazelden, 1986).
4 Thich Nhat Hanh, *Anger*, 103.

References

Beattie, Melody. 1986. *Codependent No More: How to Stop Controlling Others and Start Caring for Yourself*. Center City, MN: Hazelden Publishing.
Lorde, Audre. 1984. "The Uses of Anger." In *Sister Outsider: Essays and Speeches*, 124–133. Freedom, CA: Crossing Press.
Nhat Hanh, Thich. 2001. *Anger: Wisdom for Cooling the Flames*. New York: Riverhead Books.

15 Diving Into the Body

Trauma, Care, and the Path to Embodied Healing

Teacher Lila Kate Wheeler said in a meditation retreat titled *Mindful of the Body*: "May we know that arriving in our bodies is the ultimate pilgrimage" (Insight Meditation Retreat, March 6, 2015). Your basic and most intimate refuge is your body. Yet, too often it is not treated with the respect it deserves. You cannot sustain wellbeing or care of others if your own basic needs are unmet. Although this advice sounds simplistic, my clients—like me—struggle with self-imposed and external pressures that override physical needs. Proper nutrition, regular movement, and sufficient sleep are non-negotiable. Ignore them too long, and consequences will surface.

As Anushka Fernandopulle reminds us in the same retreat, "the stability of the body supports the stability of the mind." The tools and exercises below are regular psychotherapy interventions and guided meditations. They are not culturally universal, but they are offered with humility and adaptability. I have used them in my practice and in my own life. Some are widely available, but simplicity should not be mistaken for lack of depth. Use what resonates with you when it feels right.

A Healthy Diet

As much as you can, make healthy eating choices. Our bodies are nourished or broken by the foods we eat and the liquids we drink.

> *Do not assume you cannot change your habits:* Taste is flexible if you give yourself time. Experiment with a variety of fresh fruits, veggies, and nuts. Consider buying a blender to alternate the texture of your fruit and veggies intake by drinking it. Leave it on your counter where it's easily accessible. Also, keep a wooden chopping board and a nice knife nearby. Leave some prewashed fruit and veggies on top of the chopping board for easy access. Cut it into small slices and eat the morsels raw; learn to slowly chew it and savor it.
>
> *Notice when food becomes emotional regulation:* Use smaller bowls; eat slowly. Your brain needs time to process fullness.
>
> *Eat without screens:* When you eat, just eat.

DOI: 10.4324/9781003648703-20

Create an environment that supports healthy choices: Do not keep processed snacks in the house. Talk to those you live with.

Pause before emotionally eating: When an urge to emotionally eat arises, try a pause. Make tea, write a paragraph describing what is triggering the urge. Name the emotion. You can still eat afterward, but with more awareness.

Use a Thought Record if needed: If your thoughts drive the urge to eat, consider using a Thought Record or a Nine-Lens (described in Chapter 20).

Begin again after overeating: If you overate at lunch, do not abandon the rest of your meal plan. Begin again.

Hydrate: Drink water throughout the day.

Drink alcohol with awareness: Drink alcohol, if at all, with full awareness and no excuses.

Meditations

Not everyone is ready or able to practice meditation or other body-focused techniques. If you can, bring attention to your body and your breath. Some may find this extremely unsettling. You decide. You can stay with the space around you, or use visualizations or imagine something else entirely.

Raisin Meditation

This five-minute meditation builds mindful attention. The *raisin meditation* is a simple practice that helps you think more mindfully about food. Commit this time to a sense of playfulness, allowing yourself to proceed unrushed. For this brief time, put aside any worries or tasks. You can come back to those things after these five minutes pass. If you can, buy dry raisins specifically for this meditation.

Place a raisin in your hand, and examine it closely. Give your attention to the details of the shape, texture, color, and weight. Notice how it feels between your fingers, and if it has any smell. Press it against your lips, then taste your lips. Put it into your mouth, but don't bite. Contemplate how it feels on your tongue and the sides of your mouth. Move it around and consider whether the increased salivation changes your experience. Resist biting into it for a while. Place it between your molars and press. Notice how the taste might change. As you continue to bite, mull over the change of texture and taste, and how your mouth engages in this experience. As you swallow, examine how you feel. Take a moment to experience the taste as it lingers and disappears. Consider whether this experience has also changed the way you feel emotionally, the quality of your thoughts, or your breathing, as well as any other feelings you may have. You can learn how to focus this type of attention and pleasure to any other experience you like. An audio file of this exercise is on my website: www.leideporcu.com.

Movement Meditations

Daily movement supports health: digestion, sleep, and mood. Commit to some level of movement every day. Commit to a daily feasible unit of exercise, like a 20-minute walk. Or start small: Take the subway one stop further; take one more flight of stairs. Park your car a bit farther away from your destination. Movement with a buddy adds accountability. If you do sedentary work, make sure you get up every hour and move around and stretch. Or dance, especially to familiar music from one's culture of origin. Below are three simple movement meditations that can help you connect with your body and calm your mind. Walking slowly, or gentle Qigong (see below) can support calming without intense body focus. You can find accompanying videos on my website.

Walking Meditation

Walking meditation consists of connecting to your body by walking very slowly and focusing your attention on slow movements and sensations as you put one foot in front of the other. There's no need to be outside in an amazing landscape. As long as there's enough space to move back and forth, this meditation can be done in a small area, preferably with bare feet so that you can feel the floor. Notice how your mind clears as you focus your attention on your feet.

Shaking (Qigong)

Stand up, unlock your knees, and gently bounce up and down. As you do so, let your arms float "like two ropes."[1] Let your chin bob and your body become looser. Imagine your arms like two wet ropes dripping water as you shake. Imagine that the water falling from your hands is tension leaving your body. Let it fall, droplet by droplet to the ground. You can also imagine a shower of water falling onto your head, and let this water wash away all the tension and stress from your body. Let your stressful thoughts and your tiredness go down the drain. After a few minutes, or whenever it feels right, stop. Now, notice the tingling in your hands, and any other feelings you may have. You will feel lighter and more relaxed.

Crane (Qigong)

The crane meditation is a Qigong practice that consists of mimicking the poses of a crane, a bird that in China is among the most revered and sym-bolically rich. It represents, among other things, grace, longevity, and good fortune. Imagine how it feels to be a tall, elegant bird flying in a beautiful natural environment of your choice. In practice, though, you are flying on the surface of the ground, stepping forward, on your feet, not flying high like real birds or Superman. Use your imagination, like children do, when they play at being birds, but do that on a slow, harmonious tempo. For a better experience, I would suggest you look at a video tutorial, but here I want to lay out the basic idea. The crane meditation proceeds with a flowing slow movement and not a staccato movement. It requires and fosters deep concentration. In this meditation, you are doing many things at once while keeping balance. Start by standing still, with arms down and your feet slightly apart. After a few centering breaths, the crane takes flight. That is, the crane/you, simultaneously breathe in slowly, while lifting one leg and foot from the floor, as if you were about to take a step forward; at the same time, you spread your wings, that is, you slowly bring both arms up. The arms lift laterally, from both sides of your body, as if you were a bird flying. Your leg is still up, mid-air, at the end of your inhalation. As you breathe out, you slowly bring your lifted leg down gently, one small step in front of you; your arms come down again from the sides of your body. All this movement with practice becomes harmonious, without breaks or much wiggling. You repeat breathing in by lifting your wings again and also lifting up your other leg, and then slowly and harmoniously as you breathe out, you bring that leg down, stepping a small step in front, while lowering the arms. Imagine you are a crane in its natural environment in all details and sensory aspects: What color is the sky? What quality has the breeze? How does it feel on your plumage and wings? Which sounds surround you? Experiencing the scene in your body and senses with your imagination helps. Repeat, alternating your legs. You can also fly while standing in place and instead of stepping in front, you can place each foot down back in the same place. Paying attention to the gestures while keeping balanced helps you to feel focused and grounded. Qigong Masters engage with their postures beautifully and with precision. Each posture they take and each inch of their body has its own aesthetic, symbolic, and energetic reason. I am aware I may be saying something equivalent to heresy here, however, for you or me, the precise position of hands and fingers are secondary to the power of the visualization and the slowing down of your system as you sync your breath and movements. You can find various versions of this exercise on YouTube, as well as my version on my website. You can always perfect your style with the help of a Qigong Master, if that pleases you.

Sleep

We all know that proper sleep is fundamental for our health. Sleep helps the body repair at the cellular level; it affects hormonal balance, the immune system, and heart health. It also helps regulate mood and mental health. Developing proper sleep habits serves you well. Proper sleep habits—otherwise called "sleep hygiene"—mean maintaining roughly the same schedule of wake and bed time, thus helping maintain the internal body rhythm. It means sleeping a sufficient number of hours continuously to feel rested, having a sleep routine that helps you unwind and transition from a busy day to a calm night, and signals to your brain that you are about to transition to sleep.

When sleep habits are not maintained and the sleep/wake cycle is irregular and disturbed, insomnia kicks in, and with it, a pernicious form of anxiety: fears of more sleepless nights. It's a vicious cycle that only perpetuates itself. Worrying about the quality of the sleep you will have, about not being able to sleep, or the fear of waking up tired only makes restful sleep even more elusive. Here are some tips for navigating insomnia and improving your quality of sleep:

- Say to yourself: "If I have a bad night of sleep, I will still try to have an okay day. I will continue to implement healthy sleep habits so that, little by little, I will get back into a good rhythm."
- Maintain the same wake-up and bedtime, approximately, each day. Sustaining a schedule will eventually help.
- Do not hit the snooze button and stay in bed indefinitely. Get up, even if you haven't had enough sleep. Accumulate tiredness during the day and go to sleep that night with a "hunger" for sleep when bedtime comes.
- Turn your clock to face the wall or cover it. Do not spend the night peeking at your clock and calculating how many hours you have lost or how many hours remain before you get up.
- Make your room comfortable, cool, and dark.
- Create a bedtime routine that gives your body the cue that it is time to sleep. This can include slowing down, drinking an herbal tea, changing to bedtime clothes, brushing your teeth, and listening to calm music. Create a predictable, slow pattern that tells your brain you are getting ready for bed.
- Do not watch the news or exciting or upsetting shows before bedtime. The keywords here are: *Wind down*.
- Close your screens and put your phone on airplane mode 30 minutes before going to bed.
- If you feel that your phone needs to be on because you must be on call for loved ones all night, but it's interfering with your sleep, consider whether anxiety and worry are part of that need, and whether you can really be helpful to anyone if you continue to lose sleep.
- Alcohol does not help you sleep. Limit caffeine intake to mornings.
- Hydrate all day, but limit drinking a few hours before bedtime, so that you avoid getting up to go to the bathroom.
- Exercise, stretching, and movement meditations are fine and recommended, but do not do strenuous exercise late in the evening. For most of us, strenuous exercise wakes us up.
- Use the walk or drive after work to wind down and create a boundary—a liminal space—between work and home.
- Going to sleep anxious, frazzled, and hyper won't help you sleep. During the day, spend a few moments every few hours to check in with

yourself and process what's happening. Find moments of relaxation and breaks to process your emotions and the day's events.

- Nothing causes sleepless nights more than trying to solve problems in your mind or revisiting old grudges. Your mind is not sharp and logical at night, so trying to solve problems or rewrite history is a waste of time and only feeds your worrying and brooding habits.
- Expose yourself every day to sunlight. Do not remain indoors constantly.

The Projector Technique

If you experience thoughts and restless energy racing through your mind and body at night, visualize a thick velvet curtain covering your window. Then imagine projecting those thoughts outward from yourself, like a movie or shape of energy, onto the curtain. See these scenes shift from color to black and white; then hear the volume decrease, little by little. As the scenes shift and volume slowly quietens, let them fade away, absorbed by the thick curtain, as if they were falling outside the window and dissolving into the space outside. This idea comes from H. E. Stanton, in Corydon Hammond's *Hypnotic Suggestions and Metaphors.*[2]

The Importance of Self-Care

When our body works well, we have more energy to do all sorts of things. Taking care of the body in fundamental ways also helps us manage our feelings. When we are tired, thirsty, have overeaten, or we are hungry or hungover, we become irritable, sluggish, and unproductive. A healthy body can help us feel empowered. Once we have taken care of our body at a basic level, we will have extra energy and attention to focus on additional self-care efforts, such as the following:

- Being able to be still. Calming the nervous system through meditation and breathing.
- Checking in with our internal speedometer and slowing down, in case we are speeding up, or activating ourselves if we feel sluggish. It is better to notice and troubleshoot early on, before we devolve into extreme sadness, or become frazzled or disconnected.
- Asking ourselves in a non-judgmental voice: How am I feeling? How do I express my emotions? Do I bottle them up? When and with whom do I tend to respond with joy and openness? When do I respond in inhibited, passive-aggressive, or overly angry ways? Where do I feel my emotions in my body? What is the history of the particular emotion that I am feeling right now? Does it remind me of any other interaction?
- Being more present in the situation.

Tools to Anchor the Mind and Body

Below are some more tools using your imagination and the external environment to promote relaxation and centering.

- Name 5 things you can see, 4 you can hear, 3 you can touch, 2 you can smell, and 1 you can taste.
- Focus on a soothing object (a plant, landscape, candle, or artwork).
- Do a soothing place visualization (the word "safe" can be inaccessible for some; ask what word feels more resonant—perhaps "place of rest," "calm place," or "place you can be;" the goal is not safety as an ideal, but a moment of reduced threat).
- Imagine a protective figure, including a religious/spiritual figure or a pet that brings comfort. Picture a loving gaze or smile.
- Visualize a boundary, like a protective bubble all around you, or the image of home or another place that brings an "okay" feeling.
- Listen to calm music or poetry.
- Watch a movie or even old home country advertisements on YouTube.
- Call someone from back home who speaks your mother tongue.
- Recite a mantra, prayer, or comforting word (e.g., from one's own language or childhood); gargling or humming.
- Sing (Marsha Linehan once said in a lecture that singing "Shalom" had become her highest form of meditation).
- Write, draw, color, collage, read, journal, or engage in another type of creative expression.
- Do grounding tasks, like cleaning or cooking.
- Have water experiences, such as washing dishes, taking a bath, sitting by a fountain in the park or museum.
- Read something light, calming, or sacred.
- Hold or look at a meaningful object (stone, cloth, photo).
- Touch a soft blanket or other comforting texture.
- Engage in aromatherapy (if you find scent soothing and non-triggering).
- Engage in tapping (if you want to try out tapping on your own, I recommend following a video or audio tutorial).[3]
- Be in the company of people (or pets) that are safe and that you enjoy, and do things together: a walk, cooking, knitting, or eating together.
- Take a trauma-informed yoga class or other body activity with people who are knowledgeable about trauma.
- Notice your breath; notice your belly; with a hand placed on your belly, notice if it is rising as you breathe in and falling as you breathe out or if your belly is tense and unmoving. Breathe at a count of 4 breaths in, and 4 breaths out, or explore *coherent breathing*,[4] slowly filling your lungs in for a count of 5, and breathe out for 5, if it feels ok.

Explore what brings calm. Stay curious.

To Clinicians

Multiple Trauma, Safety, and the Body

The field of trauma across psychology, neuroscience, and psychoanalysis is vast and evolving. It cannot be fully summarized here, but it must remain present in your clinical awareness, especially when working with immigrants. For many, trauma is not a single event but a layered thread woven through premigration, the journey itself, postmigration life, and often in the recursive loops of onward migration or return. Trauma can also be transgenerational, passed down unconsciously and non-verbally across decades and borders. In Chapter 16, we will encounter Charlie, a client of Irish heritage whose family immigrated generations ago. Despite the passage of time, unhelpful cultural patterns and transgenerational trauma continue to affect him.

Some immigrant patients come from settings shaped by war, trafficking, systemic violence, or profound poverty. For them, the body may have been a site of fear, punishment, or shame. Pain may emerge not through the Western mind–body split, but through numbness, somatic complaints, or unexplained illness. Emotional language may be inaccessible.

If the body has been a site of violation, pain, or cultural taboo, patients may not want to focus on it. Do not rush them toward *reembodiment*. Honor their pacing and protect their agency. Reclaiming the body after trauma is not always safe or even desirable. Move slowly. Be still in their presence, so that eventually they may loosen the defenses that were once necessary for survival. The feeling of safety—if and when it comes—must emerge organically. It cannot be imposed or suggested with words like "relax," which are well meaning but frustrating and alienating for many traumatized individuals. The therapeutic frame itself—its rituals, boundaries, and predictability—already does much to foster calm, as does going slowly in the work. As the old psychoanalytic saying goes: "Avoid scratching your nose, if you have an itch." If you need to get up, even to open a window, let them know beforehand, especially if you need to pass behind them. Pre-narrate your actions. This is not only a psychoanalytic principle; it is also a tenet of trauma-informed yoga.[5] I also understand that going slowly in therapy may not be a financial possibility for many patients, therapists, and clinics. When that is not a possibility, mindful, trauma-informed homework may be a useful integration, and for that I mean practices like the ones suggested in this book, which may support the patient between sessions, fostering emotional regulation, self-knowledge, and understanding of their position in larger dynamics.

Agency, Collaboration, and the Frame

Clients who have been invalidated or harmed, by people or by systems, need to be witnessed, but more than that, they need space to experience agency. Our role is not to rescue or fix, but to cocreate a process that honors their pace and perspective.

Therapy must balance psychoeducation with attuned listening to the client's emotional, physical, and historical narrative. Ask regularly: What do you need from me? What are your goals? How would you like to be supported? These are not just intake questions, they are foundational to a collaborative stance.

Be curious about what the client's body knows, what their history reveals, and what their insight offers. The more you center their dignity, the more space they have to reinhabit their experience with power and choice.

The Layers of Trauma, Intergenerational Examples: The Potato Famine and Slavery

Psychologist Jennifer Mullan reminds us to fully attend to the meaning of migration and what caused it:

> Many people are forced to migrate, whether they are conscious of it or not. You may often hear phrases such as, "There are more opportunities in America/Britain..." or "I came here for a better life." Although these phrases are true to that individual and perhaps to that affected community, there is a deeper root cause to the migration.[6]

Jennifer Mullan reminds us that to accompany our patients fully, we must be present to not only individual suffering but the transgenerational and collective histories that shape it. Together with our patients, we must attend to their family histories, to the transgenerational transmission of trauma, and to collective traumas, both historical and ongoing. To ignore these dimensions is to amputate the work.

Among the examples Jennifer Mullan discusses in her book, the example of the Potato Famine in Ireland (yes, England's first colony), stands out. History affects the present in an insidious and powerful way and often goes unacknowledged or dismissed. History lives in our minds and bones, if not in our genes. Sometimes patients arrive to us with a clear awareness about their present and historical oppression and how it is connected to their malaise. Other times, it is up to us to open a space for a conversation about these determinants without making abstract lectures. These determinants will become apparent from patients' history and the language of their malaise. At the time of the Potato Famine (1845–1849),[7] the Irish people were starving. However, at the same time, goods were being shipped from Ireland to England. It is striking how, in many places, people are poor while the land is rich.[8] Isn't that an interesting contradiction? Often people are blamed for their incapacities to rule themselves and prosper, while they are, indeed, oppressed and exploited often under the guise of helping them. These global dynamics of power and exploitation affect the oppressed individuals and the generations that follow, who find themselves impoverished, devalued, and at times also unsafe. As Mullan remarks, "In Ireland, the colonizers may not have created the plant blight that infected the crops, but their policies and demands led too many to die from starvation."[9] At that time, the Irish had to resort to mass migration on unsafe boats—an image that recalls the Africans leaving for Europe, fleeing countries rich in resources in search for a better life. They too traveled on unsafe boats, often drowning, like the film *Io Capitano* [10] shows.

Mullan encourages therapists working with people of Irish descent to keep in mind the following questions, which can be adapted to any patient from colonized or historically oppressed backgrounds:

- How have colonialism, White supremacy, and patriarchy influenced Irish people's current emotional health?
- What are the correlations between Irish people's wellbeing and generational abuse and colonization?
- What may be some of the intergenerational expressions of what was described above for Irish descendants today?[11]

In an extensive vignette, the author demonstrated how the experience of colonialism can show up in the session, as therapist and patient explore the history of the emotion, in this case, rage, anger, and hunger, passed down consciously and unconsciously for generations in individual families and collectively.[12] The trauma of the Irish potato famine, for instance, may live on in family rituals, in heirloom recipes passed down with pride. But alongside the pride, trauma too is transmitted unconsciously. On an unconscious level, our grandmothers and grandfathers pass on what was not metabolized in their time. Much may be omitted from the official history. However, what is omitted, as psychoanalysis has taught us, comes back with a punch. Gradually, with our patients, we must bring into the clinical space the layered histories of trauma, including the broader traumatic effects of capitalism, colonialism, slavery, and patriarchy. These do not exist apart from the individual; they are embedded in our bodies and psyche. Trauma is geologically stratified. Our ways of seeing are contextually formed. We must unpack its layers because knowledge is empowering and access to it should be a fundamental right.

Behavior, Resistance, and the Role of the Clinician

Mullan warns against reducing behavior to dysfunction without acknowledging context. Rage, withdrawal, hallucinations, or resistance may reflect survival strategies: responses to prolonged injustice or inherited grief. She gives examples of Black youth who are failed by the system, including clinicians, who label their behavior in damaging pathologizing terms instead of providing a true pathway for self-knowledge, collective empowerment, restitution, healing, and social accountability. One's disruptive and oppositional behavior and one's hallucinations sometimes make sense when they are in response to a history of oppression, exploitation, devaluation of one's homeland, groups, and identities. In those cases, emotions, bodily responses, and behaviors require attention through multiple lenses because *there is logic in the madness.*

Ethics and Survival in Clinical Work

In the face of trauma and injustice, we must ask ourselves difficult questions: How can we provide or conjure up healthy alternatives, especially when, as therapists, we often work in isolation and rely on bureaucratic exploitative systems we cannot dismantle? We must be present with the reality we are embedded in, contending with insurance companies that reimburse us for our patients' treatment and also indirectly pay for our mortgages and our own medical insurance. Of course I am not justifying destructive social behavior. A history of violence and oppression is not a justification for violence. However, what we can do, at the very least, is help our patients connect all the strands of their lives. In doing so, we can foster their healing and promote clarity—and perhaps open space for advocacy, or, at the very least, help them pursue a more strategic way of being in the world.

As clinicians, no matter whether we are willing to be called by our first name and are not interested in highlighting a hierarchy, we are privileged compared to many of our patients. Even new clinicians working in under-funded clinics, who are poorly paid even if insurance companies are billed at high rates, may still hold significant privilege. New clinicians, as I hear from my students, want to change the world. And yet they are already suffering. Some young clinicians are hoping to "climb the ladder." Ironically, climbing that ladder often means becoming more integrated into systems of exploitation. Even by accepting private insurance—often itself an exploitative system—we risk reproducing the very inequalities we hope to undo. We may be exploited by the system, but we are also complicit in it. Even this book, which has cost me blood and tears and has taken up all of my free time to write, is not exempt. It offers help to immigrants but it is also built on the pain of others. We need to come to terms with how we are implicated in systems of exploitation. These systems affect many, but particularly immigrants, who might never have migrated if it were not for these forces that have been shaping and damaging their environments, depleting their natural resources, interfering with their national politics, and falsely marketing global capitals as dream destinations.

I do not know how to resolve these big issues apart from doing pro bono work and talking about them, even when talking does not feel safe at all. However, not talking would be equally catastrophic. Let us not forget Bion. During the Blitz, when bombs were falling on London and analysts remained unflinching, he stood up and interrupted the talk. He said something along the lines of: "I just want to point out that bombs are falling." Acknowledging reality is necessary, even when we cannot change it. A vivid example comes from the 2025 class I was teaching, Social Work Practice with Immigrants and Refugees, where we could not move forward with the assigned readings without naming the elephant in the room: the current immigration policies. These policies were disrupting our classrooms, our communities—and most tragically, putting our clients' lives at real risk.

Our personal, social, and clinical view is not neutral but marked by our positionalities and the ideologies inherent also in our training. To keep the world outside of the consulting room and pretend that we are "neutral" would be a kind of *folie à deux*—a shared denial. Yes, there may be moments when creating a quiet island is helpful, especially early on, to calm a patient's agitated nervous system. But we must position ourselves—and, when warranted, also share it with patients—to build trust. We must also name the roots of suffering, when the suffering is not just "in their heads."

Recognizing our position in the web of relations that shape our patients' lives—and may also shape our own—must also emerge in the session. It cannot be deflected with a reflexive question. The screen may remain, but we cannot pretend it is blank. Trust is built also in these exchanges.

The Clinician Position: Strike One Side and Then Strike Another

In his book, *The Practice of Everyday Life*, Michel de Certeau[13] made a distinction between people with considerable power, who own land, resources, and knowledge, who can afford having a "strategy"—a forward-moving plan. The less powerful must rely on "tactics;" they find themselves in the terrain of the other and they exploit whatever openings they can find, moment by moment, step by step. Immigrants often don't have the luxury of having a full strategy. When they immigrate, they may have a few pieces of a plan, perhaps a school placement or a job offer, but rarely the full map. Even in the best-case scenarios, they rely on tactics; they need to hone a capacity to be nimble in the new land; to see clearly, build connections, and quickly seize opportunities in real time when they open up.

Therapists may see themselves as a source of strategies, and others may seek them out for these. After all, they are experts; they have masters, PhDs, licenses, and certifications. They have walked the walk and have gone through their own therapy or psychoanalysis to get here. However, no matter the expertise of therapists, clinical work is complex; the terrain is always shifting. It is no wonder that so many therapists never feel competent and acquire training beyond the continuing education credits required—me included. Therapists also need to be nimble. They may identify themselves as primarily trained in one orientation. But when working with immigrants in particular, a strong holistic approach is needed. I am not suggesting a training that is "a little bit of this, of that, and of everything." I am advocating for a lifelong learning mindset, a commitment to humility and openness, a willingness to collaborate across healing traditions beyond psychotherapy. As clinicians treating immigrants, we can no longer hold the stance that our school of thought is the best, and all others are antiquated or simplistic; this happened during my training. When it came to the orientation of choice for treating patients there were two warring factions, CBT and psychoanalysis. At that time, it was taboo to combine them, and so both sides regarded me with suspicion. That kind of insularity limits us. We are all, more or less, incompetent. What saves us is our awareness of that fact and our willingness to reach beyond our silo, in the same way our immigrant patients must do in life.

All our certifications and licenses are based on frameworks rooted in the Western canon, even though many of our tools have been enriched, adapted, or even appropriated from theories and practices developed elsewhere. And while some of us have dipped our feet into culturally informed approaches, our capacity to hold, understand, and help people from all walks of life remains profoundly incomplete. This side-dish approach to cultural mindfulness, as seen, for instance, in how cultural idioms of distress are categorized in the DSM, is not enough. But it is a beginning. My recommendation is to work with multiple systems in mind: learn the Western canon as much as you can in all its facets because there is good in all approaches and you need depth to develop both yourself and a comprehensive toolkit. Be open to healing modalities your patients embrace and those from their countries of origin that may have been devalued and forgotten over time. Be ready to have consultations not only with psychiatrists and family members but also with other healers and spiritual figures, if helpful or requested.

As clinicians, we must walk an ambiguous path side by side with our patients. Even if it feels messy, we must strike one side and then strike another. In other words, you need to think within the box and outside of it. Even if some theoretical approaches appear incompatible, they may work together in practice. I have combined psychoanalysis, psychodynamic therapy, and CBT even when putting them together were viewed by many as mixing oil and water. But now these modalities speak more and more to one another, and that is a good thing. Use your judgment when combining methods, even if current ideology does not support it. However, please do not work in isolation. There is strength in numbers. Find a supervisor or a group of like-minded colleagues. Share ideas. Listen to your patients and their symptoms: Are they getting better or worse? Ask yourself, is the modality I am using congruent with my patient's worldview? Refer out if you are not helping. Also, be aware that certain modalities and tools have been tested with immigrant populations and show evidence-based effectiveness. Among these are:

- Narrative exposure therapy (NET)
- Trauma-focused cognitive behavioral therapy (TF CBT)
- Cognitive behavior therapy (CBT)
- Solution focused brief therapy (SFBT)
- The cognitive behavioral intervention for trauma in schools (CBITS)
- Eye movement desensitization and reprocessing (EMDR)

Above all, remember: it is not the technique but attunement that heals. Many immigrant patients have had to ignore their bodies in order to survive. Reconnection, if it comes, will come in relationship—at their pace, in their way. Be with them there.

Notes

1 An expression taken by the master Robert Peng, my Qigong teacher. You can find out more at www.robertpeng.com.
2 H. E. Stanton, "Dumping the 'Rubbish,'" in *Handbook of Hypnotic Suggestions and Metaphors*, ed. D. Corydon Hammond (New York: W. W. Norton, 1990).
3 Parnell, Laurel. *Tapping In: A Step-by-Step Guide to Activating Your Healing Resources Through Bilateral Stimulation* (Boulder, CO: Sounds True, 2008).
4 Richard P. Brown and Patricia L. Gerbarg, *The Healing Power of the Breath: Simple Techniques to Reduce Stress and Anxiety, Enhance Concentration, and Balance Your Emotions* (Boston, MA: Shambhala, 2012). This book also provides audio instructions.
5 Inhale Exhale, *Train the Leader Program: Trauma-Informed Yoga Certification*. Taught by Joyous Pierce (Silberman School of Social Work, CUNY, 2025).
6 Jennifer Mullan, *Decolonizing Therapy: Oppression, Historical Trauma, and Politicizing Your Practice* (Berkeley, CA: North Atlantic Books, 2023), 54.
7 Mullan, 52.
8 The same can be said of Sardinia, where I come from, a land exploited for its minerals by outside powers since ancient times.
9 Jennifer Mullan, *Decolonizing Therapy*, 52.
10 Matteo Garrone (dir). *Io Capitano* (Italy: Archimede, Rai Cinema, and Pathé, 2023), film.
11 Jennifer Mullan, *Decolonizing Therapy*, 53.
12 It is worth reading the full passage; please get the book or get the verbatim session and note the ways she brings the history into the present. But, if you can, continue reading till the end for more examples. Mullan, *Decolonizing Therapy*, 56–59.
13 Michel de Certeau, *The Practice of Everyday Life*, trans. Steven Rendall (Berkeley, CA: University of California Press, 2002), xix.

References

Brown, Richard P., and Patricia L. Gerbarg. 2012. *The Healing Power of the Breath: Simple Techniques to Reduce Stress and Anxiety, Enhance Concentration, and Balance Your Emotions*. Boston, MA: Shambhala.

de Certeau, Michel. 2002. *The Practice of Everyday Life*. Translated by Steven Rendall. Berkeley, CA: University of California Press.

Garrone, Matteo (dir). 2023. *Io Capitano*. Italy: Archimede, Rai Cinema, and Pathé.

Inhale Exhale. 2025. *Train the Leader Program: Trauma-Informed Yoga Certification*. Taught by Joyous Pierce. Silberman School of Social Work, CUNY.

Mullan, Jennifer. 2023. *Decolonizing Therapy: Oppression, Historical Trauma, and Politicizing Your Practice*. Berkeley, CA: North Atlantic Books.

Parnell, Laurel. 2008. *Tapping In: A Step-by-Step Guide to Activating Your Healing Resources Through Bilateral Stimulation*. Boulder, CO: Sounds True.

Stanton, H. E. 1990. "Dumping the 'Rubbish.'" In *Handbook of Hypnotic Suggestions and Metaphors*, edited by D. Corydon Hammond, 313–316. New York: W. W. Norton.

Part V

Exploring Your Unconscious

Albert Einstein is often credited with saying, "Problems cannot be solved by thinking within the framework in which the problems were created."[1] This section offers tools that, to more scientifically inclined minds, may initially seem a bit "out there." If you are one of these people, I invite you to have an open mind and try these exercises with a curious attitude, if not one of expectation. I remember as an anthropology student I was fascinated with the story of a childbirth healing ritual performed by a Shaman of the Cuna Indians. It was documented in the essay, "The Effectiveness of Symbols" by Claude Lévi-Strauss (1949/1974).[2] The story and the interpretations of Lévi-Strauss and of the anthropologists who followed are complex and beyond the scope of this book. However, there is something about this story that for me aligns with all the meditations that are described within these pages. For instance, I can't help but draw parallels to the crane meditation, which was presented in the previous chapter, "Diving Into the Body."

Lévi-Strauss talks about a difficult and life-threatening childbirth. The shaman is called in to save the mother and the preborn baby. The shaman performs an incantation, a ritual that tells the story of a parallel, spiritual world where the spiritual beings are in disagreement about going through or blocking a passage. The story also includes the use of statuettes representing these beings, as if it were a puppet show, but with the gravity and power of a ritual that brings to life the mythological history and its power in the present. It's as if the events being narrated are unfolding both in a mythological realm and in the woman's body, while also taking place in her imagination.

This story spiritually mirrors the woman's current gynecological condition: both in reality and in the narrative, a crucial passage is blocked and not functioning properly. The shaman resolves this by performing a ritual that directly connects to the present issue. Through this connection, the shaman invokes a mythological dimension within the woman's body, which becomes the stage for healing. The shaman's words depict a battle against evil spirits that have overtaken the woman's soul, describing the encounter, the fight, and the victory over them. As the symbols and words take effect,

DOI: 10.4324/9781003648703-21

the gynecological blockage is released, and the baby is born and is healthy, as is the mother.

We could ask ourselves: How does it work? Is it a religious or spiritual intervention? Is it psychological? A placebo effect? Is the woman simply relaxing into the story, allowing the tension in her body to release? Is it the power of symbols at play? These questions could be debated for decades. However, for our purposes, the Cuna story is significant for two reasons: First, it highlights the idea that, in similar ways, engaging both the imagination and the body, as occurs through guided meditations and hypnosis, can create profound changes, although their impact is more mundane than miraculous. This incantation may not seem relevant to everyday life; however, as we'll see below, with Charlie and Dada, powerful images and visualizations can be used in our daily lives to bring our projects to life, energize ourselves, heal, and overcome obstacles. By visualizing and embodying the movement and form of our current state, we give it shape and meaning. Through further movement, free association, and narrative, we transition toward the positive state we wish to achieve. This process can help shift our emotions and help us regain focus.

It is worth restating, as explored in Chapter 15, that as therapists working with immigrant populations, we must recognize that a strong foundation in mainstream Western therapy is not enough to effectively support our clients from other cultures. We need to approach our work with cultural humility. Our Western-based methods may not universally apply, and before speaking from a place of blind authority or imposing our views, we must remain open to diverse cultures, contexts, and individuals—not only having knowledge of them but allowing them to shape and inform our understanding and practice. This requires taking a step back and truly listening to our clients in a comprehensive way, including being curious about their culturally specific healing practices. If a client wishes to collaborate with a Shaman, Curandera, or other native healer, our openness and willingness to create a synergy between practices can greatly enhance the success of the treatment.

If you're an immigrant in therapy and feel hesitant to mention other practices you use for your wellbeing, consider bringing them up with your therapist. See if you both feel comfortable discussing this aspect of your life as part of your treatment.

Notes

1 This quote is widely attributed to Albert Einstein, although no definitive source confirms he actually said or wrote it. I requoted from Feldman and Levin, who had quoted it from Pound (2004), but I was not able to verify Pound. Anatol G. Feldman and Mindy F. Levin, "The Equilibrium-Point Hypothesis—Past, Present and Future," in *Progress in Motor Control*, ed. Dagmar Sternad (New York: Springer, 2009), 724.
2 Claude Lévi-Strauss, *Structural Anthropology*, trans. Claire Jacobson and Brooke Grundfest Schoepf (New York: Basic Books, 1974), 186.

References

Feldman, A.G., and M.F. Levin. 2009. "The Equilibrium-Point Hypothesis—Past, Present and Future," in *Progress in Motor Control*, edited by D. Sternad, 699–726. New York: Springer. doi:10.1007/978-0-387-77064-2_38.

Lévi-Strauss, Claude. 1974. *Structural Anthropology*. Translated by Claire Jacobson and Brooke Grundfest Schoepf. New York: Basic Books.

16 Healing with Symbols and the Imagination

Sometimes I wake up in a panic, sweating from dreams that all my things are gone—furniture, clothes, even books—just vanished. In the dreams, I search storage rooms or unfamiliar places, trying to find them. But what I am really looking for are things I no longer have: my grandmother's scarf, the toy train from my old bedroom, the photo albums we left behind. I think the fear is not really about losing stuff—it is about losing the life I once had and the people tied to it.

—Anonymous contributor

The Tree with Deep Transnational Roots

Barbie, a patient of mine, was struggling with a sense of loss, fatigue, and futility. She felt that no matter what she did to improve her life—working long hours, attending evening classes, and applying to school—she continued to fall short of her goals, as if she were swimming against a tide. She was battling an impulse to "screw things up," to go to a bar the evening before a qualifying exam for graduate school, rather than prepare. Together we created a meditation to help her find strength. I led her into a progressive relaxation technique that combined elements of a guided meditation that I learned in a Hypnosis Level 1 course at the NLP Center of New York with Steven Leeds and Rachel Hott.

I helped her visualize a tree and all its details. She internalized the qualities of the tree: its stability, energy, vitality, durability, and strength. And during this process, she seamlessly shifted to a sense of calm. Next, I led her on a journey, in which she experienced the changes of the seasons, which allowed me to inject an element of time, movement, and continuity. We finished with a loving kindness meditation (available on www.leideporcu. com) to evoke self-love and acceptance.

When the meditation was completed, she said, "I visualized a tree with deep roots in the ground. The roots kept the tree erect, but the leaves were all gone, in the cold winter." In that moment, we both learned something: we both understood that those fallen leaves were a clear representation of her depleted, sad, self.

DOI: 10.4324/9781003648703-22

Then Barbie continued:

> At some point during the meditation, something shifted. I felt a strong feeling of warmth inside. I knew that the leaves had fallen but would come again and adorn my branches. The roots went deep into the dirt and that made me feel a connection to my country and my relatives. I thought, "I may feel the winter now; bare, and cold. But I feel the spring will come."

In her everyday life, Barbie has to blend in and underplay cultural traits, such as her accent, because her culture is stigmatized in the United States. Despite that, during the meditation, she was able to connect with and find sustenance in her culture and family. Her disposition shifted drastically; I could feel the spring sprouting within her as her strength and determination began to increase. Her posture changed. She looked more erect and energized. I realized that we had just cocreated a new tool for transnational healing—I call it the Tree with Deep Transnational Roots. The next day, she took the exam and passed.

Visualizing powerful images, such as the deep-rooted tree, can facilitate a path forward that clears the way for healing and renewed energy for life. When you are feeling stuck or anxious, take a quiet moment to locate where the malaise rests in your body. Try to identify its physical location. Pay attention to its shape, energy, and movement. We're not aiming for scientific validity in this exercise. Consider the experience more of a dream, fantasy, piece of poetry, or an artistic representation coming from your imagination.

Describe in detail how this malaise feels; use all your senses. Consider the energy of it. Mimic the movement with your hands. Is it a spiral movement? Or circular? Is there a sound? A buzzing, perhaps? Does it have weight? Describe its shape and material. Is it gaseous? Sticky? Solid? Liquid? Is it the consistency of Play-Doh? How defined are its borders? Are they fuzzy or neat?

Once you have considered the discomfort in great detail, engage it and notice what happens if you interact with it? Can you touch it, move it, breathe into or play with it? Perhaps you can change it or reverse it and in doing so, perhaps you can change the way you feel.[1] Below are some examples of playful explorations of this kind. May they serve as inspiration for your own explorations.

The Big Potato

Charlie is not a recent immigrant. Although his family's emigration from Ireland goes way back, he tells me he still feels the effect of what he calls a "lace curtain" culture of his heritage, which he identifies, among other things, with a propensity for impeccable appearance, emotional reserve, and unavailability. One day, his feelings of isolation and sadness felt unshakable.

I asked him if he was game to try a new exercise. First, I led him in a meditation to experience his body in a rich sensory and imaginative way.

This meditation, which I learned from Anushka Fernandopulle and Kate Lila Wheeler, teachers in the insight meditation tradition, helps to gradually rediscover one's body creatively, in all its layers (you can also find this exercise on my website).

Beginning with his feet, I invited Charlie to notice the feeling of weight and the experience of the floor. Then, we moved his attention to the parts of his body that were clothed, and those exposed to the air. We lingered on their different temperatures. Then I led him inside, very slowly, layer after layer, from the skin to the fat underneath the skin; then, slowly, to the muscles, organs, nerves, veins, and arteries. Next, we traveled to the bones, continuing the exploration until he reached the bone marrow. This imaginary journey was slow, allowing for a full body awareness.

Once Charlie was relaxed and inwardly focused, I shared that sometimes it is helpful to experience pain as an object, to have a sense of its energy and movement. I asked him to imagine activating his x-ray capability and to focus on the exact location of the pain in his body. I said, "Notice what's there as you delve inside. It's not important during this exercise to make logical sense. Whatever comes to mind—an image, shape, movement, or energy—is good. The objective is to get a sense of what the pain feels or looks like and to engage the poetic version of your internal landscape. You can interrupt the experiment at any moment if you feel uncomfortable."

After some time spent exploring his pain, the following exchange occurred: "It's in my chest, it has no clear boundaries, but it sits in my chest," Charlie said.

I asked: "Can you stay in the meditation, and also softly open your eyes, and tell me if you can imagine taking it out of your chest and holding it in your hands in front of you?" I gestured as if taking an object from my own body. He followed. We faced each other. I mirrored his movements as he removed with his hands the unwanted imaginary pain from his chest.

"It feels as if I was yanking it out and holding it in my hands," Charlie said.

I asked, "What do you notice now that it is in your hands?"

Charlie manipulated the imaginary substance, and I continued to mimic his gestures, to catch a bit of what he was feeling and be with him in the experience.

"How is it?" I asked.

"It is like a giant potato. I don't like potatoes," he said.

"A giant potato," I repeated, honestly surprised. "How does it feel in your hands?" I asked, and, after some waiting, I volunteered: "Does it give like Play-Doh? Is it as hard as stone, or is it spongy?"

"It's yellowish-white. I used to hate them when I was little. They have a revolting rotten smell. We used to make colcannon mash with them."

I imagined his characterization in my mind as I continued, like him, to take time to explore the imaginary potato, the version of it that took shape in my mind and hands. I asked, "Can you imagine playing with it? Move it around, or move it from hand to hand, or whatever makes sense to you? Sometimes these pains have a certain energy or movement. Notice what comes to you." We both moved our hands, while facing one another, each of us exploring our imaginary big potato. I asked, "How can we change it in some way? If you squeeze it, what happens?"

"It changes into a nerve ball; it is like squishy foam," Charlie said. "Then it's bigger again but less dense. There is air in the nerve ball. But it's getting more malleable now." He continued to manipulate this imaginary nerve ball. "It's not boiled potato-like anymore because if you squeeze a boiled potato it would be obliterated and turn into mush. Not this one. This one is different. It is changing and it's not so smelly anymore."

"What's the feeling for you now?" I asked.

"It's very satisfying." He continued to knead this substance with absorption until I asked again, "What is going on?"

"It feels more like a pie crust dough; I want to roll it, cut it, and put it into a pie dish. I am crinkling the crust now."

I was following his experience and started crinkling imaginary pie crust as well, mirroring him. He proceeded to sprinkle sugar and put the pie into an imaginary oven. Charlie is an accomplished cook, and I could see his satisfaction from this experience. Baking is a meditative practice for him. But that day in the session, he made new use of cooking skills, perhaps we could call it *play*. He transformed the toxic internal experience, a shapeless dreaded thing that was overcoming him and sapping his energy, into something positive. He felt empowered.

"The pie," he said, "is bringing up good memories of the days when my grandma and I would bake."

His teen years with his grandmother were without conflict, danger, or loss. What a lovely way he had found to comfort himself and transform the rotten, smelly big potato into a mighty apple pie. In this experiment, he engaged negative historical experiences, and while using his body and movements in ways that were evocative and empowering, he connected with positive experiences from his past. He was able to experience each moment (past and present) in the present, and to share the experience with me. Charlie loved the exercise, and he added it to his battery of tools. And I learned something more of what it means to be him.

The Attention-Seeking Dog and the Mighty Lion

Dada, an immigrant on a working visa, worked in the American branch of a European-based firm. In his current job, he felt secure against layoffs. His bicultural competence and native language skills were assets, but over time, he grew frustrated. As often happens, the parent company leadership sometimes made strategic decisions that made sense for the parent company, but not in the context of the U.S. branch.

Recently, the parent company made decisions about the U.S. market that undermined Dada's department and his success. To make things worse, The U.S. branch of his company gave promotions and offered compensation that were not in line with those of other American companies. They were lower than American companies and equivalent to those of the parent company, where the standard of living is much lower. "In my job," he said, "I feel like a dog... neglected... overworked... forgotten like an old dog."

Dada had outgrown his role at the U.S. branch of his company, but he felt uneasy about leaving since it was through this job that he had gained legal status in the US. Although he had lived in the US for some time and had already secured a green card, the connection to his company still weighed on his decision. He had only worked for this company, which was based in his country of origin. He had not ventured into the American job market because he felt that the American work culture, unlike his home culture, would not provide adequate protection against layoffs; this was a scary prospect for a foreigner without an appropriate safety net. He also thought his experience and English language proficiency were not up to par. Thoughts of leaving his job made him anxious, and thoughts of staying frustrated him. He felt stuck, and unable to decide. However, by not making any decision, he did in fact make one, he chose safety over growth. Dada had previously drawn much pleasure, meaning, and identity from his job. But he began to feel heavy and unmotivated and to experience headaches.

In our sessions, our work was to identify and modify his self-distortions. Dada tended to see himself as a less competent, less desirable candidate than he was. We worked to identify areas where he could grow and expand his opportunities.

We began by addressing his avoidance and isolation. He needed to speak more English and increase his networking activity. We then built a savings plan to provide a financial cushion in case something went wrong during the transition from his current position. We also worked on his history of feeling "dog-like," which was connected to early family dynamics. Becoming aware of these feelings marked a positive shift, indicating that he was beginning to question and outgrow behaviors and patterns that no longer served him. In a session, he shared a dream in which a caged dog was being ignored. The image of the dog reminded him of when he was a child, an attention-seeking youngster in a world of busy adults. As he connected to the image in the dream, he said, "I felt forever like a dog, a bit sad, faithful, always available to fetch someone else's stick for them. But there are times, I feel like a lion."

We were both struck by this new image of a lion. I decided the material that was emerging in the session would make a good focus for a meditation. I asked him what kind of animal qualities he wanted to channel and what animal he would want as a protector in this imaginary animal-themed journey. He chose to use the dog as the subject of the meditation and the lion as the protector. I led him and the dog, the animal he most identified with, into a deep relaxation.

In our cocreated imaginary journey, I guided Dada, but he also guided me by offering feedback on what he experienced internally. He described a dog in an office, one of those tall, glass-walled buildings in downtown

Manhattan, similar to the U.S. branch of his company. The dog lay bored on the floor. As the meditation deepened, a metamorphosis occurred: Dada told me the dog was beginning to feel uneasy, and this unease grew; he described the sensations in his body. Gradually, he gave feedback that a different energy was emerging within him—he was beginning to feel more like a lion.

Dada described these sensations as originating from his body, identifying with the lion and "becoming" it. The lion grew restless, feeling tight, irritable, and uncomfortable in the glass structure. From inside, he could see the bustling world outside but couldn't participate—much like how Dada felt, day after day, in his glass skyscraper office: disconnected from the tactile world below. As the meditation progressed, Dada sensed the lion's strength building; he could feel the feline's chiseled muscles stretching beneath his skin. Like a lion awakening from a long slumber, he yawned and stretched unapologetically.

Approaching the glass pane, Dada reported "live" that the lion gave an effortless push, and the glass opened wide to the outside. Perhaps it had always been unlocked, waiting for a push, but only now did the lion discover it. The lion stepped out into the open air without looking back, with a fierce swagger, his mane caressed by the sun and the gentle wind. He trusted his instincts, even without knowing his destination. He walked away proud, confident, and calm.

These images reflected the transformation occurring within Dada. Visualizing the change helped him embrace these emerging aspects of himself, as he increasingly identified with the lion. He began to consider that perhaps his own "pane of glass" could be unlocked. Shortly after, Dada quit his job and began working for an American company where he felt valued and had a leading voice. Although he had been worried about his accent and status as a foreigner, in the end, they didn't matter.

Note

1 I leaned this technique, the "Reverse Spin," from Hypnotist Melissa Tiers in a video training. But it is also available for free on YouTube. Melissa Tiers, *Anti Anxiety Reverse Spin* (YouTube video, published January 4, 2018), Melissa Tiers channel. Demonstrates the "reverse spin" technique—a neuro-linguistic programming (NLP) and integrative hypnosis tool used to shift emotional states by reversing and collapsing anxiety patterns. www.youtube.com/watch?v=LVYN5OSKMXc

Reference

Tiers, M. 2018. Anti Anxiety Reverse Spin. *YouTube*, January 4. Melissa Tiers channel. www.youtube.com/watch?v=LVYN5OSKMXc.

17 Interpreting Dreams of Displacement and Belonging

> While I was sleeping, my grandmother who passed years ago crossed the veil to sit beside me. She said nothing, but I woke up with the feeling that she had come to check on me.
>
> —Anonymous contributor

In your journey to know yourself better, do not ignore the guidance your dreams can provide. Dreams can tell us so much about what we are feeling deep down. Sigmund Freud once said that "The interpretation of dreams is the royal road to a knowledge of the unconscious activities of the mind."[1] While we do not have to get too technical, our dreams offer us stories, symbols, and emotions that reflect what is happening in our lives. Dreams give us a way to talk to the parts of ourselves that we do not always pay attention to. By looking at our dreams, we can get to know ourselves better. In the following pages, I will share some simple and practical ways to help you explore your own dreams and what they might mean. While I often talk about dreams with my patients, I want to show you how you can start thinking about your dreams in a meaningful way. Dream analysis is not for everyone. Some people do not remember their dreams, and others do not feel they are important. But for many, dreams can be a helpful way to gain insight into their lives. Little by little, as you begin to explore your dreams, you might notice that different parts of yourself come through—your thoughts, emotions, memories, and even things society has taught you. All these things can come together in your dreams and help you understand yourself better.

How to Start Engaging with Your Dreams

When you wake up with a dream in mind, take a moment to think about it. What stood out to you? What emotions did you feel? Sometimes, it is the little details or feelings that can be the most revealing.

Here are some simple steps to help you reflect on your dreams:

1   *Think about the dream:* After you wake up, think about your dream. What do you remember? What parts felt most important or meaningful to you?

DOI: 10.4324/9781003648703-23

2   *Connect it to your life:* Does the dream remind you of anything happening
    in your life right now? Sometimes, our dreams reflect what we are dealing
    with emotionally, even if we are not fully aware of it.
3   *Explore your feelings:* Ask yourself, "How did I feel during the dream?
    Did I feel scared, happy, or confused?" These feelings can give you
    clues about what is going on inside.
4   *Notice recurring dreams:* If you have the same dream or similar dreams
    over and over, take note of them. Recurring dreams often show us patterns
    in our lives that we need to pay attention to.

Example: Flor's Dream

Here is an example of a dream from one of my patients, Flor:

> I dreamed I was sleeping on a straw mat by the entrance of a large,
> creaking wooden lodge. The place had many levels, but I was left near
> the door, exposed to wind and footsteps. Laughter and voices echoed
> from the upper chambers, yet no one noticed me. I felt ashamed to be
> seen like that, half-awake in public view. My grandmother passed by
> and whispered, "We must go—they've piled all our belongings in the
> hearth room." She walked off into the shadows of another corridor, and
> her voice faded. I strained to hear her, but the silence grew thick. I
> awoke trembling, gripped by a fear I could not name.

Even though you do not know much about Flor, you can probably feel her
fear and confusion. She feels out of place, uncomfortable, and unheard.
Now, if this were your dream, what might it be saying about your life?
Maybe you have felt like you are stuck somewhere you do not belong or
perhaps you have struggled to be heard in certain situations. The dream
gives us a way to explore those emotions.

When Flor and I talked about her dream, we realized it was connected to
her immigration journey. She was feeling unsettled and insecure because she
was not sure if she could stay in the US or would be forced to leave. Her
feelings of being out of place in the dream mirrored her real-life concerns
about not having a secure home. Her present feelings were also reinforced
by old feelings we had not yet processed in therapy about the ways she had
also felt unsafe and abandoned as a little girl.

Dreams as Guides for Self-Reflection

When you reflect on your own dreams, remember that they are like stories
from your inner world. You do not need to analyze them like a professional;
instead, just stay curious. Ask yourself what the dream might be saying about
how you feel or what you are going through right now. You can even ask
yourself, "What is this dream telling me about my life?" This approach can

help you connect the dream to your own life and emotions. Much like a song or a poem, dreams can resonate with you in unexpected ways.

Common Immigrant Dreams

Many immigrants have dreams that reflect their unique experiences of living between two worlds. Common themes include:

- *Feeling torn between two places:* Dreams of being "here" and "there," or not fully belonging to either place.
- *Nostalgia dreams:* Dreams about returning to childhood homes or reconnecting with loved ones left behind.
- *Anxiety dreams:* Dreams about being unprepared, lost, or overwhelmed, often mixing details from different times and places.

For example, a patient named Maya dreamt she was on a train passing by her childhood home in Greece. She was filled with joy when she saw her old house, but she woke up realizing it no longer existed. This dream reflected her deep longing for a home that was gone, and how, even though she had built a life in the US, part of her still felt connected to her past.

Phases of Immigration Dreams

As shown in Flor's dream above, themes related to the immigration experience itself often show up in the dreams of immigrants. For example, people may dream of being torn between two countries or about feeling they do not fully belong anywhere. These dreams might include memories of home, family, or even feelings of loss and grief. I spoke with my colleague, Carlos Padrón, a psychoanalyst who immigrated from Venezuela to the US, and he shared some of his own dreams during his adjustment process. At first, his dreams were filled with anxiety, often showing natural disasters like floods, which seemed to reflect the emotional turbulence of his immigration. Over time, his dreams shifted, showing more of his longing for home, such as dreams about walking through his old neighborhood or visiting family. Eventually, his dreams became more rooted in his new reality in the US. Carlos's experience shows how our dreams can change as we adjust to a new country. They can move from feelings of chaos and confusion to a deeper understanding of where we are in life, both mentally and emotionally.

Example: Laura's Dream of the Bruco Mela

Dreams often reflect how we feel about our current life situation. Here is an example from a patient named Laura:

I had a dream that I was on vacation, back in Italy. I wanted to take the fast train to the main city, but instead, I ended up on a small roller coaster. It wasn't the kind of thrilling, adult roller coaster you'd expect, but one of those slow, caterpillar-shaped ones for kids that goes through a giant apple—what we call the *Bruco Mela* [Apple Worm] in Italy. There were no proper safety belts, and the landscape was all green hills. As we rode, I noticed a fire in the distance, with trees burning in the valley. I shouted "Fire!" and we had to get off the ride. The firefighters were already there, and someone warned us not to speak so we could hide safely. I was worried about my dad, thinking, "He takes the fast train to work every day. I need to make sure he's okay."

When Laura and I discussed this dream, we realized it reflected how she felt about her life in New York City. In the dream, she wanted the fast train, a symbol of what she thought her life in the US would be, the American Dream, but she ended up on the *Bruco Mela*, a much slower, less exciting version. She had come to the US with high expectations of "making it big," but instead, she felt stuck and diminished, just like on the kiddie ride.

The fire in her dream symbolized both her fading opportunities in Italy and her concern for her aging parents. Her Italian connections now fading, given the years passed since her emigration, Laura had missed the faster, better jobs she was offered in Italy. The dream reflected her disappointment, as well as her underlying fear of losing her parents while being far away from them. At the end of our session, Laura summed up her experience with a line that perfectly captured her disillusionment and her constructive self-shielding humor: "I started my journey in the US thinking I'd be riding on the Business Class Acela, and instead I'm on the *Bruco Mela*."

Laura's dream provides a vivid metaphor for the gap between our expectations and reality. If this were your dream, what might it be saying about how you feel in your current life? How might your thoughts and feelings connect to the symbols in your dream?

Note to therapists: When patients share metaphor-rich dreams like Laura's, resist the urge to decode them too quickly. Invite the patient to explore the emotional texture, the humor, disappointment, and hope, at their own pace.

Mourning Dreams

For immigrants, one of the hardest parts of living far from home is not being able to be with loved ones when they pass away. Often, the distance makes it harder to fully process the loss. You might find yourself dreaming about the person who has died, feeling like you never got the chance to say goodbye. It's common for these dreams to reflect the disbelief and guilt that many immigrants feel when they cannot be present during a loved one's final moments.

One of my patients, Gabriel, shared a dream after his brother passed away. Gabriel had been living in the US, far from his family in France:

> I dreamt I was back in my parents' home, where I grew up. My mother greeted me at the door, and we sat down to eat. My brother was there too, looking healthy and just as he was before he got sick. We were chatting and laughing, and I felt happy and at peace. But then I woke up and remembered the painful reality—my brother is gone. The dream left me feeling sad and alone, as if I hadn't fully said goodbye.

For Gabriel, this dream was a way of holding onto his brother, especially since he had not been there for his death. It's common for immigrants to feel this lingering sense of incompleteness after the loss of a loved one. Dreams can offer a place where we reconnect with those who have passed away, but they can also bring up deep feelings of sadness and longing.

How to Honor and Process Mourning Dreams

If you have lost someone important while living far away, and you find yourself dreaming about them, it is helpful to create space to honor these dreams. Here are two exercises that you can try alone or with loved ones who share your grief:

Exercise 1: A Memorial Tablecloth

Gather a small group of family or friends who knew the person you have lost. On a special occasion, like a holiday or an anniversary, ask everyone to bring a personal story, a poem, or a memory about your loved one. Have a white tablecloth or large piece of fabric on hand, along with markers that will not wash off. As each person shares their story, invite them to write or draw something on the tablecloth in memory of the person. This might be a special word, phrase, or symbol that represents your loved one. Over time, this tablecloth becomes a shared tribute to the person you have lost, one that you can bring out each year to keep their memory alive.

Exercise 2: Shared Memory Exchange

This is a great activity to do with family and friends, even if they live far away. Take a piece of paper and divide it into sections, like a grid or four squares. In one section, write down or draw a favorite memory of your loved one. Then, mail the paper to a family member or friend, asking them to fill in another section with their memory. The paper gets passed along until all sections are filled. When it comes back to you, make copies or take a picture and share it with everyone who participated. This creates a shared keepsake that brings everyone's memories together, no matter how far apart you are.

If your dreams are bringing up memories of a loved one who has passed, it is important to recognize that this is a natural part of mourning. Dreams give us a way to reconnect, but they can also stir up emotions that are hard to face. Take your time and allow yourself to feel what comes up, whether it is sadness, guilt, or longing. These feelings are all part of healing. These exercises help create space for your grief, while honoring your loved ones in ways that feel meaningful and supportive. Over time, your mourning dreams may evolve, but these practices offer ways to stay connected to those you have lost, even from a distance.

Trauma Dreams

For some immigrants, the experience of trauma, whether it happened in their home country, during migration, or after arriving in the new country, can lead to disturbing and repetitive nightmares. These are known as trauma dreams, and they are common among people with *posttraumatic stress disorder* (PTSD). One example comes from a former combat sergeant who fled to the US as a refugee.[2] He had recurring nightmares of being chased by ghosts, which symbolized the guilt he felt for the soldiers who had died under his command. Through therapy, he confronted these "ghosts" in his dreams and found that they were his fallen soldiers simply asking him not to forget them. With the help of his community, he performed rituals to honor them, and his nightmares stopped. In another case, a refugee woman had a recurring dream of her deceased grandmother, which caused her panic. She feared that her grandmother was coming to take her away, but after exploring the dream in therapy, she began to see her grandmother's presence as a form of support rather than a threat. This shift in perspective helped in calming her nightmares.

A note for immigrants: If you are having trauma dreams or nightmares, it is important to seek help from a therapist who understands trauma. It is also important to choose a therapist who can understand or is interested to learn how dreams are seen in your culture.

A note for therapists: Dream interpretation is not for everyone. With some immigrant patients, when dreams come up, an integration of their tradition on dream interpretation and ritual use may be helpful to process their emotions. *Imagery rehearsal therapy* (IRT), also called *nightmare rescripting*, is evidence-based to help patients with PTSD and it may be helpful with some immigrants.

Interpreting and Transforming Dreams

Dreams can reflect our inner struggles, but they can also show us how we are growing and transforming over time. Sometimes, the same types of dreams repeat, but as we work on ourselves, these dreams can change, showing us new strengths and progress. One of my patients, Eddie, had a series of dreams that mirrored his journey of personal growth. Eddie had a difficult childhood in Asia, where he felt unwanted and inadequate. Later, he moved to the US and became very successful, but some of his old feelings of self-doubt followed him. He often had dreams where he felt lost or incapable, especially before important meetings at work. For example, Eddie frequently dreamt about being back in school, unable to find the exam room or being given the wrong test, leaving him feeling anxious and out of control. These dreams were always mixed with elements from his new life in the US, like American buildings or places from his home country. Over time, these dreams began to change as Eddie started to gain confidence.

Eddie's Dream Theme of Cars

One major theme in Eddie's dreams was cars. At first, he often dreamt that he was a passenger in a car, lacking any control and having scary rides. This symbolized how he felt in his waking life, like he was not in control of where he was going. But as Eddie started working on his self-esteem, his dreams began to shift.

In later dreams, Eddie was the one driving the car. At first, he struggled to control the vehicle, having trouble finding the brake pedal or steering. This showed that while he was starting to take charge of his life, he still needed practice managing his emotions and responsibilities. As time went on, his dreams became more positive. He began to dream of negotiating where to go with the people in the car, instead of just following their directions. In another dream, he stood up to his parents, who were telling him where to drive. He raised his voice and insisted on making his own decisions. Eventually, Eddie dreamt of riding a motorbike—a symbol of freedom and independence. Although he worried about not having the right paperwork for the bike, he confidently explained himself to the police in the dream, and they let him go. This marked a turning point where Eddie began to feel more secure in his decisions and more in control of his life.

As Eddie worked on his self-confidence and sense of worth, his dreams shifted from feelings of helplessness to a growing sense of control. In the beginning, Eddie was always the passive passenger, but by the end, he was confidently in the driver's seat of his own life. His dreams became a mirror of his real-world progress as he stopped trying to please everyone and started taking charge of his own path. For example, in one of his final dreams, Eddie was driving a beautiful convertible, feeling completely at ease. He was no longer worried about others' expectations or rushing to meet anyone's demands. Instead, he drove at his own pace, feeling free and confident. This transformation in Eddie's dreams showed how far he had come; his dreams reflected how he felt in his life. He no longer felt the need to be perfect, and he began to trust his own judgment and enjoy life more fully. His driving the convertible in his dream captured not only how much control he now felt over his life, but also his sense of ease, his pride in his transformation, and how much he was enjoying it.

Dreams often change as we grow and heal. If you are noticing patterns in your dreams, pay attention to how they evolve over time. You might start with feelings of fear or confusion, but as you gain confidence in your waking life, your dreams can shift to reflect your inner strength and growth. If you are going through a tough time, remember that your dreams can be a tool for understanding what is going on beneath the surface. They can show you where you feel stuck and also where you're starting to move forward.

Dreams can be a powerful way to explore your inner world, especially if you are dealing with big changes like immigration or trauma. They can help you understand what is going on beneath the surface and guide you toward healing. As you work with your dreams, remember that they are a tool for self-discovery. Whether your dreams reflect anxiety, longing, or healing, they are showing you something important about your emotional world.

How to Use Your Dreams for Self-Discovery

You can start using your dreams to learn more about yourself by doing these simple things:

- *Write down your dreams:* As soon as you wake up, jot down your dream or record it as a voice memo. This will help you remember the details later.
- *Reflect on your emotions:* How did you feel in the dream? What might those feelings be telling you about your life right now?
- *Connect the dots:* Think about whether your dream is connected to any recent experiences, emotions, or challenges you're facing.
- *Stay open:* Sometimes, even if a dream does not seem to make sense right away, it can still offer insight if you give it time.

When you have your dream written down, take a moment and ask yourself these questions:

- What is my dream telling me about my life right now?
- How do the emotions in the dream connect to what I'm feeling during the day?
- Does this dream remind me of anything that is happening in my life?
- What are the recurring themes in my dreams?
- What might I learn from these patterns?

By engaging with your dreams, you can discover more about yourself and your inner world. Just like any journey, it takes time, but each dream can offer a new piece of the puzzle.

The Dream Circle, a Group Dream Exercise

The Dream Circle is a practice that I have learned from Jill Hammer, a Rabbi in New York, but it has been practiced by therapists and healers across different traditions. You gather in a circle, with the shared intention of supporting one another and also learning about yourselves. You volunteer a dream without offering personal associations or referencing their history, current life, or future concerns. You repeat the dream, so everyone has a chance to absorb it. Then, have each person in the circle share their thoughts about the dream, starting with, "If this were my dream, this dream would be about…" They then describe how they interpret the dream as if it were their own. To keep it safe and respectful, they do not analyze or interpret your dream or ask personal questions. Instead, participants reflect on what the dream would mean for them personally, if they had dreamt it; they mention a feeling, an image, a song, or anything that the dream has brought up for them. This keeps the exercise non-intrusive and safe for you, and shifts the focus onto each group member's personal discovery.

How to Try This on Your Own

Even if you are working by yourself, you can still apply this technique to your own dreams. Here's how:

1 *Write down your dream:* After you wake up, take a few minutes to jot down the dream while it's still fresh in your mind.
2 *Reflect on the dream:* Step back from your own dream and look at it as though it belongs to someone else. Then, ask yourself, "If this were my dream, what would this dream be about?"
3 *Explore new perspectives:* This distance helps you notice new meanings or connections you might not have seen before, giving you fresh insight into your emotions or life situations.

By doing this, you might discover layers of meaning in your dreams that were not obvious at first, and it gives you a respectful way to work with dreams in groups or on your own.

Tonight, as you prepare for sleep, you might set an intention to welcome any dreams that wish to visit you. Whether you remember them or not, trust that your mind is speaking to you in the language of images, feelings, and symbols.

Notes

1 Sigmund Freud, *The Interpretation of Dreams*, trans. James Strachey, in *The Standard Edition of the Complete Psychological Works of Sigmund Freud*, vol. 4 (London: Hogarth Press, 1953), ix–627.
2 This and the following dreams are taken from Joseph Westermeyer and Jerome Kroll, in "Handling Cultural Differences Between Patient and Clinician" in *Migrant*

Psychiatry, ed. Dinesh Bhugra (Oxford: Oxford University Press, 2021), 459–465. Dream of the sergeant and the ghosts: 460–461. Dream of the woman and her grandmother: 461.

References

Freud, Sigmund. 1953. The Interpretation of Dreams. Translated and edited by James Strachey. Vol. 4 of *The Standard Edition of the Complete Psychological Works of Sigmund Freud*. London: Hogarth Press.
Westermeyer, Joseph, and Jerome Kroll. 2021. "Handling Cultural Differences Between Patient and Clinician." In *Migrant Psychiatry*, edited by Dinesh Bhugra, 459–465. Oxford: Oxford University Press.

18 Mindfulness and Creative Tools for Immigrant Healing

Focus Lens Exercise

In 1987, the photographer Bernard Plossu took a black-and-white picture called *Sur l'île de Stromboli*.[1] Take a pause from reading now and search this picture online. Take the time to explore the picture, without distractions. What do you see? How do you react to this picture? Consider the way the artist created its composition, notice the effect it has on you. What story can you make of the mother and child, based on the composition? Chances are, a lot of what you see in the picture speaks of yourself, your sensitivity, history, point of view, and, perhaps, of your fantasies, fears, and desires. If you do this exercise as a group, what other people see in it may also be interesting and useful to you.

After examining the photo and free associating to it, you could also consider this interpretation. I'm not offering it to direct your thoughts, but to provide another perspective. An observer might notice that, although the photo depicts a landscape, it's formatted vertically, like a portrait. The focus is on a tree-covered mountain, with volcanic smoke or clouds in the sky. In the foreground, on the far right, a blurred woman and child stand at the guardrail of a ferry, facing the camera. The sea separates them from the mountain. The viewer might wonder why the mountain is sharply focused, while the people are blurred—who is the real subject here?

The woman and child seem suspended between places, neither here nor there. In an online Narrative Medicine class I attended, the focus was on this picture. Many students, including myself, saw it as a metaphor for immigration and being between worlds, reflecting on family history and heritage. Does this interpretation resonate with you? Use the image as a way to reflect on immigration and dual belonging. What might the woman be feeling? Does she remind you of anyone? Add this perspective to your toolkit for exploring art and situations in new ways.

Alternatively, instead of using a ready-made image, you can create your own collage or drawing of your own immigration experience. Consider its temporal and geographical dimensions and ways of expressing emotions visually. Use scraps and images from your country of origin and the US.

DOI: 10.4324/9781003648703-24

Place yourself within the collage in a way that makes sense to you, that is, pushed to the corner, front and center, either whole or in pieces. Where should you put the elements from your land of origin/heritage and the ones from the land where you live now? What should be in focus and what should be fuzzy? Who is there with you and who isn't?

You can also decide to explore this collage/drawing as a work-in-progress, with representations of your past, present, and future—a type of vision board related to your present and history.

Hands-On Experiment: The River of Life

This exercise is designed to help you locate yourself in the world and understand how your life is embedded in family, cultural, and social dynamics. You can do it alone, with a partner, or in a group. Each person should work individually and then set aside time to share their reflections with others.

Start by drawing a winding river (Appendix B). Imagine your life as a river, beginning at a mountain or lake and flowing downward. What rivulets or springs fed your river in its early stages? What rocks, rapids, dams, tributaries, lifeboats, forks, or hidden undercurrents have shaped your course? Add dates and a short phrase next to each feature, if helpful. Note the emotional or historical events they represent. Who were the important people at each turn? What broader social or political forces were at play? The River of Life uses symbols of nature to represent both events and emotions, reminding us that life is fluid and ever-changing. It shows us that while the path may be winding and difficult, as long as there is water, there is life—and where there is life, there is possibility. See Figure 18.1 for Jennifer's River of Life.

Alternatives to the River of Life Exercise

The Life Map

If rivers are not your metaphor, you might try creating a Life Map. Your Life Map does not need to be linear. You can use drawing, collage, photography, even real maps. Follow your intuition. Let images, routes, places, and landmarks come together in a way that expresses your journey.

The Soundscape

You can also build a Life Soundscape, using not only words but also music and sound bites. Are there songs that marked important chapters of your life? What sounds would go into this soundscape that remind you of home, of migration, of grief, or joy? Creating your soundscape may give you new access to your story.

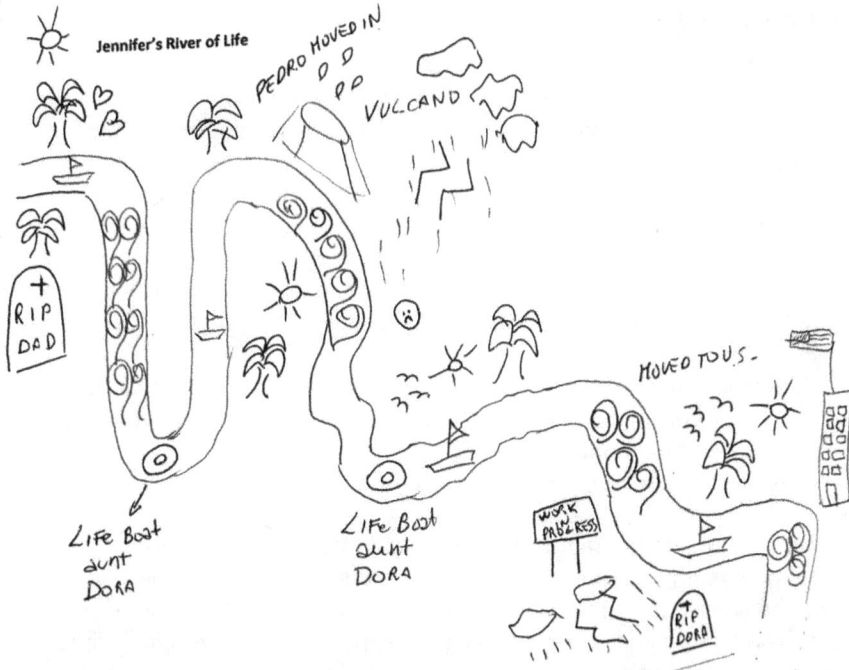

Jennifer, a 21-year-old Mexican woman, drafted her "River of Life" at the start of therapy. She marked significant events that shaped her journey. Her life began in a "sunny place," but her father's death at age three created a "waterfall" of grief that deeply affected her family. Her aunt's arrival brought temporary relief, but things worsened when her mother started dating an angry, controlling man. When her aunt left, Jennifer felt alone, angry, and scared. A "life boat" came when her aunt returned after the man left, allowing Jennifer to thrive in school and with friends. However, the river took a sharp turn when Jennifer, her mother, and her aunt immigrated to the U.S., leaving behind her community. She faced many challenges, including language barriers, bullying, and financial hardship. Eventually, a new period of comfort came, with support from older Mexican immigrants and a nurturing teacher who helped her regain confidence. But another "waterfall" appeared: her beloved aunt passed away, leaving Jennifer in deep mourning. She currently feels stuck, unable to envision a future.

Figure 18.1 Jennifer's River of Life. Jennifer Is a Young Mexican Immigrant

The Tactile Lifeline

If you prefer a more physical experience, you can try building a Tactile Lifeline, as used in *narrative exposure therapy* (NET)[2]. Lay out a long rope to represent time. Place symbolic items, such as stones, flowers, photos, objects, along the rope to mark life events. You may move around to create it and invite others to do the same. This turns your story into a temporary sculpture.

Where trauma is present, NET reminds us that our personal stories are also political. Creating and sharing your lifeline can offer both emotional relief and testimony. What happened to you matters. Witnessing and being witnessed are powerful acts of healing—and resistance. An account of witnessing that attests to what has happened or is happening might help hold people accountable and may help prevent this from happening to others.

Culinary Biographies: The Dish and Soundscape Ritual[3]

This is a multilayered creative process that engages all the senses, as well as both the conscious and unconscious parts of the mind. I experienced it as part of a group project whose ultimate goal was to create a sensory meal that tells a story—a story that transcends language and can be shared not only by the person who creates the dish, but by all those who experience it.

As Adele Madau, the creator of this project, said in the workshop: "Without senses we would not have memory; each dish is a tiny dramaturgical work." This process helps us reclaim our memories and offers a way to process and share them with others. Each participant was invited to:

- Develop a recipe that reflects a part of their personal or cultural story.
- Create a corresponding soundscape: a mix of recorded sounds, music, and spoken elements.
- Prepare and share the dish with the group.

Unlike a traditional narrative, no one told the story in words. Instead, the story was expressed through taste, smell, color, texture, and sound. The shape of the food, the spices used, the way it was served, alongside the audio accompaniment, created an immersive and layered experience. The resulting ritual was deeply emotional and transformative. Emotions flowed freely and were shared in a space that moved beyond language. Each soundscape was carefully attuned to the story behind the dish. The soundscapes varied but included the following:

- The sounds of cooking or preparation.
- Field recordings—such as fishermen casting their nets or rice farmers singing traditional songs.
- Voices of loved ones.
- Poetry recited in one's native language.
- Music that evoked a place, a time, a loss, or a celebration.

I can imagine this process being adapted for families in grief, or for groups of immigrants processing nostalgia, love, longing, and loss. I first experienced it in a group setting, but I believe it could also be facilitated one-on-one. Because this process engages multiple emotional registers at once, it must be guided with care, especially when trauma is present.

A Word on Process and Safety

As you work on these exercises, check in with yourself. If your journey holds deep grief or trauma, you may want to pause and process. Take breaks. Ask for support. There is no need to rush. You can return to the exercise at another time. If a memory feels too difficult, you can mark it with a symbol and revisit it later, when you feel ready.

Note for individuals with trauma: Especially if your trauma involves food, family, or sensory input, this activity may feel intense or even triggering. You may wish to approach it gently, with flexibility, or skip it entirely in favor of other expressive methods like drawing, music, or collage.

Group Example: Martha Bragin's Life Map Exercise

My colleague Martha Bragin, who works with migrants around the world, uses a version of the Life Map in her group work. Martha covers the floor with poster paper and distributes chalks and crayons. Participants are teen-agers and adults, and each person draws their map with the paper in front of them. Each member presents their story by stepping into the center of the room, then invites the next person to do the same.

Three Worlds of Values Exercise

As a person living between cultures, the values of each culture may have become more visible to you. This exercise will help you clearly identify which values are most important to you, what is important to retain from your country of origin and what is important to integrate into your new adopted country. Take a piece of regular size paper and fold it vertically into three columns. Now open it. On the left, create a list of the most important values in your culture of origin. On the right, list the most important values of your culture of adoption. Circle in both columns the most important values for you, and reflect upon why they are important to you. Now, record those circled values in the center column. If there are any values you want to add that are not very important in either culture, but are important to you, also add them in the center column. From this center column, you can create a statement of purpose in which you state to yourself what's crucial for you.

You may be aware of many values, some that have been consciously imparted in each culture. There are the values you absorb unconsciously, only recognizing them when they clash with new ones or when the two cultures collide. There are also values in each culture that cause you pain. You often become aware of these values within a culture only when you feel their impact. Those are the values that may not work well for you. You need to figure out how to approach them so you can be more comfortable. For instance, a value that I am becoming increasingly aware of is how youth is praised and old age is disparaged in the US. Given that aging is unavoidable, I am in the process of figuring out how to age happily despite the cultural disparagement of aging and diminishment of older adults in the country. The more you become bicultural, the more the values of each culture will become visible to you. The more you have a grasp on these values, the more you will be able to negotiate where you want to place yourself in relation to them.

Now consider whether you are living according to your most important values. If not, what are the impediments to doing so? Are the impediments internal, external, or both? This internal dialogue about values can become an ongoing topic of reflection, helping you to live in accordance with your values.

Table 18.1 shows a *Three Worlds of Values* exercise completed by Tiffany, one of my second-generation Asian American patients. This reflective work began in session and was later continued as a take-home assignment. In it, she explored her experience of living between cultures—navigating life as the daughter of immigrants, among other immigrants and U.S.-born Americans.

The exercise invites patients to articulate the values they associate with three spheres: their culture of origin, the dominant culture they live in, and their personal emerging identity. Notably, at the time we discussed the exercise, some columns were more fully developed than others, highlighting where Tiffany's attention and internal conflicts were most active.

This type of values work is open-ended and can be revisited or adapted over time. The next step in the process would be to craft a values-based statement that feels authentic to her, and to begin exploring how to live those values in everyday life. This process often helps patients clarify priorities, reduce internal conflict, and begin to feel more aligned in both cultural and personal dimensions of identity. See Appendix C for a template that you can use.

Tiffany's *Three Worlds of Values* exercise revealed the internal tug-of-war many second-generation patients experience as they navigate inherited, dominant, and emerging values. On one side, she carried the expectations of her Asian heritage—putting family first, providing financial support, conforming to strict gender roles, and avoiding open discussions about mental health or emotions. On the other, she was surrounded by American cultural norms that prioritize individual independence, emotional openness, and personal choice. As she began to name her own values, Tiffany found herself somewhere in between: wanting to honor her family but also needing space to define her own boundaries, beliefs, and ways of being.

What struck me in our discussion was how the exercise helped Tiffany begin to separate what she was taught from what she truly believes. It was not about rejecting her culture, but about making space for complexity—recognizing that some inherited values no longer fit, and others need to be reimagined. The chart was uneven at first, with some columns fuller than others, but that imbalance gave us a starting point. Over time, Tiffany began shaping a more coherent and authentic sense of self, grounded in her lived experience and evolving identity. Exercises like this are open-ended by design; they offer not just insight but direction for how to live more closely aligned with one's values, even when those values span multiple worlds.

Table 18.1 Tiffany's Three Worlds: Asian, American, and Personal Values

Cultural Heritage Values	My Values	American Values
Putting family first no matter what circumstance you're in	Prioritizing own financial responsibilities	Parents in nursing homes
Being family's financial support when you finally become financially independent	Placing financial boundaries with friends, family, and boyfriend	Independence (out of parent's home as soon as possible as adults)
Sending money to relatives at home	Making own choices about that	
Parents want their children to be doctors, nurses, engineers, or professors	Parents can give counsel, but children should be able to have a say	Careers in arts and music are ok
Catholicism, religion. Poor mental health = not close enough to God	I don't believe in God. Resentment toward religion; Inability to open up about not being religious around family	
Not pro-choice	Pro-choice	
Mental health doesn't exist	Mental illness is not due to lack of religious beliefs and should be treated like physical injury; parents should take their children's feelings seriously	Mental health is proper
Women always doing household chores. Mom scolding me for not cleaning enough but always cleaning after my brother	Household chores and responsibilities are to be equally split	
Beauty standards: Pale skin, thin body. No muscular figure. Body shaming, colorism		
Blunt communication		
Always respecting authority		
Parents are authority figures, not friends. No talking to their children about their feelings		
Acts of service		

Often, it is hard to think of values in the abstract. Therefore, I use "value cards," with my patients; you can purchase them or get free printable versions online. These cards help patients reflect on whether the values in the cards are present in each of the cultures to which they belong. Often, my patients add values that are not included in the original printouts. I add these patient-found values to my deck, and my other patients often appreciate those fresh contributions. I often use value cards with couples in therapy. I give each of them a set of cards, ordered by numbers, so we are all on the same page, and I keep one set for myself. Then one of us names the value on the cards and each of them puts the card in one of four pre-established columns: 1) Very Important, 2) Important, 3) Somewhat Important, or 4) Not Important. We all become aware of the choices of each partner. Then we go to the next card on the deck, until we finish the whole deck. We may add additional personal values.

Then, by looking at the overall composition of the rows, we can have a clear visual of what is important for a person and how invested they are in their values. There are people, for instance, who end up with a very long list of "very important" and almost nothing that is unimportant. They are very passionate about everything. However, it is useful to identify top priorities among all those values. No one can focus on everything at once. I usually ask them to reduce the list to the five or ten most important values. This is done by comparing two cards at a time, selecting one, or choosing the card that best reflects their values to help narrow down the choices. Alternatively, I may ask them to build, out of the multitude they have selected, a few sets that contain values with similar characteristics, such as family, love, giving, commitment, faithfulness.

Lastly, they create a statement that defines who they are and what they want to do in the world based on their values. The experience sheds a critical spotlight on what is really important for each person. A deeper understanding of one's own most and least important values (as well as those of a partner) helps assess whether the individual or couple are living in alignment with their values. If they are not, it is useful to ask why not. This exercise reveals why conflicts may arise and addresses misalignments.

As you move through these exercises, notice what comes up emotionally, physically, or imaginatively. Whether you are doing this work for yourself or in the company of others, these practices are an invitation to connect more deeply with your own story and values. For therapists, they may offer new ways to meet patients where words fall short. For immigrants and all those in transition, they can be a reminder that your path matters, your voice matters, and even in silence, you are not alone.

Facilitating These Exercises in Practice—For Therapists and Facilitators

If you are guiding others through these exercises, whether in individual therapy, a group, or a community setting, consider the following guidelines to support safety and emotional integration:

- Create a safe container. Let participants know that they can pause at any time, use symbols instead of direct disclosures, or skip elements that feel overwhelming. Be clear about confidentiality and pacing.
- Prepare clients emotionally. Some exercises may evoke memories, grief, or complex feelings. Offer grounding tools before and after, and allow time to process whatever emerges, verbally or non-verbally.
- Follow up after creative expression. Ask open-ended questions like, "What was that like for you?" or "What surprised you?" Allow meaning to emerge organically rather than interpreting too quickly.
- Stay attuned to trauma responses. Watch for signs of dissociation, shut-down, or overwhelm. If trauma surfaces, slow the pace, reorient to the present, and offer containment. Adapt or pause as needed.
- These practices are not about completing a task; they are about making space for exploration, connection, and healing.

Reflect and Integrate

Reflections for Immigrant Readers

Having done these exercises, reflect on them by asking yourself the following questions:

- What did I learn about myself through these exercises?
- Which medium (visual, tactile, sensory, verbal) felt most natural? Most surprising?

Reflection for Therapists

If you are a clinician or facilitator, what ideas from this chapter might you bring into your work and with whom? You might also consider how your own frameworks influence your work. As therapists, we each carry implicit models of time and story, which are often inherited from our culture, training, or personal experiences. Do you imagine life as a straight line? A circle? A spiral? A journey with milestones? A series of disruptions? These frameworks can unconsciously shape the way we listen and what we expect from a patient's story. Take a moment to reflect on the following questions:

- What metaphors of time do I gravitate toward?
- How do these affect my understanding of progress, healing, or integration?
- Am I open to stories that do not resolve?
- Can I sit with a patient's sense of being stuck, fragmented, or suspended?

Notes

1 This photo can also be found in Bernard Plossu, *L'odyssée des petites îles italiennes* (Paris: Édition Textuel, 2024), www.editionstextuel.com/livre/lodyssee_des_petites_iles_italiennes. The exercise using Plossu's photo was introduced in a Narrative Medicine Program Zoom class, taught in Italian by Carly Slater on March 6, 2021, hosted by Columbia University's Department of Medical Humanities and Ethics, www.mhe.cuimc.columbia.edu/education/narrative-medicine.
2 *Schauer, Maggie, Frank Neuner, and Thomas Elbert. 2011. Narrative Exposure Therapy: A Short-Term Treatment for Traumatic Stress Disorders. 2nd revised and expanded edition. Göttingen: Hogrefe Publishing, 43.*
3 I learned this process in August 2024 at a yearly retreat for Sardinian immigrants and people of Sardinian Heritage, *Disterraus* (www.disterra.us), created by Valeria Orani Creator and Creative Producer (https://valeriaorani.com) and held in the village of Rebeccu, Sardinia. The workshop *Biografie culinarie suoni e sapori* was created and facilitated by Adele Madau, chef, musician, and composer (www.instagram.com/adelemadau), with the collaboration of Cristina Marras, podcast producer and radio journalist (www.cristinamarras.com).

Reference

Plossu, Bernard. 2024. *L'odyssée des petites îles italiennes*. Paris: Édition Texturel.
Schauer, Maggie, Frank Neuner, and Thomas Elbert. 2011. Narrative Exposure Therapy: A Short-Term Treatment for Traumatic Stress Disorders. 2nd revised and expanded edition. Göttingen: Hogrefe Publishing.

Part VI

Reframing and Organizing

Sometimes I feel like a juggler in a windstorm—just as I manage to catch one ball, another slips through my fingers. I rush to keep everything in the air, but the more I try, the more the chaos grows. It is exhausting to hold it all together.
—Anonymous contributor

19 Challenging Biases with CBT Therapy

"People generally see what they look for and hear what they listen for," Harper Lee wrote in *To Kill a Mockingbird*. This is vividly illustrated in the story of Sofia, a South American woman in her 30s who came to see me in therapy. She told me:[1]

> Last week I was so down and anxious, I could not even sleep. My boss removed me from the team even after one of the teammates had asked specifically that I be added. He told me to work on another project all by myself. When he said that, my heart sunk. "What's wrong with me?" I thought. "Am I such a bother to the group? Am I slowing them down? Is it my English?" I thought I was put on a bench and was gonna be fired anytime. I could not sleep for days. Then I mustered the courage and asked him why. He said that the other team did not need that many "Unicorns." He said he assigned me to the other project because I can work independently. I don't need to be babysat. I am coming to realize it's true I have wrong assumptions. Good thing I asked.

In Sofia's initial interpretation, she assumed she was about to be fired. This fear was amplified by her lingering insecurity about speaking English as a second language and by prior experiences of being overlooked or excluded in professional settings as an immigrant. Like many who migrate, she had learned to brace herself for bad news and expect dismissal. However, in this case, her assumptions did not reflect the facts: Her manager had actually shown how much he trusted and appreciated her. Previously, she would have withdrawn into despair, but this time, she was able to confront her manager. Sofia demonstrated significant progress.

To help Sofia reach this milestone, I used CBT, which helps people gain an objective interpretation of the facts. CBT focuses on the connection between thoughts, feelings, and behavior. These three elements feed into one another in a reinforcing loop. When thoughts become bleak, mood goes down, and as a result, behavior becomes increasingly unaccommodating. Therefore, it is important to question the validity of your thoughts, by using an objective, rigorous, simple framework. If there are distortions, reframe

DOI: 10.4324/9781003648703-26

them. If there is no distortion and the thoughts are accurate, then work on acceptance, by creating a doable plan to change what can be changed. The more you look at your thoughts in a systematic way, the easier it becomes to recognize distortions, reframe your thoughts, and lift your mood. For best results, practice examining your thoughts as soon as you notice a negative shift in them; by doing so, you persuade the logical and benign parts of yourself to enter the ring before the harsh and biased parts become too strong.

When I met Juana, a Latina patient, she was depleted, depressed, and in a relationship with someone she felt was sucking the life out of her. Additionally, her family of origin expected her to do most of the emotional labor; that is, she was expected to understand, manage, and accommodate everybody's emotions. Also, she had two demanding low-paying jobs. She was frustrated but continued to operate on automatic pilot.

Through our CBT work, she took time to stop, feel, and think about her predicament. When she spoke about her situation aloud to me, she also, for the first time, listened to herself speak about the circumstances; she heard it clearly. And when she journaled about it, she saw it in black and white. She had grown so accustomed to impingements that she felt they were the status quo. But after a careful objective look, she began to feel how burdensome the weight that she carried was and decided that she did not like the trajectory of her life. Some of those demands could not be easily changed. For instance, she needed to continue to work at a strenuous pace because she needed the money and lacked qualifications for higher-paying work. However, she had family and cultural obligations for which she needed to find a workable compromise.

More realizations were revealed through our work. She had always thought of herself as a giving person, but she discovered that her generous spirit was only part of the story. In fact, she learned that with her generosity, she was attempting to control her loved ones, ensuring they would never leave her. Her fear of abandonment and need to accommodate and please were responses to childhood trauma. After considerable time and work in therapy (with CBT as well as with other modalities), Juana stopped justifying unconstructive behavior. She expressed a desire to learn a new way of relating to others. In turn, she reclaimed her space. She set boundaries, left the mismatched partner, and set what she considered reasonable limits in relation to her family of origin.

Some of the time that she regained was spent on strategizing ways to increase her income, and to do so with a fulfilling job. Her family protested. They were comfortable with old Juana, not this new "disrespectful" and "self-centered" Juana. But Juana had decided her terms, for herself.

It's important to note here that Juana took significant risks in setting these new boundaries with her family. She risked losing them and being isolated from the family and culture that she loved. They protested, claiming that she was becoming "stand offish" and "different." Needless to say, she did not want to be alone. But, if we think about her situation as if it were a garden, Juana was like an unkempt garden, where people stepped without care. She wanted to be a cherished plant among other plants; therefore, she needed more soil and sun to prosper. Her energy and mood improved. She eventually met a new loving partner. Her family, also, eventually came to appreciate her even with her new independence. She began tending to her life like a garden: clearing space, protecting what was growing, and choosing what to nurture.

Note to the Therapists

While CBT has been shown to be effective with some immigrant populations, it may not be appropriate for everyone. In particular, patients from cultures where spiritual, communal, or hierarchical values influence one's sense of agency may not resonate with CBT's emphasis on individual autonomy and personal empowerment. Let the patient explore if CBT is right for them and if it supports their goals and values. Juana was already navigating life between cultures and had begun to question some traditional expectations. She embraced CBT and benefited from having her feelings about multiple demands and expectations explored and validated. Ask yourself the following as you consider using CBT with some of your immigrant patients:

- Have you noticed resistance to CBT in your cross-cultural work? How do you typically respond?
- What assumptions do you carry about agency and autonomy?

Takeaway Exercise

Whether you are new to CBT or familiar with its tools, this metaphor may help you reflect on your mental and emotional climate. The image of gardening can be helpful when taking charge of your mental health. Think of your mind as a garden you can tend. There is the soil, with its riches and limitations. There are also external elements to contend with, such as the weather or predatory bugs, but you can still navigate these factors. For instance, if you automatically lean toward negative distortions, such as catastrophizing or thinking in simple terms of black and white, become vigilant and check your inner weather forecast often. If necessary, prepare your garden for heavy rains and freezing temperatures. If your mood or behavior changes for the worse, for example, you find yourself overeating or oversleeping, examine the content of your mind to check what you are reacting to and ask yourself these questions:

1   Are the negative thoughts increasing?
2   Am I doing new and more challenging projects?
3   Am I associating with toxic people?

4   Are there things I can weed out, or fences I should install?
5   How about some burlap to protect my plantings from the cold winter?
6   Do I need to water or boost the soil with some friendly outings, therapy, or meditation fertilizer?
7   Has my garden been exposed to pests?
8   Do I need sticks and raffia to sustain my new, healthy habits?
9   Is my garden getting enough sun exposure?

Acknowledge to yourself, and to others, the good things that are happening in your garden. And remember to tend to your garden regularly.

Note

1 Harper Lee, *To Kill a Mockingbird* (New York: J. B. Lippincott & Co., 1960).

References

Lee, Harper. 1960. *To Kill a Mockingbird*. New York: J. B. Lippincott & Co.

20 The Nine-Lens Reflective Tool
A Culturally Aware Framework

For Therapists

As Aaron Beck, the founder of cognitive therapy, noted, "The Stronger person is not the one making the most noise but the one who can quietly direct the conversation toward defining and solving the problem."[1] Although this chapter is primarily intended for immigrant readers, therapists may find the sociocultural and historical extensions of the Thought Record, which is a core cognitive therapy tool, particularly valuable in broadening clinical insight and cultural responsiveness. This culturally expanded version of the traditional Thought Record—what I call the *Nine-Lens Reflective Tool*—adds critical reflections on history, family, and society. The traditional Thought Record includes structured prompts for identifying the situation, emotional responses, automatic thoughts, cognitive distortions, alternative perspectives, and reevaluated emotional intensity.[2] The Nine-Lens tool builds on this cognitive foundation by incorporating historical/psychodynamic dimensions, such as formative relational patterns, sociocultural contexts, including systemic pressures and cultural identity, and a final action plan to support meaningful change. These additions allow for a more layered and contextually grounded reflection, especially useful in therapeutic work with immigrants and others navigating complex experiences of displacement, identity conflict, or marginalization.

Consider how you might integrate cultural awareness into standard CBT techniques and how to support clients in recognizing both internal psychological patterns and external sociocultural forces. This broader lens can help clients reframe distress in ways that honor their lived realities, not just their thoughts.

Our thoughts can easily spiral out of control, especially when we're faced with stress, anxiety, or overwhelming situations. Unchecked, these thoughts can distort our perception, cloud our judgment, and fuel negative emotions. That's why having a tool to organize and manage them is crucial. The Nine-Lens Reflective Tool is a powerful way to bring structure to your thoughts and emotions, helping you make sense of them when they feel chaotic.

There are many versions of the Thought Record, but the modification presented here is adapted from the work of Judith Beck, with additional

DOI: 10.4324/9781003648703-27

insights on family, history, and sociocultural influences (see Table 20.1 and Appendix D). The key to its effectiveness lies in writing it down, rather than simply thinking through the process in your head. Putting your thoughts into words provides clarity and structure, allowing you to approach overwhelming emotions more calmly. The Nine-Lens Reflective Tool offers several important benefits:

- *Creating order:* It helps you organize your thoughts and feelings, breaking down the complexity of emotional experiences into clearer, more manageable parts. This structured process can act as a grounding tool when emotions start to feel out of control.
- *Providing a tangible reference:* Having a written record gives you something concrete to refer to when you feel lost or overwhelmed. This physical format helps you make sense of emotional storms, offering stability in the midst of chaos.
- *Challenging distorted thinking:* Writing down your thoughts allows you to see where biases or cognitive distortions might be influencing your feelings. This process helps you step back and view situations more objectively, enabling you to reframe your thoughts with greater clarity.
- *Focusing on solutions:* By separating irrational thoughts from real concerns, the Nine-Lens Reflective Tool allows you to focus on the key issues that need addressing. This clarity empowers you to take meaningful steps toward solutions, rather than getting stuck in unproductive rumination.
- *Exploring external influences:* This version also encourages reflection on how family dynamics and societal pressures shape your thoughts and emotions. It helps you to recognize that while these external factors may contribute to challenges, they may also provide potential solutions.
- *A self-guided tool:* Although it can't replace a therapist, the Nine-Lens Reflective Tool provides a framework that mimics the therapeutic process. It gives you a structured way to work through difficult emotions when professional support isn't immediately available.

The Nine-Lens Reflective Tool is formatted on a page structured in nine rows to help sort out experiences in a systematized way. Same as a traditional Thought Record, in the first three rows you: (1) document the situation, then

Table 20.1 Nine-Lens Reflective Tool

Situation	Feelings/ body sensations	Immediate thoughts	Investigating & reframing	Family history	Intersectionalities/sociocultural realities	Balanced perspective/new mantra	Updated feelings/ bodily sensations	Action plan

(2) indicate your feelings, and (3) record your thoughts and images related to the situation_that is, your immediate interpretation of what occurred. In the fourth, fifth, and sixth rows, you switch gears. Step back and, at some distance, suspend your full immersion in your thoughts and feelings, and seek out evidence of your immediate perception as if you were an external investigator, a defense lawyer (4). The next two columns are an expansion of the traditional Thought Record. You expand beyond the cognitive inquiry— as a social scientist, you weigh the situation from multiple perspectives. You then reflect on the family and transgenerational history (5), to grasp what dynamics have contributed to your ways of seeing and behaving. You consider the sociocultural realities (6) that influence your perceptions, emotional responses, the barriers you face, and areas where you may feel stuck. In the seventh, eighth, and ninth rows, you reassess and create a new coping strategy and action plan.

Let's do a Nine-Lens Reflective Tool together (use the template in Appendix D). However, at the beginning, if you are new to this type of work, I suggest you start with the classic version; that is, do rows 1, 2, 3, 4, and 8 (skip 5, 6, 7, and 9).

After you become adept with the basic steps of reframing (4), you can add the other rows for a wider view that connects your experience with your family dynamics, history, and society. Pause for a moment and consider a situation that causes you sadness, anxiety, or other bothersome feelings; then sort out your experience into these nine rows:

Situation (Row 1)

In the first row, note the date and time, and write a brief description of the event that triggered the negative feelings: what, who, when, and where.

Feelings/Body Sensations (Row 2)

In the second row, enter the feelings and body sensations (with a rating of 1–100) that are associated with this event. Is there a stomachache, butterflies in the stomach, or other feelings?

Thoughts and Images (Row 3)

In the third row, enter the thoughts and images you experienced during the event. Because of their emotional intensity, negative thoughts feel believable and real; moreover, images can be even more powerful than thoughts, as they can make you feel as if you are in the imagined situation. For every thought, enter enough material to describe what was occurring in your mind and to recall the issue in the future. You want to clearly document the experience so that you can compare your entry to subsequent entries in the Nine-Lens Reflective Tool. You want to discover patterns and record change.

Investigating and Reframing (Row 4)

Below are the types of questions you ask to yourself in Row 4. The fourth row is where big change starts to take place. Use the questions below to inquire into the thoughts reported in Row 3 and respond here in Row 4:

- What's the evidence this thought is true?
- What's the evidence of the contrary?
- Could there be an alternative explanation?
- What's the best, worst, and most likely scenario?
- If the worst-case scenario happens, would I be able to survive it?
- If it were my friend, partner, or child in my place, thinking this way, what would I tell them?
- Are these thoughts helping me reach my goals?

Relevant Family History (Row 5)

In the fifth row, record any relevant family history that has helped shape your way of thinking and behaving. In essence, consider how you see your current struggle as connected and perhaps also, at least in part, determined by your history and family dynamics, including the previous generations that may have had issues of mental illness, poverty, trauma, addiction, stigmatization, and subordination, to name a few. Reflect on how your family of origin and early upbringing affect your feelings, your thoughts, and your choices. For example, you can note here if you have a temperament similar (or contrary) to your parents. Ask yourself when else, apart from the event in question, have you felt the same way. Reflect on what comes up for you, in your history, in this situation. This row helps to keep you from blaming yourself and helps you distinguish past from present, so that you do not collapse or ignore your history. It helps you become alert to the ways in which the past lives in the present. You will recognize, for instance, patterns and the ways in which you repeatedly engage in acts of self-sabotage.

Note to therapists: Consider how intergenerational trauma and family structure shape cognitive patterns. Are you attuned to these when helping clients reframe?

Intersectionalities/Sociocultural Realities (Row 6)

The sixth row helps sort out where you stand vis-à-vis intersectionalities and sociocultural realities. It highlights how your situation is embedded in larger social dynamics. How are your thoughts, moods, feelings, actions, lifestyle, success, and general wellbeing interrelated with the place you occupy in society and the ways your family raised you? In this row, reflect on how social factors, such as health, age, identity, beauty, race, gender, religion, country affiliation, and relationship status, affect the ways in which you express agency, how you show up, your sense of belonging, and your values in the world. These social and material circumstances affect your psychology, and your power, or lack thereof. For instance, if you are pegged in a way that does not represent you or represents you unfavorably, if you feel invisible, if you are stereotyped or marginalized, then some of the rage, shame, anxiety, depression, or sense of paralysis you feel is legitimate and not abnormal. Your feelings of powerlessness and alienation may make a lot of sense if who you are is being denied, if the groups you identify with (or other people identify you with) are denigrated or exploited.

This is not an invitation to riot or place blame but an opportunity to take stock of your social position within historical happenings and global dynamics more clearly. It is an invitation to strategize; to find alliances and support. It is also an invitation to have compassion for yourself and reevaluate internal voices that may tell you, "You should be different," "You should already have achieved this or that milestone," "If only you had more willpower," or "You are such a wimp." There are visible and invisible structures and discourses that disempower us. Intergenerational transmission involves not only trauma but unhelpful unconscious patterns. Society expects a lot while taking away the means for achieving. So, before interpreting personal inertia and bad moods as personal flaws, understand that psychological malaise is also often a social malaise.

Note to therapists: How do you help clients explore the link between cultural positioning and internalized shame or helplessness, without imposing your own assumptions?

Balanced Perspective/New Mantra (Row 7)

In the seventh row, create a new coping statement and a modified point of view that is more objective, that can support you, and that takes into consideration and reframes cultural and family influences. This new mantra or personal statement helps you to maintain a balanced outlook. Use it to stay on your path when you are triggered, to remind you who you are, and to hold onto a positive feeling and direction. You can take a picture of it and carry it with you. Leave a copy on the bathroom mirror and on the refrigerator door. The more accessible it is, the more you rehearse it, the less you will be bogged down by negative, inaccurate thoughts. The mantra can be a long statement, one line, or part of a song or poem that captures your message.

Updated Feelings/Body Sensations (Row 8)

On a scale of 0–100, indicate here whether your mood and feelings have changed.

Action Plan (Row 9)

In the ninth row, now that you are unencumbered by extreme feelings and distortions and aware of social and family dynamics, devise an action plan to improve the situation that considers your needs, strengths, weaknesses, and the difficulties of the terrain. This plan allows you to formulate concrete, actionable strategy within the same reflective framework so that insights do not remain abstract or theoretical but translate into specific, grounded steps. This ninth row extends the Thought Record format into actionable territory.

You want to clearly document the experience so that you can compare your entry to subsequent Nine-Lens Reflective Tools and see how the problem, emotion, or cognition is changing (or not). Start filling in a Nine-Lens Reflective Tool the moment you notice your mood is deteriorating (or the moment your headache starts, if, for instance, you get headaches that are emotional in nature).[3] The longer you wait, the harder it will be to return to the feelings and thoughts associated with the event. If you feel okay now but still want to try out filling in a Nine-Lens Reflective Tool, bring to mind a painful past situation in all its details to make it come alive and activate your feelings. Start with one situation only. It is best to zero in on a specific situation and examine it through the lens of the Nine-Lens Reflective Tool. You want to clearly document the experience so that you can compare your entry to subsequent Nine-Lens Reflective Tool entries rather than to pile up several situations as they string together in your mind. For this exercise, if you let your mind roam freely, you run the risk of feeling overwhelmed and unfocused, which may lead to inconclusive results.

Common Cognitive Distortions in the Immigrant Experience

At any point, as you complete your Nine-Lens, and especially during the reframing, spend a moment looking at your thoughts. In true CBT style, it is helpful to put a label on your thoughts, to find a name that defines their negative essence. This way you can eventually quickly recognize them and dismiss them as unhelpful distortions of reality. For example: "Oh, here we go, I am catastrophizing again!" This may help you not to attach to your unhelpful thought too seriously.

While cognitive distortions often reflect unhelpful thought patterns that can be gently challenged or reframed, it is important to acknowledge that for immigrants, some of these thoughts are grounded in real social experiences.

For example, a thought like "They think I am ignorant because of my accent" may not be irrational—it may be based on repeated encounters with condescension or exclusion. Similarly, "I do not belong" may reflect systemic barriers and social alienation, not just internal struggle.

The purpose of this list is not to invalidate those realities, but to help you recognize when such thoughts become overly generalized, self-attacking, or emotionally paralyzing—especially when they overshadow resilience, nuance, or supportive experiences. We need to hold both truths: the reality of social injustice and the possibility of reclaiming agency, dignity, and complexity in how one sees oneself.

Here are a few, taken from the Beckian tradition[4] and accompanied by thoughts my patients often bring me:

> *All-or-nothing thinking:* "If I cannot succeed completely (in this new country), I am a failure." Black-and-white thinking is common in high-stakes adaptation and in navigating conflicting cultural standards.
>
> *Catastrophizing:* "If I lose this job, I will be deported, my children will suffer, and everything will collapse." This can reflect both real precarity and exaggerated anticipatory fear.
>
> *Mind reading:* "They think I am ignorant because of my accent." Immigrants often assume judgment from others, especially when language or cultural signals differ.
>
> *Should statements:* "I should be further along by now. I should not need help. I should be grateful." Internalized pressure from both the host society and one's culture of origin.
>
> *Discounting the positive:* "Yes, I got a promotion, but it is only because they needed diversity." Achievements are dismissed, often due to imposter syndrome or racialized experiences.
>
> *Overgeneralization:* "No one here understands me. I'll never belong." One or a few painful experiences get generalized to all contexts or people.
>
> *Negative labeling (self and cultural):* "I'm lazy." "My people are backward." Internalized stereotypes and harsh self-judgments rooted in dominant cultural narratives.
>
> *Emotional reasoning:* "I feel like I do not belong, so it must be true." Feelings are mistaken for facts, particularly around belonging and value.
>
> *Survivor's guilt / comparative guilt:* "Others are suffering more—who am I to complain/seek therapy?" Not traditionally listed as a distortion, but very common and cognitively disorienting for immigrants.

While you label your thoughts, consider what may stem from distortion, what reflects personal vulnerability, and what arises from real power dynamics. As mentioned in Chapter 15, De Certeau reminds us, the "weak" do not always have strategies—but they do have tactics.[5] Proceed with awareness and tactically reclaim your ground.

Emi's Nine-Lens Reflective Tool

To illustrate how the Nine-Lens Reflective Tool works, let's return to Emi, the Ivy League Asian grad student I discussed in the section on Impostor Syndrome. Emi was feeling sad and anxious, and her anxiety was heightened by an upcoming presentation for which she needed to prepare. She was so anxious that she procrastinated to no end, which of course created a vicious cycle. As her thoughts spiraled, her anxiety increased and was compounded by a sense of failure and feeling not good enough. She developed a *downward spiral*, as we call it in CBT, a chain of thoughts feeding into one another, which became increasingly darker and more paralyzing. We decided to do a Nine-Lens Reflective Tool, to see if we could shake up the situation and view things from another perspective.

In the first row, Emi wrote: "Incoming presentation at school April 18." Although the presentation was not an event happening at that moment, but in the future, it triggered a series of thoughts and feelings of anticipation in the present.

In the second row, she noted: "Anxiety 50; knot in the stomach (manageable but not eating much)." Anxiety then turned into an increasing sense of sadness (55%) and hopelessness in response to her increasingly dark thoughts. "Feeling tired, weighed down, and unmotivated. Shame 80%."

In the third row, Emi recorded thoughts and images that came up for her when thinking about her upcoming presentation. She objectively rated the subjective truthfulness of her thoughts in that moment on a scale of 0 to 100:

1   I will do poorly: 60%.
2   No one will understand me because my accent is so thick: 80%.
3   My work will not be up to par, and I will be judged: 70%.
4   I will not be able to graduate: 40%.
5   I will never get a good job: 30%.
6   My life will be horrible. I have an image of me and in it I look like my parents: badly dressed and hunched over. I will not be able to make it and will be toiling all day in someone else's shop for very little money, disrespected, stuck, and destitute, like they were: 70%.
7   What's even the point of trying? I am not cut out for academia. I am not going to do the presentation. I am dropping out from school: 30%.
8   I will lose face with my professors and classmates and also back home: 30%.

Notice how Emi, before engaging in the Thought Record, is anxious and the more she strings her thoughts about her presentation together, the more her thoughts become depressive and helpless. She has entered a downward spiral. In fact, Emi became so dejected by the end of her train of thoughts that she turned off her computer and spent the rest of the evening binging on Netflix and popcorn, distracting herself to chase depression away. Obviously, this strategy, though offering some relief, was counterproductive. That's why it is important to challenge the negative thoughts the moment they start. If you let them go unchecked, they will fester. The Thought Record is the gold standard for it. It is a great tool because it allows you also to do some good work on your own. To help Emi emerge from the narrow perspective of her negative thoughts, Rows 4, 5, and 6 came to the rescue. In these rows, she analyzed the situation and her thoughts, sought an objective perspective, and documented facts.

In Row 4, Emi picked apart every single thought expressed in Row 3, by posing the relevant questions outlined above. Here is how she did it:

- For the thought, *I will do poorly*, Emi asked: What's the evidence that this thought is true? Evidence she presented:

  "If it takes me forever to start, I get so scared, and I procrastinate instead of working solidly. Also, in my early school years, I did not do so well in school."

- What's the evidence of the contrary? Here's the evidence she presented for the contrary result:

  "I have done okay so far at school. True, in my early years, I had a hard time learning to read and write. But that was a long time ago. I generally get very scared, I procrastinate, but at the last minute I catch up. Also, some of the schoolmates' presentations I have attended so far in my classes were far from perfect and a bit below my standards. But no one raised an eyebrow and the conversation that followed was still good and productive. Summing up, I have no evidence I will be doing poorly. I have a lot of evidence I will do okay."

- Next question: What's the best, worst, and most likely scenario?

  "If my presentation is perfect, I will be very pleased. If my presentation is not perfect, I can survive that. I did quite a few good presentations so far, so if I have an occasional bad one, it is not the end of the world. The worst-case scenario is that my presentation is really bad. But it is not very likely."

- Next question: If the worst-case scenario happens, would you be able to survive it?

  "Even if that happens, one presentation, even if poor, will not condemn me or define me."

- Next question: If it was your friend, partner, or child in your place, thinking this way, what would you tell them? She said:

  "I'd tell them that one bad presentation would not define them and that they tend to worry but usually do okay."

- Finally: Are these thoughts helping you reach your goals? Her answer:

  "These thoughts are not helping me. They interfere with my concentration and energy."

In Row 4, Emi also labeled each thought to indicate the type of thought it was. A list of various labels to categorize types of negative thinking, such as "catastrophizing," "black-and-white thinking," "magnifying," "perfectionism," and "minimizing," can be found in the Appendix E. Labeling helps to quickly identify and categorize the type of thought. Emi wrote: "fortune-telling, catastrophizing, black/white thinking, and discounting the positive."

Row 5 brings insight to family and early dynamics that are activated in the present situation. Emi noted the historical elements of her family's poverty and humiliations in early school years. When reframing her thoughts, she recorded the following bullet points, as insight in Row 5:

- My family was poor and extremely busy "to make ends meet." They were not so involved with me or good with emotions. It was all about making sure I was fed; no one taught me about emotions. That's why I feel so unprepared.
- My mom did not believe in herself or in me. She was very anxious, like me.
- My dad wanted and still wants me to achieve all the things he would have wanted for himself but could not achieve; Dad looked down on me and Mom because we are women. Dad was perfectionistic and critical.
- I grew up with the pressure of having to do big things and at the same time had the message that I was not good enough.
- Food is the way I soothe myself since childhood because it was the only way emotions were dealt with back then, and it stayed with me.

In Row 6, where we consider intersectionalities sociocultural realities, Emi wrote:

- Immigrant family; coming from a poor uneducated family and not having examples in my family that are in academia.
- Not speaking good English.
- Being an Asian woman, as well as one who diverges from people's stereotype of what an Asian woman in academia should be.
- Having to adjust to new expectations and speak up.
- Not belonging.

In Row 7, for her coping statement, Emi wrote the following:

> I tend to get triggered when I have big assignments. My family was not warm and fuzzy, and being an immigrant, a minority, and a woman makes it difficult for me to march forward with a puffed chest. But there is no evidence I will do poorly beyond remedy. I can do a good enough job. I need to extend to myself the kindness and good disposition I have for others. I hold myself to unreasonable standards and that bogs me down. I tend to be perfectionistic. I hear the perfectionistic and misogynistic voice of my dad as if he is talking inside my head. This stops

me in my tracks. I need to recognize that voice when it starts yapping and lower its volume or let it stay in the background, if it does not want to leave altogether. It is not easy for people like me, coming from an immigrant family with no formal education and low social status, to make it in a new country and the Ivy League. Not feeling entitled is quite literal for me; I and my family do not have a graduate degree or any other title. Of course, I am scared, insecure, and have a hard time seeing a path in front of me. It is not because I am weak or too emotional. The path I chose is so different from the path behind! This is what I want to keep in mind to help and sustain myself:

- Even if I *feel* I cannot do it, I have no *evidence* of that. To the contrary, I have accomplished a lot. My grandfather did not even read or write, my dad only finished grammar school, and yet I am here now.
- I need to separate historical facts (my school problems as a child) from present facts.
- I need to recognize how historical and social facts play in my life and create barriers.
- Good work does not need to be perfect.
- Perfectionism is the enemy of good work.
- I cannot compare my language proficiency to native speakers. But I can communicate in two languages, which is a plus, and I will troubleshoot to make my presentation understandable.
- The more I do presentations, the easier they will become.

After she finished working on Row 7, I asked Emi how much on a scale between 0–100 she believed her initial thoughts, at the present moment. Her negative beliefs, as well as negative feelings, decreased. She added the new numbers in Row 8, to highlight the change.

In Row 9, Emi listed her strategy to improve her situation:

- I will take a look every day at my Book of Success and let it really sink in.
- I will divide the preparation for the presentation into small manageable chunks. I will do them one by one, like putting one foot in front of the other. Since they are in small pieces, I will not get overwhelmed by the magnitude of the work. This way, I will be able to accomplish a good enough presentation.
- For my pronunciation, I will speak slowly and prepare a page handout about the key points of my presentation to help people follow. I can chew some gum before the presentation to release my jaw from tension. I can pause and ask people if they are following.
- I will remind myself of my tendency to imagine bored and critical faces. I may anticipate a hostile environment, but I have no evidence of that. I choose to imagine and rehearse images in my mind in which my presentation will be well received.

- My schoolmates and professors may have a "resting scholar face"[6] (quoting the video "resting scholar face" by Tom Mullaney from YouTube), but I will remind myself not to read anything negative into it.
- On the presentation day, I will engage in small talk with a few people before starting the presentation, to make a connection and dissipate any lingering feelings about separation, judgment, and negativity.
- I will wear my "power suit" and pretty but comfortable shoes (even in a Zoom talk!), planting my feet down to make me feel powerful and grounded.
- I will spend a few minutes every day meditating and imagining all the people who support and love me surrounding me in a "circle of love." I will also add to the circle some of the historical and religious figures that inspire me, including women and people from my own country and my loving grandfather, all around me and sustaining me, sending me beams of love, words of strength, and an embracing sense of warmth. I want to learn to feel their presence in my life in an ongoing way, as if I had a squad of guardian angels.

See Table 20.2 for Emi's Nine-Lens Reflective Tool.

This was not Emi's first use of the Nine-Lens Reflective Tool. It was the product of a great deal of work together that allowed her to connect past and present and to see her distortions more easily. For you, at the beginning, the Nine-Lens Reflective Tool may be hard to write and may not move this quickly, which may feel discouraging. Initially, it can be hard to discern specific thoughts and images and to name feelings. If this is the case, be patient and continue to observe. One thought to dissect is enough; you do not have to have a Nine-Lens Reflective Tool as full and complex as this one from Emi.

It is often painful to realize how your thoughts misrepresent reality and how your mind mistreats you, but do your best to distinguish between the ways in which you are at fault so you can better prepare for the issues that come from society. You may experience disappointment if all of your entries of the Nine-Lens Reflective Tool look the same. You may feel stuck, like a broken record. You may feel ashamed and think you are boring and wrong. But it's not like that. If that happens, consider that out of the vast array of existing psychological problems, you have only a few issues to change. You will repeat and repeat the same types of Thought Records as if you were lost in an intersection, going around and around looking for an exit. This is the way everybody's mind works; it's hard to change our habitual ways of being, even if we have learned they are wrong. But at some point, you will find the exit.

In the meanwhile, negative feelings may still be strong even after you complete many Thought Records. Logically, you know that the thoughts and images are distortions, but this knowledge does not make you feel better or fully endorse the new realizations. Do your best to not let those lingering negative feelings stop you from continuing the good work and eventually making changes. Continue to reframe your thinking.

Table 20.2 Emi's Nine-Lens Reflective Tool

1.	2.	3.	4.	5.	6.	7.	8.	9.
Situation	Feelings / body sensations	Thoughts and images	Reframing	Family history	Sociocultural realities	New mantra	Updated feelings	Action plan
Upcoming presentation (Apr 18) at school. Anticipatory anxiety activated by academic pressure and fear of public speaking.	Anxiety 50%, sadness 55%, shame 80%. Body: knot in stomach, fatigue, low appetite, difficulty focusing, internal pressure.	1 I will do poorly (60%) 2 My accent is too thick (80%) 3 My work is not good enough (70%) 4 I won't graduate (40%) 5 I'll fail in life like my parents (70%) 6 No point in trying (30%) 7 I'll lose face (30%)	I've succeeded before despite fear. Others' presentations are imperfect too. I procrastinate but catch up. I catastrophize. Perfectionism is a block, not a virtue. One event doesn't define me. My inner critic echoes Dad.	Mom was anxious, unavailable; Dad critical, perfectionistic. Little emotional support. High pressure to achieve but little affirmation. Shame and self-doubt run deep. Food was my comfort. Same old story in new form.	First-gen immigrant, Asian woman, low-income background, Ivy League pressure. Accent and gender bias shape experience. Feel out of place. Must push against cultural stereotypes and underrepresentation.	I deserve to be here. My accent reflects bilingual strength. Good enough is enough. My path is valid. Perfection is not the goal—progress and courage are. I speak kindly to myself when I falter.	Shame ↓ to 45; Anxiety ↓ to 30; Sadness ↓ to 25. Belief in catastrophic thoughts has weakened. Feel more grounded, less overwhelmed.	Break prep into steps. Create visual aids. Rehearse aloud. Wear grounding clothes. Meditate daily. Review Success & Missed Catastrophe books. Imagine support circle. Approach challenge as growth, not test.

Interlude for Therapists

When a client seems stuck in a repetitive cognitive-emotional loop, try gently naming the cycle and acknowledging the protective purpose behind their current coping strategies. Help them name the underlying fear, such as judgment, failure, or shame, and collaboratively choose just one distorted thought to explore, at a gentle, manageable pace. For clients with trauma histories, pacing and containment are critical. Working through all nine rows in one sitting may not be feasible; instead, move gradually, returning over time with safety, trust, and flexibility.

Interlude for all Readers

Working on Thought Records, as frustrating as it might be at times, is not the hardest part of the work. For many, the hardest part is exposure. Exposure requires us to get out of our hideout, show up, and fight avoidant tendencies. Indeed, once you have reframed your thoughts, you need to practice the new perspective you have acquired. You need to expose yourself to fear-provoking things and prove to yourself that you can do it and the world will not fall. You need to experience that getting out from your hiding place makes you feel better. It makes you succeed. But do so in small, manageable doses. You need to connect to people and go out, even if you are in a funk. When dealing with shame, it's best to microdose your exposure to it. In this way, you let small doses of fear and shame inoculate you and help you gradually build tolerance. Move out of paralysis; if even by taking the smallest move, step out of your comfort zone. In this way, you expand the areas in which you feel safe and capable. You also become more competent. The more you retreat, the harder it is to emerge from your hideaway. When overcome by shame, about what you said or did, remind yourself that making mistakes and making a fool of yourself is sometimes part and parcel of learning and existing. If you expose yourself, you will make some mistakes. But that should not destroy you; it is part of living and acting in the world. Little by little, expand your tolerance for discomfort. It is important to build tolerance in small steps, so you are not flooded by emotions. You can also work on a Thought Record with a trusted friend, who knows your background, and who can provide objectivity. But take special care to pay attention to each other's feelings, as this could be a painful process. If negative feelings are entrenched, do not sit with them. A therapist or medication can make a difference.

The Nine-Lens Reflective Tool not only highlights your unhelpful thinking but also helps identify real problems that need to be addressed in order for you to move forward. Sifting through distortions may expose a kernel of truth that needs to be addressed. In the case of Emi, alongside her perfectionism, self-doubt, and anxiety, her Nine-Lens Reflective Tool also exposed that there was a concrete problem of organization and time management that needed attention. She required better ways of tackling big projects and managing her time. Having an action plan improved her outcomes and her feelings.

Emi and I worked for over four years on her anxiety and perfectionism. I helped her relieve her struggles with communication and improve her classroom and conference presentation issues. She initially wanted to get rid of her feelings and push them away, but over time she understood that she would need to accept some discomfort and at least entertain the thought of being okay with the discomfort as a possibility to get to where she wanted to go in life. About a month into the treatment, she wrote the following coping statement:

> I want to train myself to be okay with being less than perfect. Tiny bits of discomfort here and there will increase my tolerance. Apart from elementary school, I have been always praised and produced great projects. It is hard for me to manage feedback that is not stellar. I need to build resilience with lukewarm feedback.

In this statement, she also added four bullet points with the name of the works she was able to accomplish well. In this statement, she was stating her intention. This statement functioned as her compass. She could remind herself of what her intention was when she was feeling weak and ready to hide and avoid doing what was good for her. This statement helped her stay the course. By affirming to herself that she was competent and listing evidence of competence, she was also preparing a quick rebuttal for those engrained thoughts that would hijack her mind all of a sudden and try to reinstate those negative thoughts and feelings that she had already debunked.

Regarding her presentations, she became increasingly diligent in preparing and rehearsing. She trained with imaginal exercises that induced calm and rehearsed the presentation as already happening successfully; she trained herself how to breathe to lower her agitation and practice relaxation techniques every day. Also she created a Book of Success where she listed all the positives, compliments, thank you notes, and grades that were accumulating. She also created a Book of Missed Catastrophes (see next chapter), where she listed all the things that she had feared but that then turned out okay. These are all excellent tools that come from the Beckian tradition of CBT. By looking at these books and seeing them grow she became increasingly convinced that maybe she was not as bad as she had thought after all. Emi graduated and was accepted for a fellowship where she needs to do a lot of presentations. She remains a bit anxious, but she is managing.

Therapists may find this expanded structure particularly useful when working with immigrant or marginalized clients, as it allows for contextualized exploration of internal and external barriers, and opens space for both emotional and systemic insight.

Notes

1 Aaron T. Beck, quote on official biography page, Beck Institute for Cognitive Behavior Therapy, https://beckinstitute.org/about/dr-aaron-t-beck.

2 For a classic example of Thought Record, see Judith S. Beck, *Cognitive Behavior Therapy: Basics and Beyond*, 2nd ed. (New York: The Guilford Press, 2011), 195.
3 It is important to emphasize that any ailment, even if you believe it is fully psychological or spiritual, needs to be also checked out by a medical doctor to rule out a serious medical condition.
4 See for instance, Beck, *Cognitive Behavior Therapy*, 195.
5 Michel de Certeau, *The Practice of Everyday Life*, trans. Steven Rendall (Berkeley, CA: University of California Press, 2002), XIX, 29–42.
6 For a detailed explanation, listen to Tom Mullaney here: www.youtube.com/watch?v=kEEYBG5Duds

References

Beck, Aaron T. n.d. Quote on official biography page. Beck Institute for Cognitive Behavior Therapy. https://beckinstitute.org/about/dr-aaron-t-beck.

Beck, Judith S. 2011. *Cognitive Behavior Therapy: Basics and Beyond*, 2nd ed. New York: The Guilford Press.

de Certeau, Michel. 2002. *The Practice of Everyday Life*, trans. Steven Rendall. Berkeley, CA: University of California Press.

Mullaney, Tom. Why the World Writes Chinese with an English Alphabet. *YouTube*, February 4. Stanford University Press channel. www.youtube.com/watch?v=kEEYBG5Duds.

21 Tools to Manage Ambivalence, Worry, and Self-Doubt

When I got here, at the beginning, I felt I could do anything. I felt the world was mine. But then it changed. I lost it. Now I think of all the things I could have done in all these years. I don't know how it happened that I lost it. I stopped following the things I liked. I joined the mainstream, did what was expected of me—I started my career—but stopped doing the things that I really liked. I should have better utilized the past years. I should have gone the uncharted way, but it was scary. I feel stranded now.

—Gael, a French green card holder patient

When Paralyzed by Ambivalence, Fear, and Self-Doubt

In addition to the Nine-Lens Reflective Tool and gradual exposure techniques, the following four exercises can help manage and organize your thoughts and feelings, fostering greater objectivity and momentum:

- *The Folded Page exercise* is a CBT tool designed to combat insomnia. It helps redirect your mind to a rational path of thinking, allowing you to manage nighttime worries and resume sleep—acting as your evening compass.
- *The Book of Missed Catastrophes* is where you log instances when you feared the worst, but it didn't happen. Inspired by a patient, this tool helps challenge catastrophic thinking by proving yourself wrong about potential disasters that never came to pass.
- *The Worry Container* provides a space to engage with, contain, and quarantine your worries, keeping them from overwhelming your thoughts.
- *The Chair Exercise* is designed to help sort through ambivalence and conflicting emotions, offering clarity in decision-making (see Appendix G).

These exercises, when used in combination, can greatly improve your ability to manage thoughts and feelings effectively.

DOI: 10.4324/9781003648703-28

Interlude for Therapists

You might invite clients to keep a folder of these tools or reflect together on which one resonates most with their current needs. Encourage gentle experimentation rather than pressuring "correct" use. As this book illustrates, some tools are rooted in established clinical traditions and evidence-based frameworks, which offer us authority and grounding within the field.

However, others emerge from the clinical encounter itself. We may adapt or tweak known techniques, or we may develop new ones based on what our clients bring us: their language, their imagery, their cultural and emotional logic. In honoring our professional traditions, we must also remain open to what works in the here and now.

Remaining open to what works in the here and now requires humility, curiosity, and deep attentiveness. We are not simply technicians or executors of method. We are clinicians who accumulate experiential knowledge, listen carefully to our clients, their languages, their cultures, and allow creativity to flow from within the therapeutic relationship. Feel free to explore and develop your creative and intuitive capacities, always in dialogue with the client, like-minded colleagues, and with careful ethical reflection.

Folded Page Exercise[1]

To the reader: Don't do this exercise too close to bedtime because it can be overstimulating. The best times to do it are just before leaving your office or before you start the transition from work to personal time. This exercise helps you examine your thoughts, create a roadmap for the night, and better equip yourself to problem-solve whatever is worrying you.

Take a piece of paper and fold it in two vertically so that you have two long columns. In the column on the left, list the thoughts you think might arise and bother you at night. In the right column, write the first step toward the solution of the problem.

When nighttime worries and thoughts come up, do not attach your emotions to them and start writing a novel of negativity and worry. Instead, at their first inception, when your worries are still weak, remind yourself that the prefrontal cortex, the logical part of the brain, is asleep at night, while the more primitive parts of the brain that are biased toward the negative, light up. This function is nature's way of protecting us. Our brains are designed to ensure our survival, even when we're sleeping. Remind yourself that no good, logical solution can come from debating your own thoughts at night. You risk getting stuck in a black-and-white, catastrophizing mode that will solve nothing. Remind yourself instead that you took the best first step toward the solution of your problem when your mind was still fresh, and logical thinking was intact. Use your Folded Page as a sleep aid (see Table 21.1 and Appendix F). This simple visual

Table 21.1 Folded Page Sleep Aid

Immediate Thought (Left Column)	Grounded Response (Right Column)

tool is designed to be folded and kept by the bedside. It offers gentle prompts and reminders to support relaxation and sleep onset.

You can take it from there when you wake up the next day. Below are two examples, from Maria and Luis Miguel.

Maria's Folded Page

Maria, a graduate student suffering from anxiety, shame, and insomnia was worried about her upcoming school presentation. She used the Folded Page as a way to transform harsh, perfectionistic thoughts into compassionate, practical steps. We processed and organized her thoughts and feelings in a Folded Page. In the left column, Maria wrote: "Tomorrow is my difficult class, and I am totally unprepared. I will make a fool of myself and learn nothing." She did not let herself spiral by attaching this thought to darker, more anxiety-provoking fears. She stopped there and then looked objectively at what she had written and began to debate and reframe her thought using the logical reframing she had learned through her use of the Thought Records and Nine-Lens tools. She asked herself:

- Am I really so unprepared?
- What is the evidence that this is true?
- What is the evidence to the contrary?
- Am I catastrophizing?
- Am I being a perfectionist?

After reflecting on each thought, a more balanced and truthful entry in the right column began to take shape. In the right column, she wrote: "Yes, I am not as prepared as I would like to be, but I actually know something about this topic from another class, so I may be able to follow the conversation." She added, "It is okay if, just this once, I do not speak much." She devised the following plan: "I am going to wake up at seven, spend one hour skimming through the material, and prepare a comment or two based on my readings. I will do my best with the time I have. That will do for tomorrow." She then wrote, "I am not happy about not being prepared. But it is okay to be unprepared occasionally; I do not have to be perfect to succeed. My focus on performance takes the pleasure out of my life and does not help me to do okay." As a final note on this matter, she wrote, "I want to create space and a system that allows me to prepare most of the time."

Maria recognized that indeed she was really not that prepared, so she put a note to herself to monitor herself in the following weeks and reflect on why this is happening. Without judgment or blame, she wanted to understand what got in the way and identify changes she could make to prevent the issue from becoming a pattern.

Plan for the Coming Week

Maria's action plan for the coming week was as follows:

- Understand what is getting in the way of doing my work optimally.
- Make sure this remains occasional, not habitual.
- I will ask my classmate Ana to meet midweek to touch base and exchange ideas on the readings and notes. That will help me stay on track.
- I will set aside 30 minutes a day for reading, so the workload is more manageable.

Coping Statement

Her coping statement was as follows: "Tomorrow, I may not be as prepared as I would like, but one off day will not affect my overall grade. I am working toward making school a priority in my busy schedule." By confronting her initial fear and constructing a grounded response, she was able to reduce her anxiety and regain focus. Table 21.2 shows Maria's Folded Page.

The Folded Page lent Maria a hand at night, when fears often became more pronounced. As worries began to creep in, she did not engage them. Instead, she reminded herself that her "night mind" was primitive, prone to black-and-white thinking and catastrophizing. She had already considered her predicament earlier in the day, when her mind was clearer and more capable of constructive problem-solving. So she gently told herself, "My best thoughts are in the Folded Page on my nightstand." Then, she shifted her focus, almost as if she were removing the worry from her body and placing it onto the page. That small gesture helped her sleep more peacefully.

Table 21.2 Maria's Folded Page

Immediate Thought (Left Column)	Grounded Response (Right Column)
Tomorrow is my hardest class, and I am totally unprepared. I will make a fool of myself and learn nothing. I am falling behind and I am not cut out for this.	I am not as unprepared as I think—I have read parts of this material before in another class.
I am going on and on in this spiral of thoughts, feeling more and more helpless and desperate.	I will wake up early, skim the readings for an hour, and prepare one or two comments to share. It is okay if I do not speak much this time.
	One less-than-perfect class will not define my performance.
	This did not happen for no reason. I've been overwhelmed.
	I will ask Ana to check in midweek on readings, so we stay on track.
	I'll set aside 30 minutes a day for coursework, so it feels more manageable.
	Tonight, I will rest, knowing that I have a plan.
	My Folded Page is on my nightstand to remind me in case I wake up anxious.

A Folded Page for Luis Miguel: Sleeplessness, Fear, and Powerlessness amidst Uncertainty

Luis Miguel, a 27-year-old naturalized U.S. citizen originally from Venezuela, came to me overwhelmed by anxiety and sleeplessness. He shared that one of his uncles, who helped raise him, had recently lost his temporary protected status and is now undocumented. They live together, sharing an apartment with five other individuals, which, in Luis's words, multiplies the likelihood of an ICE raid sevenfold. After hearing rumors of nearby ICE activity, Luis began having trouble sleeping. His thoughts would spin late into the night: "What if they come tonight? What if I lose him? What if they come for me next?"

Even though Luis is a citizen, the climate of fear had settled deeply into his nervous system. He had also come across public threats to revoke naturalized citizenship. Although such policies had not been enacted, the fear felt immediate and consuming.

We could not change the broader political environment, but we could work with what was within his reach. Together, we used the Folded Page technique. I invited him to write down the raw, catastrophic thought on the left side of a folded piece of paper. Much of what he feared was possible, even if not probable. We acknowledged that reality without trying to erase it. Then, after a pause, he wrote a more balanced and strategic response on the right. We sat with both sides.

Immediate Thought: Left Side

In the left hand column, he wrote his immediate thoughts: "They're coming for all of us. My uncle might get deported. I might lose my citizenship. Everything is falling apart."

Grounded Response: Right Side

In the right hand column, he tried to put his fears in perspective: "The fear is real, but I cannot solve all of this tonight. If I bundle all my worries together, I will push myself into an unmanageable state of despair. I have protections in place. My uncle Enrique has a safety plan. Let's separate the situations, deal with the emergencies first, and then make a plan. I will stay informed— but not spiral. Tonight, I will rest. Tomorrow, with a fresh mind, I will review financial options and help my family plan."

He also devised a plan of action: "My first step will be to call my sister and speak with her son, who is studying to become a lawyer, to ask what my options are and how to best support Enrique."

Action Steps

This exercise reminded Luis Miguel that, while he could not control larger forces, he could support his loved ones and prepare. Here are a few of the steps we identified together:

1   Legal preparedness:

- Updating the family safety plan.
- Consulting with his nephew and a pro bono immigration attorney.
- Creating secure digital backups of key documents, including his naturalization certificate.

2   Tactical self-care:

- Avoiding news and social media late at night to reduce reactivation.
- Practicing grounding techniques before bed.
- Using a bedside journal as a "Worry Container" to put anxious thoughts on hold until morning.

3   Community support:

- Joining a local immigrant support group.
- Downloading a trusted community alert app and tuning in to local radio to separate fact from rumor.
- Sharing his emergency plan with a trusted friend.

4   Financial and emotional planning:

- Exploring flexible work arrangements and building an emergency savings and fund.
- Reflecting on what would most support his family in both short- and long-term scenarios.
- Repeating a calming phrase to himself: "I cannot control everything, but I can care for myself and my loved ones with courage."

See Table 21.3 for Luis Miguel's Folded Page.

This example shows how Luis Miguel used the Folded Page tool to shift from catastrophic thinking to grounded, actionable steps. The layout mirrors the format used in session: the left side captures immediate, spiraling thoughts, while the right side offers calmer, more strategic responses. This Folded Page did not eliminate Luis Miguel's fear. But it gave him space to hold that fear gently, without letting it hijack his nights. It helped him to organize his thoughts, take action where possible, and rest when needed. In times of injustice and uncertainty, clarity and preparation are forms of resilience; strengthening a network of peers and allies is too.

Table 21.3 Luis Miguel's Folded Page

Immediate Thought (Left Column)	Grounded Response (Right Column)
They are coming for all of us. My uncle might get deported. I might lose my citizenship. Everything is falling apart.	The fear is real, but I cannot solve all of this tonight. If I bundle all my worries together, I will push myself into an unmanageable state of despair.
	I have protections in place. My uncle Enrique has a safety plan. Let's separate the situations, deal with the emergencies first, and then make a plan.
	I will stay informed—but not spiral. Tonight, I will rest.
	Tomorrow, with a fresh mind, I will review financial options and help my family plan.
	If I wake up during the night, I will remind myself that it is unproductive and even harmful to start troubleshooting at that hour. The most helpful thought is already written on my Folded Page, resting on my nightstand. Tomorrow, I will look at it again and take it from there.
	Next step tomorrow: Call my sister and speak with her son, the lawyer-to-be, to ask about our legal options and how best to support Enrique.

The Book of Missed Catastrophes

If your Thought Records or Nine-Lens Reflective Tools reveal a pattern of catastrophizing, consider starting a Book of Missed Catastrophes. Catastrophizing means jumping to the worst-case scenario without evidence. For example, a pimple becomes, "I'm going to die!" or a small mistake at work leads to, "I'll be fired and end up homeless!" It is an extreme and irrational mental leap.

To use this tool, fold a page in two columns:

- On the left, write down the catastrophe you feared.
- On the right, record what actually happened.

Over time, the contrast will become evident and may help retrain your brain toward more realistic thinking. As the book grows, it becomes proof that many of your most frightening thoughts did not come true.

To therapists: You may suggest this tool to clients who struggle to trust positive outcomes. Reviewing entries together can help track cognitive shifts over time.

Worry Container

Some people believe that worrying prepares or protects them, but in reality, worry tends to multiply itself and can paralyze action. One way to manage it is to contain it. Designate a set time each day as your "Worry Time," for example, 11:00 to 11:30 am. When a worry arises, say to yourself: "I will think about this later, during Worry Time." At the end of the time slot, close the imaginary container, knowing you can revisit those thoughts the next day at the same time. Over time, you may even reduce the need for Worry Time. Containing worry helps you learn that worry is not action. It does not bring solutions—it only drains energy.

Chair Exercise[2]

When you feel torn between two opposing views or desires, try the Chair Exercise to explore your inner ambivalence. Place two chairs facing each other. Sit in one and speak from one part of yourself. Then move to the other chair and speak from the opposite part. Go back and forth as many times as you need. This practice helps you:

- Understand the complexity of your inner dialogue.
- Explore how each position feels in your body.
- Develop a wise, observing part of yourself that listens to both sides.

Over time, this internal conversation becomes more fluid, and you may gain clarity. Just remember: uncertainty is part of life, and you do not need perfect clarity to move forward. A degree of risk and loss is always present.

The Chair Exercise (see Appendix G) can be especially powerful for people who feel "neither here nor there" caught between countries, cultures, identities, or life choices. It gives form to the inner split, helps reduce paralysis, and validates both sides without forcing a premature resolution. Here are some positive outcomes of the Chair Exercise:

1 *Externalizes internal conflict:* It gives voice and space to each part—one that longs for the past, the other that wants to stay and adapt—so neither is repressed or dismissed.
2 *Supports emotional integration:* Instead of picking a side, the person can learn to hold two truths at once: *I miss home* and *I am building a future here.*
3 *Reduces shame and doubt:* People often feel guilty for wanting to go back or for staying. This exercise validates both feelings and reveals the complexity behind them.
4 *Strengthens the observing self:* By creating a third position, the "witness" can listen with compassion; it fosters insight and inner steadiness.

A draft outline for engaging in chairwork can be found in Appendix G.

Example: Elena's Decision

Elena was torn between accepting a promotion and staying in her current role. In one chair, she expressed excitement, ambition, and the desire to prove herself. In the other, she voiced fear of burnout, guilt about leaving her team, and comfort in the familiar. After several rounds, she realized that both sides had wisdom. She negotiated flexible terms in the new role, and made a decision rooted in wholeness—not panic.

Jamal's Dilemma and the Chair Exercise

Jamal, a 30-year-old engineer from Egypt, moved to the US for graduate school. After graduation, he secured a job and a work visa. But he could not stop asking himself: "Did I make the right choice?" He missed Cairo, his family, the food, the call to prayer. He wondered if he had betrayed something sacred by leaving. At the same time, he valued the intellectual freedom and professional growth he had found in the United States.

- In one chair, he gave voice to the part that wanted to return: "This is not my land. I feel like a stranger. My parents are getting older. I miss Arabic all around me. I do not belong here."
- In the other chair, he became the part that wanted to stay: "I have worked so hard for this. I feel intellectually alive here. I am building something new. But I am afraid of what I am losing."
- After a few rounds, Jamal stood between the chairs and simply listened. Then, softly, he said: "Maybe both parts are right. Maybe it is not about

choosing once and for all. Maybe I need to find ways to stay in touch with home while still growing here. It does not have to be either/or."

This shift allowed him to explore hybrid solutions:

- He began attending Arabic poetry nights with friends in the diaspora.
- He planned regular visits home.
- He applied for a job with flexible travel options.
- He also realized that part of his suffering came from feeling singled out as Muslim. He decided to seek out a community where he could connect with others who understood this aspect of his identity.
- Importantly, he learned to be selective about when and with whom he discussed his faith—preserving energy by choosing safe, meaningful conversations, and letting go of the need to always explain or defend.

Jamal did not erase his conflict. Instead, he chose to hold it with compassion, act intentionally, and give himself permission to reassess in one year. He began to feel less like he had to choose between two lives and more like he was building a life that held both parts of himself: his connection to home and his place in this new country.

Therapist note: This exercise can be particularly useful with clients who struggle with indecision, internal conflict, or a harsh inner critic. Encourage them to fully embody each part with voice, posture, emotion. Over time, they may begin to internalize the observing part and use it in everyday decision-making.

Grounding Yourself "Here" and "There"

When overwhelmed by feelings of loss or isolation, try this simple mindfulness exercise: Sit comfortably and take three deep breaths. As you inhale, imagine you are breathing in the scents and sounds of your homeland: a fragrant dish or a familiar song. As you exhale, release the tension in your body, silently repeating, "I carry my roots within me." Repeat this for five minutes, allowing yourself to reconnect with the strength and resilience your heritage brings.

For Therapists: Integrating These Tools

Whether you work psychodynamically, systemically, somatically, or with CBT, these tools are not meant to interfere with your process but to offer anchoring techniques. They can stabilize clients in acute distress, provide a sense of empowerment, make implicit fears explicit, or simply provide a shared object for reflection. You might ask, "Shall we try this together, and then see what it brings up?" The aim is not compliance, but insight and movement.

Notes

1 This tool comes from the toolbox if CBT for insomnia. I invite you to explore CBTI subfield's books if insomnia is an issue for you. Here are some references: Jack D. Edinger and Colleen E. Carney, *Overcoming Insomnia: A Cognitive-Behavioral Therapy Approach, Therapist Guide* (New York: Oxford University Press, 2008), 52; Jack D. Edinger and Colleen E. Carney, *Overcoming Insomnia: A Cognitive-Behavioral Therapy Approach, Workbook* (New York: Oxford University Press, 2008), 30.

2 I learned this exercise from trainings by my colleagues Scott Kellogg and Irismar Reis de Oliveira. You can find out more here, if interested: Scott Kellogg, *Transformational Chairwork: Using Psychotherapeutic Dialogues in Clinical Practice* (New York: Rowman & Littlefield, 2014); Irismar Reis de Oliveira, *Trial-Based Cognitive Therapy: Distinctive Features* (New York: Routledge, 2016).

References

Edinger, Jack D., and Colleen E. Carney. 2008. *Overcoming Insomnia: A Cognitive-Behavioral Therapy Approach, Therapist Guide*. New York: Oxford University Press.

Kellogg, Scott. 2014. *Transformational Chairwork: Using Psychotherapeutic Dialogues in Clinical Practice*. New York: Rowman & Littlefield.

Oliveira, Irismar Reis de. 2016. *Trial-Based Cognitive Therapy: Distinctive Features*. New York: Routledge.

22 Planning and Goal Setting for Immigrants in Transition

Creating Structures and Schedules

Steven A. Safren and colleagues observe, *"Problems with organizing and planning involve difficulties figuring out the logical, discrete steps to complete tasks that seem overwhelming."*[1] People who struggle with breaking down tasks often procrastinate or fall short of fulfilling their potential. Fundamental organizational skills are crucial for people with limited means and support systems, who still seek to excel and maintain their wellbeing. This skill is especially pertinent for those who have immigrated to a new geographical location and are transitioning to a new culture. When your attention is scattered here and there on various schemes, you risk losing track of projects and responsibilities. Strengthening your organizational skills will not only help you keep track of all the threads, maximize your assets, and improve the chances of achieving your dreams, but it will also support your mind and body against psychological, professional, and social roadblocks. Below I offer basic tips on how to remain steadfast as you continue to your objective despite the challenges.

Prepare Your Environment

If you plan to do some work that requires attention, the first step to ensure perseverance is to prepare your environment to minimize distraction. Clean your desk and reduce ambient noise. Seek out what helps you focus, either privacy or the company of others. If company is what you need, find a buddy who will hold you accountable and provide that extra little push. Ensure that you are well-rested and well-fed. Keep water at your desk. If necessary, deactivate Wi-Fi or use an app that limits internet use if that is a source of distraction.[2]

Start with a To-Do List: A Sketch and a Vision

> I have come quite a long way. I have realized the value of my work. It's not that I do not have impostor syndrome or pain around it. But I have more

DOI: 10.4324/9781003648703-29

confidence to rely on. Is this the best article ever written? Maybe not, but it's okay! I cannot waste any more time on this. I need to move on. I am tired!
—Marta, a Puerto Rican American patient

(Although Puerto Ricans are U.S. citizens, many like Marta experience cultural dislocation and identify with the immigrant journey.)

Building to-do lists and schedules is essential to helping you sort out and keep in mind all the things you need to accomplish toward your objective. Of course, these tools cannot become an end in themselves: doing and redoing lists and never starting the actual work would not be helpful. The to-do list is not a novel with many drafts, and it doesn't need to be perfect; it's just a sketch that serves as a step toward action. The *doing* might be scary. But doing things in small increments generates the best chance of accomplishing them. Address your fears with a Thought Record or a Nine-Lens, in which you reframe distortions and assess realities. Then make your to-do list. In the section on A, B, C Prioritizing, you will learn how to break your list into small action steps, and then to place them onto your calendar. As I say to patients who get lost in the vision before basic groundwork is done, "You do not put earrings and nail polish on your project before it has ears and legs." Start with what is essential and proceed step-by-step.

From the To-Do List to a Roadmap

"I know what I want but I don't know how to get there" is a sentence that I often hear in therapy. It is an especially common sentiment expressed by people transitioning from college to work or graduate school. It's also prevalent among couples who move to the US together, especially when one of the partners is the accompanying partner and has no path set in the new country yet. It's common among first-generation immigrants and also second-generation individuals navigating inherited expectations.

To be able to go from here to there, you need to build a roadmap. This roadmap is made of your hopes, values, and vision: who you are and who you want to become. However, more concretely, the roadmap is made of tools and structures like a to-do list and a simple and attainable schedule. You need to build a habit to mark your activities in your calendar and to look at your calendar often; you need to check on the time and double check what's on your calendar now, this week, and in the following week. You may initially find this process to be time-consuming, but once you become accustomed to tracking time and your tasks, you will find it gratifying to check off completed tasks. At that point, it will have become a habit. Train yourself to follow your calendar from the moment you wake up. The picture of your calendar allows you to envision your path. This is your road map. By following your calendar as closely as possible, you create new habits and a different future.

Revisit the calendar several times a day, and if necessary, set reminders on your phone to follow its contents. Let's now look at one concrete case where we applied this method in therapy.

Angelo's Story

Angelo, a second-generation European immigrant, struggled with chronic procrastination, which left him feeling stuck and unfulfilled. Although he worked for his family's industrial construction company, he longed to pursue more "interesting things," though he couldn't pinpoint what those might be. Angelo felt immense pressure from his larger-than-life father, a successful immigrant, and believed he could never measure up. This pressure left him feeling isolated from the more successful, dynamic members of his family. Since childhood, Angelo had been expected to work in the family business, which limited his ability to explore his true identity. He felt trapped in a "golden cage," afraid that despite his comfortable life, he might need to take a risky and unfamiliar path to find himself. Angelo had a passion for photography, with a large collection of photos, but he never dared to pursue it seriously, fearing failure and the unknown.

Recently, though, he began to wonder, could photography be more than just a hobby? Angelo's procrastination was rooted in deep-seated resentment toward his father, a controlling and judgmental figure in his life. Angelo did not seek out working experiences to find himself, independently from his father's company. Unlike his siblings, who actively sought to challenge their father's authority, Angelo withdrew, but stayed within the company, resorting to passive self-sabotage. When assigned tasks by his father, Angelo would delay out of a mix of spite, self-doubt, depression, and fear. He needed to address this pattern and decide whether he wanted to continue in the family business or forge his own path. Not knowing what to do about his career was part of a larger issue: finding himself. Finding who he wanted to be, finding fulfillment in a career, and improving his mood and work performance in the short term were interrelated matters. We decided to address them simultaneously. He didn't know the details of what he wanted to become. His identity had been, to some extent, imposed by birth and by definition—as a member of a prominent family with a family business. Finding himself was an ongoing pursuit. But in the short term, he was clear that he wanted to be more organized and be able to find his things. While I kept raising the possibility of consulting a psychiatrist to see if medication could help with his feeling scattered and disorganized, we devised an immediate plan. Below are the concrete steps we took to improve his current work situation with the hope that an ordered office may help him also have a clearer mind. He kept visualizing his space decluttered and clean and himself being serene and at ease in it. He started to appreciate the idea of having a different environment; he started to visualize it. But did not know how to get there.

Taking the First Steps

To improve his day-to-day performance, Angelo began by decluttering both his mind and physical environment. We started by tackling the mess of scattered papers and disorganized chaos in his space. He committed to spending 30 minutes each morning tidying up, making it a ritual by adding music. In addition, he stated he wanted to call his grandma during these cleaning sessions. Speaking with grandma was both a duty and a mild pleasure. He realized that talking to her while attending to reducing the clutter around him made him feel less restless and less annoyed at her repetitive stories and "life lessons." As we conducted our sessions via video, I could witness Angelo's progress directly, which added a layer of accountability. We were also able to troubleshoot and confront inertia in real time. I believe this step was particularly helpful at that stage, even if it may have slightly interfered with the goal of fostering autonomous decision-making.

For the first week, Angelo focused on organizing and filing the papers on his desk, breaking down the task into manageable chunks to avoid feeling overwhelmed.

Organizing Priorities

Next, we developed a consolidated to-do list. Angelo initially jotted down a long list of tasks, but then we prioritized them using the A, B, C method:

- A tasks: Urgent and important, deadlines needing immediate attention.
- B tasks: Important but can be done next week.
- C tasks: Non-urgent and can be done later.

Angelo committed to completing all A priorities before moving on to B and C tasks. For example, although he wanted to shop for a side table, it was a B priority and had to wait. He put an A, B, or C next to all items of his to-do list. He highlighted all the As to make them stand out. The As were all that mattered for now. See Table 22.1 for this to-do list.

After identifying Angelo's A priorities, we broke them down into specific, manageable steps. We estimated the time needed for each step, leaving some extra time to accommodate unforeseen challenges. Once we created a timeline for each priority—accounting for urgency and deadlines—we placed each step in his calendar, blocking the hour, half-hour, or more needed for each chunk of activity. He also added 10–15 extra minutes to each block for rest, buffer time, or transition. This process helped him *link* his internal intentions to external structures.

We filled the calendar mindfully, aiming to complete each A priority at least one week ahead of its deadline, in case he ran into delays. Angelo was a privileged person who had never followed a real schedule. The goal was not to turn him into a master of productivity. He could afford time to think

Table 22.1 Angelo's List of To-Dos: To Revise Weekly

Activity	Priority	Time if applicable
Staten Island Project	A	
Buy new side table	C	
Return call to Aunt Ida	B	
Look at a box of old prints	C	
Sort out pictures on my phone	B	
Sort out digital pics taken with Canon	A	
Go to barber	B	
Hartford Project	B	
Meeting with Tony S.	B	
Meeting with John F.	B	
Meeting with Silvio D.	C	
Family business meeting		Twice daily (or more)
Read book on organization		Daily just a bit
Meditate		Daily, ten minutes
Go to gym		Twice weekly two hours with commute
Organize apartment		Daily, 30 minutes

and to find his way. However, his financial comfort also contributed to inertia and a lack of urgency.

The deeper aim was to help him *link* his actions to a sense of inner direction and purpose—to reconnect with the rhythm of task and rest, doing and being. We were not just filling his time; we were helping him *link* his efforts to meaning and identity. His tasks needed to *link* to one another and to the outer world. He needed to experience how small steps could unfold, how structure could support rather than imprison his movement, and how his life could regain a sense of coherence.

He also needed to learn how to be "on" and "off" with intention: to work when needed, but also to rest without guilt. To be able to shift between roles and spaces without becoming untethered or overwhelmed. He needed a schedule that would not drain him, but instead allow him to end his day feeling both accomplished and whole. Gradually, this structure became a scaffolding for addressing deeper emotional and existential concerns—without postponing the improvement of his life in the here and now.

To support his difficulty with transitions and attention, we added mindful visualization exercises. Each morning, he sat with his calendar and imagined the steps of the day. He revisited this between tasks and meetings, mentally rehearsing what came next. Sometimes, he used a symbolic image, like "the ball into the hoop," to help him *link* intention with movement. This anticipatory linking helped him face inertia and reconnect with flow. Often, he would include a transition between activities, which served as a kind of palate cleanser between courses. For his being, the equivalent of a refreshing basil granita might be a Metallica song (his favorite band) or a short video call with his adorable nephew, Pino Jr.

To the reader: As you follow Angelo's story, consider doing the same. Prioritize your to-do list into A, B, and C categories, and commit to your A priorities first. Break them into small, doable steps, pair them with a reward, or build in support and accountability.

Do not focus only on the most urgent deadlines. Sometimes, major goals—like applying to graduate school or preparing for a future job—may look like C priorities because they are far away, but they are false C's: they require early attention and long-term planning. Include them. Link your now to your future.

What matters most is creating a system that helps you sort, activate, and *link* your efforts. With structure and persistence, steady progress becomes not only possible, but likely. Stay focused as long as it works for you. Then step away. Come back refreshed and refocus. That rhythm, too, is part of the work.

Example: Staten Island Project (One of Angelo's A Priorities)

One of Angelo's most pressing A priorities was preparing for a Staten Island project. We broke it down into tasks that were required to accomplish the A priority well and in a timely manner. We planned for weekly objectives; within the week, we considered how many available hours were in Angelo's calendar. Then blocked time based on time available in the calendar and his attention span. For instance, in Week 1, Angelo had five hours to accomplish a step called "Outline and develop Staten Island project." To create this project's outline, Angelo scheduled one hour on Monday morning, after meditation at 9:30–10:30am; Tuesday, he scheduled his work on the outline at 12pm, before lunch, and another hour before leaving the office, at 5pm; Wednesday he would work on it 9:30am after his meditation, and he scheduled the last hour on the outline for the week. He knew that scheduling five hours in a row would not match his span of attention and would not suit him. During the day, when Angelo finished one task or appointment, he could stretch, refresh but then he knew what he needed to do next in his calendar, in order to inch a step closer to the fulfillment of his overall project; in between chunks of activities, a transition "ritual" helped. Week 1 focused on building the foundation of the project, Week 2 on production and refinement, and Week 3 on finalization and rehearsal. Angelo's photography work spans a longer three-month arc, with initial steps scheduled in these early weeks. Table 22.2 shows Angelo's calendar over the three weeks of his Staten Island project. Table 22.3 shows a typical day in the first week of the project.

Table 22.2 Angelo's Calendar for the Development of the Staten Island Project and Angelo's Daily Schedule Routine

Week	To do	Time
1	Foundation and early planning of the Staten Island project	
	Meditation / Set intention (daily)	10 min.
	Outline and develop Staten Island project	5 hours
	Return calls	1 hour
	Begin sorting photography portfolio	1 hour
	Office cleanup (daily)	1/2 hour
2	Development and refinement of the Staten Island project	
	Meditation / Set intention (daily)	10 min.
	Flesh out Staten Island project details	1 hour
	Create PowerPoint presentation	5 hours
	Draft leaflet	2 hours
	Request feedback	1/2 hour
	Continue office cleanup	1/2 hour
	Continue organizing photography portfolio	1
	Office cleanup	1/2 hour
3	Finalization and rehearsal of the Staten Island project	
	Meditation / Set intention (daily)	10 min.
	Finalize leaflet design	1 hour
	Rehearse Staten Island presentation	1 hour
	Approve final drafts	1 hour
	Contact galleries (photography portfolio)	1 hour
	Prepare PDF of portfolio (initial version)	1 hour
	Office cleanup (daily)	1/2 hour

All this behind-the-scenes work allowed Angelo to free up mental space. Instead of constantly having to figure out what to do next and dragging himself there, he felt less stuck and more focused. Over time, the structure did not feel constraining, it felt liberating. It gave him a sense of accomplishment, forward movement, a stronger voice within the family and even freed up time to play.

Balancing Work and Personal Goals

Angelo also added personal priorities to his calendar, such as exploring whether he could turn his photography passion into a career. He planned to

Table 22.3 A Day in Angelo's Calendar the Second Week of the Staten Island Project

Time	Activity
8–8:30 am	Wake up: Meditate
9–9:30 am	Tidy up
9:30–10:30 am	Flesh out the Staten Island project
10:30–11 am	Return calls
11–1 pm	Create PowerPoint Presentation
1–2 pm	Lunch
2–3 pm	Meeting
3–5 pm	Create PowerPoint Presentation
5–6 pm	Buy ticket
6:30 pm	Meeting
7 pm	Gym

devote one hour after work on non-gym days to organizing his photo collection into a portfolio. By setting aside specific time for this, Angelo made the task more manageable and less daunting.

Angelo's journey involved learning to rely on his calendar, breaking tasks into small, achievable steps, and trusting that change was possible. These tools helped reduce his sense of overwhelm and allowed him to focus. Most importantly, they supported a growing belief that he could shape his own path: professionally and personally.

Takeaway Exercise: A, B, C Prioritizing

Try creating a calendar to help you accomplish your goals. Creating a structure may help you to feel like you are on task and less stressed:

1   Create a to-do list.
2   Sort tasks into A, B, and C priorities.
3   Focus on A priorities, setting deadlines for each.
4   Break down A tasks into smaller steps and estimate the time needed for each.
5   Schedule these steps in your calendar, allowing time to rest and recharge.
6   For complex projects, set weekly objectives.
7   Troubleshoot potential obstacles and revise your calendar as needed.

Remember, your to-do list and calendar are roadmaps that guide you toward your goals, helping you stay on track even when life throws unexpected challenges your way.

Set Your Intention: The Ball Goes in the Hoop

One way to motivate yourself is to try the following meditation, which you can repeat several times a day. I first learned this exercise during a professional development training led by athletic coach David McDuff, who taught his basketball players to center themselves, gather their concentration, and visualize the ball moving toward and sinking into the hoop.

They sync their breath in and out with this imaginary movement. Like them, you can sync your breathing to your movement from ideation and gathering of intention to your imaginary representation of your goal, already accomplished.

Start by sitting still and breathing slowly, gathering concentration. With a deep long exhale, release all stale air. Say to yourself, "I am setting the intention of..." and name whatever the goal or next step is while visualizing the endpoint.

You can then start to synchronize your breathing with a rocking movement, which can prove to be quite hypnotic. As you breathe in, flex your spine, moving your chest slightly forward and lifting your face. As you breathe out, focus inside—your silence, your stability, your energy— and slightly round your upper body, lowering your chin. (In other words, from a seated position, you flex and extend your spine, in a wave-like motion similar to the four legged cat/cow yoga pose.)

Focus on your target and imagine the presentation, the interview, or the performance ending with applause. Imagine the project accomplished, the book published, the building constructed. Let yourself feel the sense of completion and satisfaction, as if it were happening now. Visualization can activate hope and keep momentum alive, even when the external path feels uncertain.

From To-Do List to Daily Schedule: A Clear Planning Process

1 *Clarify your priorities:*

- Create and review your full to-do list.
- Prioritize using A, B, and C and identify your most important "A" priorities—what truly matters or is time-sensitive.

2 *Break down each priority into tasks:*

- For each priority, list the specific tasks required to complete it.
- Estimate the time each task will take and identify what needs to happen before you can begin.

3 *Draft a general timeline:*

- Lay out when each priority should ideally be completed.

- Build in extra time—aim to finish at least a week before the actual deadline.

4   *Plan weekly objectives:*

- Decide what progress you want to make on each project this week.
- Select a manageable number of tasks for the week based on your capacity.

5   *Translate weekly goals into a daily schedule:*

- Assign your weekly tasks to specific time blocks on your calendar.
- Use realistic chunks (e.g., 30–90 minutes), and add buffer time for transitions or delays.

6   *Include transitions and recentering moments:*

- Between work blocks, include something that resets you: a short walk, a song, a cup of tea.
- For example, one patient used a Metallica track or a video call with his nephew as a reset.

7   *Begin each day with a quick review:*

- Check your schedule. Adjust based on new demands, energy levels, or insights.

8   *Stay focused and flexible:*

- Work with focus as long as it serves you. Step away when needed. Return grounded.

Interlude for Therapists

Many of these techniques, such as prioritization systems, calendars, scheduling rituals, may be familiar or depending on your orientation you may find them not appropriate for therapy. Yet even the most practical tools can become transformative when approached as part of a shared, attuned therapeutic process.

What may look like procrastination or disorganization may be due to shame, fear, or inherited relational dynamics. When clients say, "I do not know where to start," we can help them break tasks into steps, but we can also help them to pause and free associate and to invite reflection on the narratives and emotions woven into the stuckness.

Setting an intention is an important part of the process—but on its own, it is not enough. As the saying goes, "The road to hell is paved with good intentions." Intention is the seed; it holds the vision and the spark. However, it is the ongoing practice, the repeated effort over time, that turns intention into habit and habit into real change.

Together with your client, you might explore the following:

- Whether a calendar evokes hope or pressure
- How family expectations shape career ambivalence
- What a "to-do list" might represent emotionally—freedom, obligation, or something else

In the vignette above, Angelo's shifts were not only logistical; they reflected movement in his sense of self, agency, and relational position. Behavioral tools served as scaffolding, but the change was rooted in the therapeutic relationship. These tools are offered not as protocols, but as flexible supports that can be adapted within your existing frame, whether psychodynamic, somatic, systemic, or another.

What may look like a simple time management technique is, in fact, a layered therapeutic intervention. Moving from to-do lists to priorities, from priorities to weekly focus, and from there into daily calendar blocks, with time for rest and transitions, is not only about productivity. It is about reclaiming agency, creating flow, and making space for a life that feels lived, not just managed. For many immigrants, survivors of trauma, and highly sensitive or ambivalent individuals, structure can offer containment without rigidity. Thoughtfully applied, it becomes a way to link internal intention to external action, to move from paralysis to engagement. A schedule does not have to imprison; it can become a vessel that helps hold complexity, pace, and possibility.

Returning to You

Whether you are an immigrant finding your way in a new land, or a therapist walking alongside someone through the uncertainty of transition, remember that the tools in this chapter are not only about getting things done. They are about regaining a sense of agency. With a calendar, a to-do list, and a moment of stillness to set your intention, you are not simply organizing tasks—you are quietly, steadily, shaping your future.

Notes

1 Steven A. Safren, Susan Sprich, Carol A. Perlman, and Michael W. Otto, *Mastering Your Adult ADHD: A Cognitive-Behavioral Treatment Program* (Oxford: Oxford University Press, 2005), 14.
2 The cognitive-behavioral tools developed for ADHD are valuable for anyone seeking to improve organization and focus. In my clinical work, I often draw from the structured approach outlined in Safren et al., *Mastering Your Adult ADHD*. For those who wish to explore further, I sometimes recommend *Atomic Habits: An Easy & Proven Way to Build Good Habits & Break Bad Ones* by James Clear (New York: Avery, 2018), which offers practical guidance on habit formation, structure, and momentum.

References

Clear, James. 2018. *Atomic Habits: An Easy & Proven Way to Build Good Habits & Break Bad Ones*. New York: Avery.

Safren, Steven A., Susan Sprich, Carol A. Perlman, and Michael W. Otto. 2005. *Mastering Your Adult ADHD: A Cognitive-Behavioral Treatment Program*. New York: Oxford University Press.

23 One Step, One Thread

Sewing Toward the Unknown Path of Belonging

I often emphasize the importance of organization. People are creatures of habit, and even those who tend to be less structured but want to change often struggle to commit to a more structured lifestyle. However, organization is a fundamental step toward progress. If you're hesitant about making changes, consider that organization and vision serve as your roadmap, helping you turn abstract ideas into actionable steps. This roadmap connects where you are now to where you want to be in the future, allowing you to move forward with clarity and purpose.

By staying connected to your vision and remaining organized, you create the structure needed to stay focused and on course. The roadmap marks your current position—"you are here"—and guides you toward a future that doesn't yet exist but is within reach. The concreteness of a schedule makes this imagined space feel real, bridging the gap between dreams and reality. It combines your hopes and aspirations with a realistic assessment of your time and resources. Visualization alone won't bring results; it's the structure that turns dreams into achievable objectives.

Each day, as you follow your plan, you get closer to your goal, marking progress one step at a time. If unexpected obstacles arise, you troubleshoot and adjust accordingly. Just as a journey requires a compass and a backpack filled with essentials, reaching your goals calls for the right tools: Nine-Lens, Set Your Intention meditation, coping statements, the Book of Missed Catastrophes, and the Book of Success, along with the support of loved ones. These tools help you navigate challenges, maintain focus, and keep moving forward.

Your compass—made up of mindfulness and observation—helps you stay grounded and adjust as needed. It ensures that your schedule becomes reality, guiding you from vision to execution, like securing a new job or completing a major goal. A disciplined lifestyle, balanced with pleasures, supports your progress. Change doesn't happen through hope and imagination alone; it requires work.

So, how do you link your present reality to your dreams? How do you keep going when discouraged? Tools like the ones described in this book are the guiding forces that make progress possible. Rather than viewing organization as a chore or burden, embrace it as an essential tool for success. Yet,

DOI: 10.4324/9781003648703-30

no matter how much you plan, life may take unexpected turns. You might set out for one destination and end up somewhere else entirely. While organization is key, it's important to recognize that some outcomes remain beyond our control.

Even if my words have convinced you, I know that it is not an easy task to organize ourselves. Often what drives us to get more organized is the realization of an imminent failure. If we are not too discouraged and helpless, then we seek help. Sometimes stubborn disorganization is a symptom of a medical condition, such as ADHD or depression. In such cases, therapy and medication can help. But it could also be that you may not have had helpful examples in your life and have to start from scratch with organizational techniques. Maybe, as happened to me in grad school, a new step in life requires a higher level of organization you weren't even aware existed. However, you may also be resisting organization. You may find organization boring and see it as an extra step that wastes time and adds little. It could also be that you shun organization because you experience it as an imposition and a limitation of your authority. It may be that it reminds you of old authority figures, like your parents, or your old country's governmental power structure, or you may be resisting the tight time/work structure of this capitalist country. Sometimes patients need years to dispel the psychological blocks that prevent them from adhering to a minimum of scheduling and organization. No scheduling is equal to freedom for some of them, and I get that. But from a pragmatic viewpoint, if we want to get from here to there, if we want to succeed in this country, we need to endorse a minimum of organization as it is conceptualized in this country.

The Power of Images and Visualization

One way to create a future in which you become who you want to become and achieve your dreams is to visualize it. When visualizing your ideal self, it is important to do so in the present tense, as if it were already happening. This is especially relevant for immigrants, who are often portrayed negatively in the media. Images of migrants lined up at borders, depicted as helpless or as threats,[1] dominate public perception. These representations can be demoralizing when absorbed uncritically. I am not denying the reality these images reflect; many immigrants have lived through tremendous hardship. But these portrayals are only part of the picture. Equally real, though less visible, are the millions of immigrants who sustain this country every day, keeping it running through their work, care, and creativity. Both the demonized and idealized representations reduce people to symbols and serve political agendas more than lived truth.

Visualization is not only a private act; it is also shaped by the images that surround us. That is why it is vital—for individuals and communities—to reclaim the narrative, just as artists do. *Another Way Home*,[2] a project by the Open Society Foundations, brings together eight initiatives by 13 artists and

254 Neither Here Nor There

storytellers who explore migration through documentary practice. They highlight themes of identity, community, and resilience, challenging dominant portrayals of refugees and immigrants.

Among them is *Project Luz*, a collaboration with Mujeres en Movimiento, a group of Latina women in Corona, Queens, NY. These women stage themselves doing the creative or professional work they already do or aspire to do. One woman poses as a pastry chef; another, an activist who started a school community garden, presents herself with some of the piñatas she makes and sells. Their images affirm both present strength and future aspiration. In *After Migration*, artist Walé Oyéjidé photographs immigrants in striking garments that blend African and European influences, portraying them as dignified, stylish, and fully seen. The *Vision Not Victim*[3] project supports girls and women globally by helping them step into their power. In one initiative, refugee girls work with mentors and are photographed already embodying their future careers—pediatrician, painter, pilot, teacher, fashion designer, human rights lawyer. Through these staged portraits, fantasy becomes a step toward embodiment. Representation becomes transformation.

Takeaway Exercise

Create your own *tableau vivant*: a living portrait of who you want to become. Dress up, pose with friends or children, and enact a scene from your imagined future. Take a photo or short video. Share it, if you wish, as a declaration of your evolving identity. The future starts here.

Andrei's Story

My patient Andrei's resistance to organization illustrates how difficult it can be for children of immigrants to get more organized and succeed, especially when their parents endured unfathomable unprocessed losses. Andrei is an only child, second-generation Russian American man. He comes from a chaotic family. His father is an alcoholic, and his mother suffers from depression, with a history of not protecting her son. Andrei's father wielded authority in an arbitrary and ineffective way. He was also an angry man, frustrated by the loss of what could have been a promising future had the USSR not collapsed. His life in the US had not turned out as well as he had hoped.

Andrei initially grew up either avoiding or submitting to his father, but as soon as he could, he began challenging and resisting him. This defiance extended beyond his father to include resisting many of his school's rules, workplace expectations, and society's norms in general.

Andrei had never been in trouble with the law, but he was not thriving in life either. He sought my help as a last resort after receiving two write-ups at work, realizing he was on the verge of losing his job. Although he wanted assistance, he was initially unwilling—or perhaps unable—to absorb my guidance or put any of the tools I offered into practice. Offering organizational tools was not about bypassing depth but about meeting Andrei where he was—on the edge of crisis—and using those moments as entry points into the emotional undercurrents beneath his behavior.

Andrei would come to sessions to vent, often contradicting anything I said, putting me down, and expressing anger. I realized I had to adjust my approach and allow more time for progress. Even when we worked colla-boratively, setting objectives, schedules, and strategies for his work week, he still had a rebellious inner voice that sabotaged his efforts. For instance, while interacting with his boss or team, he would undermine himself by rebelling, stalling, getting angry, or becoming short-tempered.

Eventually, through mindfulness and micro-observing his thoughts and feelings during those critical moments before self-sabotage, Andrei uncov-ered the root of his behavior. He realized that there was a voice inside him saying, "Fu@#$ it!" in response to minor irritants. However, this reaction was amplified by unresolved anger from the past, specifically his childhood experiences with his father. Andrei was reacting to present power struggles with the exaggerated force of emotions tied to his father's annihilating, overpowering, and arbitrary authority.

As he became more aware at work, Andrei noticed a feeling of power-lessness and suffocation just before the "Fu@#$ it!" moment. In those instances, he would relieve those unbearable feelings by asserting a sense of power and freedom, the power to rebel and say by words, actions, or inac-tion, "Fu@#$ you!" However, his behavior came at the cost of damaging his professional relationships. What he came to understand was that his intense anger in the present was not truly aimed at his boss or coworkers—it was directed at his father, whose anger he had silently endured as a child.

Through this realization, Andrei recognized that his past experiences, while still alive within him, no longer belonged in his workplace. The pre-sent situation was far more benign; he was not powerless or oppressed any-more. In fact, he was competent and capable, no longer the victim he had been as a child. Acknowledging this, Andrei decided he didn't want to continue harming himself with this misplaced rebellion. The anger he once felt toward his father, while justified, was now irrelevant. His father, old, depressed, and powerless, was not the same force he had once been.

What Andrei could do now was focus on healing his own life—working through his childhood trauma in therapy and taking responsibility for his future. The self-sabotage was not serving him, and with that insight, he was able to move forward.

The Strategical Self and the Emotional Self

In the example of Andrei, above, we saw how Andrei was conflating past and present, when he was triggered by issues of authority. However, even when there is no trauma or major issues of authority and control, we can be of two minds about going forward with our projects. Change is elating and exciting but also hard and scary. Change entails big sacrifices and we like our rest and pleasures. Change makes us different from the people around us, so it can also be isolating and alienating.

As we prepare the roadmap for our journey and face our next challenge, we may notice the presence of different aspects within ourselves. I call these the *strategical self* and the *emotional self*. Often, one may dominate the other. The strategical self is the mindset that plans for change, creating schedules to balance family, work, and self-care. It organizes projects, sets boundaries around worry, and takes a proactive, logical approach. This part is positive, self-assured, and can clearly map out the steps toward achieving a goal. Operating from a bird's-eye view, the strategical self builds the roadmap and tracks to-do lists, deadlines, and schedules. It thrives in the abstract, where there's safety in planning and room for hope and imagination.

Even during strategy sessions, the emotional self is present. It brings the passion that fuels your goals but also the fear and doubt that can hold you back. It wants to protect you, sometimes to a fault, and often reacts with shame, anxiety, or uncertainty. The strategical self, by contrast, plans and reasons. It focuses on logical steps and long-term goals. These two sides of the self, emotional and strategic, are both essential. But learning how to balance them is key. This is not about denying emotions or splitting off parts of ourselves. It is about learning how to let our strengths prepare the way for the parts of us that need more reassurance, so we can move forward as a whole.

What I am suggesting is this: make the strategic self work ahead of time. Let it create a plan when you feel calm and clear-minded, so that when doubt creeps in, you can trust the process already in place. You built it with foresight. When the moment to act arrives, emotions may surge. The closer you get to execution, the more threatened you may feel. The bird's-eye view of planning gives way to the tension of reality. If you feel strong, emotions energize you. But if doubt takes over, logic can be drowned out. In those moments, your job is to recognize what is happening and return to the roadmap. Trust the work your calmer mind already did. One step at a time.

Reflection for Immigrants

What if your emotional self takes over, instilling doubts and fears at a crucial moment? What would your strategic self say in that moment? Use your internal compass to navigate these challenges. This means applying the CBT tools we've discussed. When you feel your mood shift or sense avoidance creeping in, turn to the classics: Thought Records, the Nine-Lens, coping statements, the Book of Success, and the Book of Missed Catastrophes. Guided meditations that help you visualize your path can also reinforce your strength and calm your mind. Your written plan helps you stay on course, even when emotions threaten to derail you.

The roadmap you built when your mind was calm and focused will guide you. Don't surrender to the doubts and fears brought on by emotional turbulence. Trust the work of your strategical self. Remind your emotional self that the plan was created with logic and care, and that each step is feasible. Reassure yourself that you are not in harm's way.

When distractions and temptations pull you away from your goals, bring your strategical self back into the driver's seat. Decide how much you can realistically accomplish each day, even if it's just a small amount. Progress, no matter how incremental, is still progress. Sometimes just one step forward is enough. Be mindful of hyperactivity and hyperfocus: When all your energy goes into personal advancement or career development, you may become more vulnerable and emotionally impoverished. True resilience includes care for your inner world and your relationships, not just your goals.

Connect your heart, mind, and body to your vision and follow through with your commitments. In difficult moments, when your courage, energy, or self-esteem waver, practice self-compassion. Bring all your inner voices into dialogue, including the anxious, doubtful, or "lazy" ones, and let the most mature and functional parts of yourself comfort and guide the others. Don't abandon your efforts, especially under pressure. In moments of overwhelm, bind yourself to your plan. Let your strategical self, like a crew of steady rowers, guide you stroke by stroke, bringing you closer to your destination.

The Support Network

As plants need sticks and raffia for support when they are still tender and growing, you too need structures of support in your life. Waiting to feel in sync with the world before you start a project may mean waiting forever. It is by reaching out to others that you can receive support. It is by building links, not severing them further, that you feel more connected. It is by realizing your capacities and your creativity that you feel better. It is by testing negative beliefs that you learn about your distortions. It is by confronting your fears that you diminish them. And by doing and daring to be yourself, you give yourself the chance to develop your potential.

However, all the above mentioned statements are much better achieved in the presence of positive loving people that lovingly challenge you, cheer you on, and are willing to be your buddy when you are anxious or disorganized. So, connect with others. Do not wait. Make that call; join that running club; go to that meetup. Do at least a little bit to connect—to your loved ones, your community—every day. Below are some bullet points about connection:

- Maintain your community. Check in with your loved ones.
- Continue to expand a solid network. If you have not yet established a network, ask yourself: "How can I build supportive communities that sustain me, so that I am not completely or exclusively self-reliant or dependent on my partner, job, or unhealthy habits for comfort?" Search for local support or interest groups or volunteer.

- Do not underestimate or be snobbish about your community of origin. There may be judgment, envy, shame, or outdated values and ideologies you hope to leave behind, but this community might also offer valuable networking leads, mentorship possibilities, and emotional sustenance. Cultivate the connection, but do not let it confine you.
- If you cannot leave an unhealthy relationship because of financial or immigration reasons, consider the pros and cons. Reach out to your local Office of Immigrant Affairs,[4] where pro bono lawyers can give you advice. If you are emotionally dependent, go to a CoDA meeting.[5] Think about an exit strategy. Even one good new connection may offer a way out. A small amount of professional advancement, such as an online course, for example, may provide a helpful pathway to financial independence.
- Know your weaknesses and look ahead for strategies to help you handle upsetting situations that may result in impulsive and self-sabotaging behavior.
- Get a friend/buddy—even on Zoom—to help you move off the couch and onto a yoga mat or an outdoor running path.
- Connect your brain to a community brain. Don't be ashamed to ask for help or internalize and use other people's helpful ideas. Everything that is spoken, written, and accomplished is the result of the accumulation of the knowledge that preceded it. It takes a village to accomplish things, so take the village with you in your journey.
- Expand your heart to the community: If you make people your home, you will feel at home.

Seize the Moment When It Comes

As an immigrant, you have made addressing the unexpected a normal way of being. You have developed a capacity to adjust to unpredictable situations and challenges. You can take the lead when extraordinary situations arise. Observe your environment to see where you have an edge. Where can you take advantage of the qualities you developed in your *double belonging*? Where can your ability to speak and operate in various languages, cultures, traditions, and values fit and be especially valued? Where can you capitalize on your capacity to be flexible and adapt and make do?

Consider how this position gives you an edge. As an outsider, you can naturally think outside the box. Some of us don't even have the box. If you add the few simple tools presented in this book and activate the capacities you have been honing all along in your immigration journey, you could definitely increase your chances of success. Let's consider my client Flor again. She recently changed jobs. The new job is so advanced she feels she cannot find her footing. One day she started our session with the following:

I feel like a puzzle with all the pieces thrown on the table. In the past, I would have freaked out. I am more mature now. When I am getting stressed, I automatically think of the *dimmer switch* we talked about in therapy, and I manage to turn my strong emotions down a bit. I tell myself to "tone it down." At meetings, I feel so confused. They talk, and I don't understand a great deal. I sit there in silence, trying to soak it all in. Still, I have not figured out what I am supposed to do. But I also say to myself: "In three months, I will get it." I think I am really experiencing time differently. As we said last week, in the past I was flattened, bidimensional. I could not imagine movement or light at the end of the tunnel. Now I find myself saying, "Little by little, piece by piece, I will figure it out."

In these few words, Flor summarized an important part of our work together. She can use the image of a "dimmer switch" to caringly tone down her unpleasant and unproductive emotions; she can zoom out of the present difficult moment and soothe herself by knowing that no feeling or situation is permanent. The thrilling aspect of Flor's new job is that, despite her current learning curve, she has already found some opportunities that are ideal for her, including creating essential lines of communication between departments that historically have not talked (but should). Flor became the connector, the translator, the communication broker, which is a fitting role for an immigrant. She also exploited her hard-earned capacity to be okay with being in an environment with unclear and confusing rules. Her hard-earned wisdom about acknowledging the legitimacy of different points of views and working with them, and her capacity to deal with the confusion of tongues and crosstalk, are invaluable contributions that are often unique to what immigrants can bring.

Therefore, keep honing your skills; keep honoring your heritage and culture; keep being open; keep working on your roadmap and your emotional well-being. If there is a glass ceiling, keep scanning for cracks, and when you see an opening, seize that opportunity and jump in with your powerful immigrant toolset. You already possess what it takes: the grit, the adaptability, the vision. This chapter is not about becoming someone else; it is about remembering your own resourcefulness and putting it to work. Each small action you take is not only a step forward but a quiet defiance of everything that has tried to keep you stuck. You do not have to wait until you feel ready. Begin now, with what you have, from where you are. Just do it—a bit.

While many of the tools in this chapter are oriented toward action and structure, they can coexist with depth-oriented work. The reflections below are offered to psychodynamic therapists who may approach "doing" with caution.

Therapist Interlude: Bridging Depth and Action

As someone trained in psychodynamic traditions, I understand the concern that too much direction, or even visibly wishing the patient well, might interfere with the treatment. We worry that offering suggestions could heighten resistance, intrude on the patient's psychic space, or create a compliance dynamic that short-circuits deeper work. These are thoughtful concerns, born of a tradition that values the patient's autonomy and the unconscious unfolding of meaning. And yet, we might ask: When does therapeutic restraint become therapeutic withholding? There are moments, especially when a patient is paralyzed, despairing, or self-defeating, when holding hope only in our minds is not enough. A tentative invitation to "do," when attuned and collaboratively shaped, can animate the work. Offering a to-do list, a roadmap, or even a single named option does not negate the transference. In fact, it can deepen it by surfacing fantasies of dependency, failure, or rebellion.

Structure does not replace depth; it can support it. When thoughtfully integrated, concrete tools become vessels through which therapeutic insight moves into life. Practical guidance becomes not a shortcut, but a scaffold. It becomes a way of saying, "I believe in your future, even if you cannot yet."

When "Doing" Deepens the Work

Many of us have witnessed moments when a simple, shared plan, such as creating a list, setting a reminder, or writing a letter, catalyzed deeper emotional work. The doing became the doorway. One patient I worked with, for example, could not begin decluttering her apartment until she named the fear that she would erase her deceased mother's presence. Only after naming that fear could she begin organizing her space, and in doing so, she found new room in her psyche, too.

Let us not split the practical from the emotional or the behavioral from the relational. Sometimes, the smallest act—making a call, clearing a desk, writing a list—can carry the weight of profound transformation. We do not have to wait five years for movement to begin. We can invite movement, delicately, while also holding space for everything it stirs.

Whether you are a therapist or someone trying to find your next foothold, remember: doing and feeling are not at odds. They can walk hand in hand.

Reflection prompt: Where am I on the roadmap? What is one structure I could build this week to support my next step?

Closing Reflection

If you are holding this book in your hands, perhaps you are stitching the threads of your life together—slowly, imperfectly, bravely. The map you are drawing may not be linear, and your compass may wobble, but with each small act of planning and doing, you are mending, you are weaving, you are choosing life.

Let the next stitch be yours.

Notes

1 Karolina Nikielska-Sekuła, "Visual Portrayals of Migrants as Threats or Victims Are Reductive—But Can Have Far-Reaching Impact," *Migration Information Source,* March 5, 2025, www.migrationpolicy.org/article/visual-portrayals-migration.
2 Yukiko Yamagata and Siobhan Riordan, "Announcing Moving Walls 25: Another Way Home," *Open Society Foundations,* September 13, 2018, www.opensociety foundations.org/voices/announcing-moving-walls-25-another-way-home www.tpr. org/2018-10-07/stunning-photos-depict-migrants-as-theyd-rather-be-seen
3 Resistance Communications, *Vision Not Victim* (n.d.), www.resistancecommunica tions.com/vision-not-victim
   ABC News, "Vision Not Victim: Refugee Girls Create Their Future," March 8, 2016, https://abcnews.go.com/International/photos/vision-victim-refugee-girls-crea te-future-36696881
4 For New York, Mayor's Office of Immigrant Affairs, MOIA, in New York: www1. nyc.gov/site/immigrants/index.page. For instance, VAWA is a U.S. law that protects immigrant spouses and children of American citizens or lawful permanent residents who are trapped in violent or abusive relationships. Under VAWA, they can apply for legal status on their own—without relying on their abusive partner to sponsor them for a visa or green card. For more info: www.ilrc.org/sites/default/ files/2023-02/Who%20is%20Eligible%20for%20VAWA%3F.pdf.
5 Co-Dependents Anonymous, *CoDA.org,* https://coda.org.

References

ABC News. 2016. "Vision Not Victim: Refugee Girls Create Their Future." March 8. https://abcnews.go.com/International/photos/vision-victim-refugee-girls-create-futu re-36696881.

Co-Dependents Anonymous (CoDA). n.d. *Official Website.* https://coda.org.

Immigrant Legal Resource Center (ILRC). 2023. "Who Is Eligible for VAWA?" February. www.ilrc.org/sites/default/files/2023-02/Who%20is%20Eligible%20for%20VAWA% 3F.pdf.

New York City Mayor's Office of Immigrant Affairs (MOIA). n.d. *Home Page.* www1. nyc.gov/site/immigrants/index.page.

Nikielska-Sekuła, Karolina. 2025. "Visual Portrayals of Migrants as Threats or Victims Are Reductive—But Can Have Far-Reaching Impact." *Migration Information Source,* March 5. www.migrationpolicy.org/article/visual-portrayals-migration.

Resistance Communications. n.d. *Vision Not Victim.* www.resistancecommunications. com/vision-not-victim.

Texas Public Radio. 2018. "Stunning Photos Depict Migrants as They'd Rather Be Seen." October 7. www.tpr.org/2018-10-07/stunning-photos-depict-migrants-as-they d-rather-be-seen.

Yamagata, Yukiko, and Siobhan Riordan. 2018. "Announcing Moving Walls 25: Another Way Home." *Open Society Foundations,* September 13. www.opensocie tyfoundations.org/voices/announcing-moving-walls-25-another-way-home.

Appendices: About the Tools in These Appendices

The tools and worksheets in these appendices include both established therapeutic techniques—such as the Chair Exercise and the Folded Page—and original adaptations developed by the author, including the Nine-Lens Worksheet. All have been shaped through years of clinical experience with immigrants and cross-cultural themes and are presented here as reflective and practical aids for healing and integration.

These are a few selected tools and worksheets. Many additional therapeutic strategies—including narrative prompts, meditative exercises, and cognitive tools—are integrated throughout the book, tailored to the themes of each chapter.

Appendix A: Feeling Scale

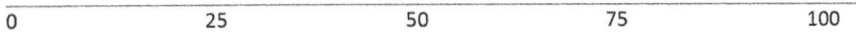

0	25	50	75	100

Figure A.1 Feeling Scale

To become more comfortable assigning a number to your feelings and creating a scale, it can be helpful to recall times when you experienced 0% and 100% of a particular emotion. What was happening during those moments? Then consider what 50% might have felt like, followed by 25% and 75%. By progressing in this way, you create personal reference points that make it easier to gauge the intensity of your emotions in the present moment.

You can use the scale by drawing a horizontal line and handwriting your thoughts or experiences next to the numbers that represent the intensity of your feelings. This exercise helps you link specific emotions—and their relative intensity—to meaningful real-life situations.

Below are two examples of how the scale can be used. For ease of reading, both have been typed and arranged vertically.

The first example comes from Lina, a South American patient at the beginning of her treatment. As she navigated the challenges of immigration and adjustment, Lina begins to identify the intensity of her emotions. She pairs each level with the thoughts and experiences that triggered them, becoming more familiar with gauging her feelings and assigning them a number.

In the second example, Juwang uses the scale to reflect on how his emotions, thoughts, and experiences shifted throughout the week. In his case, the scale becomes a tool for tracking patterns and gaining deeper insight.

Anxiety Scale

Filled by Lina, a recent immigrant experiencing adjustment stress:

Intensity (%)	Description
0	Completely calm, meditating by the sea with no responsibilities.
25	Mild tension in the chest, but able to focus—like before a routine meeting.
50	Uneasy and distracted—feeling unsure about a phone call in English.
75	Heart racing, shallow breathing—navigating a hospital form alone.
100	Full panic—missed immigration appointment, cannot speak, overwhelmed by fear.

Another Example of a Feeling Scale

Juwang: Tracking emotional highs and lows across the week:

Intensity (%)	Description
0	Saturday morning, resting in my room, and Sunday morning while jogging in the park. I feel calm and grounded, with a sense of inner quiet. No urgency, just presence.
25	Sunday evening. A wave of unease settles in as I start thinking about the upcoming week. I feel tension in my chest and pressure to fall asleep quickly, but I toss and turn instead.
50	Monday morning, just before a job interview. My body feels shaky, my mind goes blank, and a tight knot forms in my stomach. I question my ability to perform.
75	Midweek staff meeting with unexpected criticism. I feel exposed and anxious. My heart pounds, my palms sweat, and I struggle to speak. I want to withdraw completely.
100	Full panic during a high-stakes presentation at work, in an environment where I feel judged and unsupported. My chest constricts, my voice falters, and I lose track of what I am saying. It feels like my body and mind are shutting down.

Appendix B: The River of Life

If your life were a river... Which tributaries helped it grow?

What rapids, rough waters, stagnant pools, natural or artificial dams, and small islands of rest and peace made it challenging, comforting, stressful, joyful, traumatizing, or rich?

Let us pause to reflect on your journey. Seen through this visual metaphor, your story may begin to make more sense. Perhaps it will feel easier to understand how you became who you are today when you take stock of all you have traveled through to arrive here.

Take your time. Move slowly. You can always skip parts you are not ready to revisit. It is okay to protect yourself from overwhelm.

What lifeboats, travel companions, or fishing rods do you wish you had along the way? What tools can you offer yourself now?

Use words and drawings to mark the turning points, resources, losses, and moments of clarity. When you finish, look at what you have created. The river is still flowing. What might its next direction be?

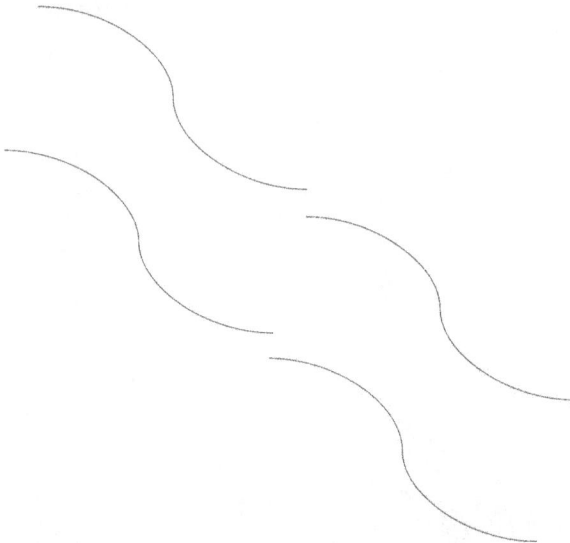

Figure B.1 River of Life, Originally Created by Joyce Mercer

Appendix C: Three Worlds of Values

For this exercise, take a sheet of paper and fold it into three columns. Use the space to reflect on and organize the values that have shaped you.

- In the left column, list the values you recognize from your country of origin, those you were raised with or that shaped your early worldview.
- In the right column, write down the values you encounter in your current context, such as those you observe in U.S. culture or society.
- In the center column, reflect on what you want to keep, adapt, or integrate from both sides. This is the space for negotiation: What feels true to you? What do you want to hold onto or transform?
- Optionally, you can add a fourth column (or mark with a symbol) for the values you wish to let go of entirely—whether they come from your past or your present.

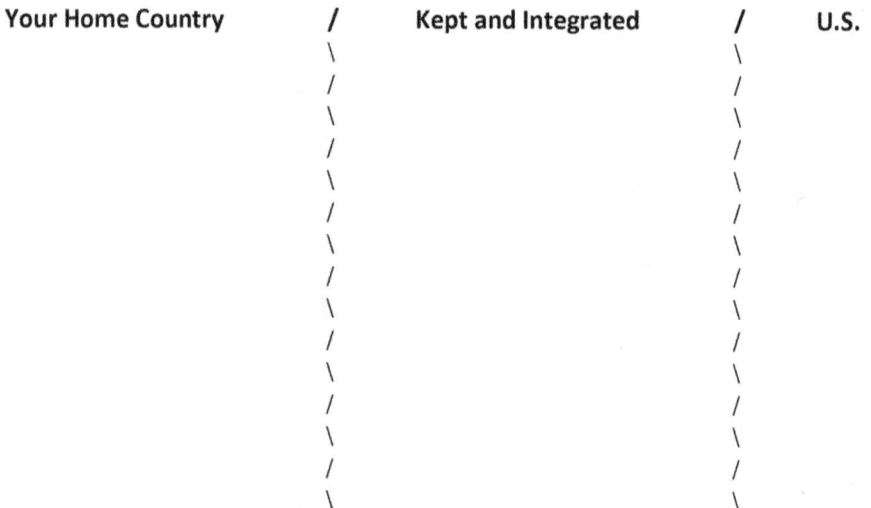

Your Home Country	Kept and Integrated	U.S.

Figure C.1 Three Worlds of Values

This exercise is not about judgment but about awareness and choice. By naming these values, you begin to map the emotional and cultural terrain that defines your life in between.

Appendix D: Nine-Lens Reflective Tool

Nine-Lens Reflective Tool—Blank Template:

1. Situation	2. Feelings / body sensations	3. Thoughts and images	4. Reframing (expanded)	5. Family history	6. Sociocultural realities (condensed)	7. New mantra	8. Updated feelings	9. Action plan
[Enter triggering situation: what, who, when, where]	[Describe emotions and body sensations: rate 1–100]	[Write thoughts/ images with truth ratings if possible]	[Examine evidence for/ against; explore reframes; label distortions]	[Family patterns, early experiences, emotional echoes]	[Key sociocultural factors relevant to this event or feeling]	[New mantra or balanced statement]	[Updated mood ratings after reflection]	[Concrete action steps informed by reflection]

The Nine-Lens Reflective Tool is a spin-off of the traditional Thought Record, expanding its scope to include sociocultural, historical, and psychodynamic dimensions. Begin by drafting your reflections to each prompt—preferably on paper—taking time to explore each lens with care. Once you have completed your reflections, condense your insights into the fields below to create a clear and integrated summary of your process.

Nine-Lens Reflective Tool:

Situation	Feelings/body sensations	Immediate thoughts	Investigating & reframing	Family history	Intersectionalities/ sociocultural realities	Balanced perspective/new mantra	Updated feelings/bodily sensations	Action plan

Appendix E: Labels for Thought Bombs
Cognitive Distortions

These labels represent recurring patterns of negative or self-defeating thoughts often found among immigrants adjusting to a new environment. Naming them can help increase awareness and self-compassion.

1   All-or-Nothing Thinking:

"If I cannot succeed completely in this new country, I am a failure."
Black-and-white thinking is common in high-stakes adaptation and in navigating conflicting cultural standards.

2   Catastrophizing:

"If I lose this job, I will be deported, my children will suffer, and everything will collapse."
This can reflect both real precarity and exaggerated anticipatory fear.

3   Mind Reading:

"They think I am ignorant because of my accent."
Immigrants often assume judgment from others, especially when language or cultural signals differ.

4   Should Statements:

"I should be further along by now. I should not need help. I should be grateful."
Internalized pressure from both the host society and one's culture of origin.

5   Discounting the Positive:

"Yes, I got a promotion, but it is only because they needed diversity."

Achievements are dismissed, often due to imposter syndrome or racialized experiences.

6   Overgeneralization:

"No one here understands me. I'll never belong."
One or a few painful experiences get generalized to all contexts or people.

7   Labeling (Self and Cultural):

"I'm lazy." "My people are backward."
Internalized stereotypes and harsh self-judgments rooted in dominant cultural narratives.

8   Emotional Reasoning:

"I feel like I do not belong, so it must be true."
Feelings are mistaken for facts, particularly around belonging and value.

9   Survivor's Guilt / Comparative Guilt:

"Others are suffering more—who am I to whine/go to therapy?"
Not traditionally listed as a distortion, but very common for immigrants.

Note: Thought Bombs are clinically called Cognitive Distortions. They often reflect unhelpful thought patterns that can be gently challenged, to help patients align with a more realistic view. It is important to acknowledge that for immigrants, some of these thoughts arise from real social experiences. A thought like "They think I am ignorant because of my accent" may not be irrational—it may reflect repeated encounters with exclusion or condescension. Labeling a thought creates a frame that allows it to be held, examined, and possibly reframed. The goal is to recognize when such thoughts—which in many cases reflect reality—become overly generalized, self-attacking, or paralyzing, especially when they begin to obscure moments of resilience, nuance, or connection. We need to hold both truths: the impact of social injustice, and the possibility of reclaiming agency, dignity, and complexity in how one sees oneself.

Appendix F: Folded Page—Sleep Aid

Table F.1 Folded Page—Sleep Aid

Immediate Thought (Left Column)	Grounded Response (Right Column)
•	•
•	•
•	•
•	•
•	•
•	•
•	•
•	•
•	•
•	•
•	•
•	•
•	•
•	•
•	•
•	•
•	•
•	•
•	•

Appendix G: Chair Exercise: Exploring Ambivalence, Shame, and Growth

Use this exercise when you feel torn between conflicting emotions, identities, or choices. This could involve fear, sadness, desire, shame, grief, or a sense of being pulled between cultures or expectations. The goal is not to resolve the conflict immediately, but to give each voice space, compassion, and clarity.

Step 1: Identify the Voices in Conflict

Ask yourself, if needed:

- Is there a part of me that feels ashamed—for leaving, for staying, for struggling, or not meeting expectations?
- Is there a part of me that is afraid or uncertain?
- Is there a part of me that wants to move forward, adapt, or grow?
- Is there a part of me that feels stuck or paralyzed?

Now write one sentence for each voice:

Voice A: _____

Voice B: _____

Voice C (optional): _____

Step 2: Enact the Dialogue

Set up two chairs facing each other. Sit in one and speak from Voice A. What does it want, fear, or regret?

Then move to the other chair and speak from Voice B. Let each part respond honestly.

If needed, include a third chair for a frozen, ashamed, or grieving part.

Repeat as needed until the voices feel heard.

Step 3: The Observer/Witness

Now stand between the chairs or take a third position. This is your wise, observing self—the part that can hold both (or all) perspectives.
Ask:

- What does each side need?
- What is the wisdom or pain in each voice?
- What might integration look like?

Reflection:

_____

_____

_____

Optional Journal Prompts

- What surprised me during the exercise?
- What did I feel in my body when I spoke from each voice?
- Did one voice feel more emotionally charged than the others?
- What would it look like to carry both truths forward, for now?

Index